The
Complete
Home Aquarium
Handbook

CHILTON BOOK COMPANY ● RADNOR, PENNSYLVANIA

The
Complete
Home Aquarium
Handbook

SALTWATER & FRESHWATER

Cleo Stephens
& Darlene Dunton

Designed by Arlene Putterman

Library of Congress Cataloging in Publication Data

Stephens, Cleo.
   The complete home aquarium handbook.

   Bibliography: p.
   Includes index.
   1. Aquariums. 2. Marine aquariums. I. Dunton,
Darlene, joint author. II. Title.
SF457.S68   1976   639'.34   76-6521
ISBN 0-8019-6432-6
ISBN 0-8019-6433-4 pbk.
1 2 3 4 5 6 7 8 9 0 5 4 3 2 1 0 9 8 7 6
Photos by Cleo Stephens

Acknowledgments

So many people have been generous with their valuable time and advice. We have been met everywhere by kindness and helpful interest.

To Ray Stephens, whose knowledge of native species and their whereabouts led us to some exciting and surprising discoveries in both saltwater and freshwater, and to Dale Dunton, whose good sense and forbearance always stood us in good stead, our love and gratitude.

Our thanks to the many aquarium shop proprietors who cleaned tanks for pictures, gave advice, and even loaned equipment for temporary experiments: Mr. and Mrs. Carl Geer of the Shell Factory in Fort Myers, Florida; John Schneiderhahn, Jim Carrol, and Leland Tate of Aqua-World West and South in St. Louis; Wayne Gmachl of Bayway Aquarium Shop in St. Louis; Jack Fournie, whose advice, analysis and up-to-date research helped immensely; Charlotte Hopfinger, expert on goldfish; and Stan Michailson, fish biologist with the Missouri Conservation Commission. Your help is deeply appreciated.

Contents

Acknowledgments   v

INTRODUCTION   1

1 COLLECTING WATER CREATURES   3

2 SETTING UP YOUR AQUARIUM   21

3 AQUARIUM PLANTS   52

4 MAINTENANCE   60

5 LIVE FOODS   62

6 SALTWATER CREATURES   71

7 FRESHWATER CREATURES   119

8 THE GARDEN POOL   181

9 DISEASES AND PARASITES   189

Useful Books   204

Index   205

General Topics   207

Saltwater Animals and Fishes   209

Freshwater Animals and Fishes   211

The
Complete
Home Aquarium
Handbook

Introduction

We see so much beauty and magic that is fleeting, unattainable; see it and lose it, except for the memory-treasures we can store. A few things can actually be caught, held, and observed at our leisure. A whole world can be ours, a glass-enclosed universe where life goes through its processes.

The variety is virtually infinite. There must be as many kinds of aquarium setups as there are fishkeepers, and each rules his own version of an orderly, beautiful, magical world.

The child coming home frustrated and intimidated from a hard day on the playground, the executive trying to forget business pressures for a few hours, the housewife who loves cleanliness and order: people who have a need to create and care for something beautiful all find an answer in the aquarium hobby.

No book could possibly discuss all the varieties of fishes that are excellent for an aquarium, for they are legion. But as long-time fish fanciers, we can share with you our experiences with fish and other aquarium animals we have known.

Each little creature became to us an individual character, with mannerisms which prompted the choice of its name. There were the sea horses Citation and Sea Biscuit; the puffer Big Mouth, so named because we caught him gulping down baby sea horses; the crawdad Snipper; Mrs. O'Leary, the snail, such a diligent cleaning woman; Hitch Hiker, the remora; and many others, all named for their eccentricities.

Our experiences with these fishes and animals ran the gamut of emotion—joy, sadness, and frustration, yet with a feeling of success most of the time. They've never been dull, never without excitement and compelling interest.

The Dunton family maintains several aquariums year round, while the Stephens family enjoys freshwater fishes when at home in Missouri and saltwater aquariums during an annual three-month stay on the Gulf of Mexico and the Atlantic in the winter. We usually release our collection into its original habitat when we leave, or turn it over to school science projects, where the kids can learn about birth and other life processes first hand. Sea horses, with their conspicuous pregnancy and birth of live babies make a fine and exciting demonstration for youngsters.

There are, of course, problems in keeping fish for pets, but what pet does *not* create problems of some sort? Once an ice storm cut off our electric heat. We frantically transferred our fish from their aquariums to jars with battery-powered airstones. Then we rushed to board our finned pets with a neighbor who was blessed with a hand-fired coal furnace.

Sometimes diseases must be recognized and dealt with, and an occasional fish grows more rapidly than his peers and begins feasting on its roommates. Fish are nevertheless among the most trouble-free of pets and some of the most decorative. Once an aquarium is properly set up, there's little extra work or expense involved.

At one time, keeping fishes meant little more than buying a bowl and some goldfish or guppies at the variety store, but in recent years the aquarium has become an integral part of home decor with large, 20–150 gallon (80–600 liter) tanks, many of which are built into the wall, forming living pictures.

The living room or family room is an ideal location for the aquarium, for this is one place the family gathers in a relaxed atmosphere. The fishes seem to enjoy this togetherness and become little showoff hams, conscious of the people around them and vying for attention.

Certainly the most important considerations in setting up an aquarium are selecting the proper equipment to provide a suitable atmosphere for your finned friends, then keeping everything in good working order.

The initial question of many people considering setting up an aquarium is, "But isn't the purchase of all those fish terribly expensive?" It can be, but it need not be. An aquarium can be supplied with a wide variety of most interesting fish by the simple and healthful expedient of collecting your own. Some of the happiest times we have experienced were wading Midwest streams capturing interesting creatures, floating the saltwater bays in our canoe, or wading and dipping through sea grass for the amazing types of aquatic animals lurking there.

Our methods of collecting are discussed in detail in chapter 1 and we urge you to look into the fun of bring-'em-back-alive safaris.

1 Collecting Water Creatures

SALTWATER NATIVES ●

There are dozens of methods you can use to collect saltwater aquarium critters: wading the shallows in sneakers, dipping with a homemade net; scuba diving or skin diving over coral reefs or among rocks, using a plastic mesh collector's net; floating in a small boat or canoe, scooping among the grasses with a long-handled dip net; seining little bays; pulling a dredge behind a boat; and more. The method you use is largely a matter of preference and locality.

In the winter we flee cold Missouri for sunny Florida, park our travel trailer on Pine Island, launch our canoe, and putter off into the bay. With its 6 horsepower motor, the canoe can take us anyplace we want to go in Pine Island Sound (Fig. 1-1).

The first matter of business is to catch a couple of redfish, snook, or sea trout for the table; the second is to stock our saltwater aquarium. Each year we are delighted and amazed at the variety of creatures we manage to come up with. Plenty of them are familiar species, but we always discover some that are new to us.

Much is written about "aging" aquarium water before putting in fish, but we have found this unnecessary when we use clean natural sea water scooped up far from the pollution of a marina. We include some of the shells and/or rocks to be sure we have the natural algae. We plug in the pump with its under-gravel filter and airstone, and immediately add the sea creatures as we bring them in. After all, it is the same environment they were in; the water is the same temperature, and the shells and rocks provide appropriate algae for those fish who should have it.

But you should understand that if you are establishing a marine aquarium far from the sea, and if you must use artificial saltwater, you'll have to take special precautions with your setup. Moreover, fish purchased from aquarium shops have often been kept in artificial saltwater and, if they are to be shifted to natural seawater, they must be acclimated to it gradually. More about these considerations later, once you've been more fully introduced to a number of the methods of fish collecting.

FLOAT DIPPING

Float dipping is simple and ideal for shallow water. You drift in a canoe or small boat, allowing the wind to carry you along. Then, with a long-handled hand net you dip up clumps of the grasses that float along the bottom (Fig. 1-2). Use a fine-meshed net if you want small fish. Then sort through the grasses and drop the specimens you want to keep into a bucket of aerated seawater.

Fig. 1-1   A canoe is ideal for floating the shallows when you want to dip for fishes.

There are many areas where this type of collecting works well. Even when the water is murky and other kinds of collecting would not serve, the creatures hiding in the grass can be easily captured.

Low tides and light breezes provide ideal conditions for this kind of collecting. In bays on the Gulf of Mexico the water is usually crystal clear, but strong winds make the bays choppy, making it hard to see beneath the surface from above. This holds true for Atlantic bays and, indeed, any large, shallow body of water. Among the islands along the California coast, even a moderate wind can bring on a strong, high chop and murky water.

A glass-bottomed bucket or box such as an Aqua-scope aids underwater viewing (Fig. 1-3). These devices are sometimes hard to find in stores. After much searching, we found this one in a shop on Marathon Key.

Fig. 1-2   Long-handled, fine-meshed nets are used to scoop through grasses in the saltwater shallows.

Fig. 1-3   A glass-bottomed bucket, box, or plastic viewer is an aid for studying water life in wind-rippled or muddied water.

Fig. 1-4   Carry along a small bucket as you wade and collect.

WADING

When you wade in the shallows to collect, carry along a net and a bucket (Fig. 1-4). The inside section of a minnow bucket can float along tied to your belt.

Remember that there are bad guys in these waters! There are likely to be stingrays, prickly sea urchins, and even the Portuguese man-of-war lurking out there and it is wise to wear heavy shoes or plastic waders. You'll want to take care, too, not to tread on a catfish's spine; that can be painful. A good plan for foiling stingrays, which are plentiful in southern waters, is to scoot your feet along the sand. The stingray (Fig. 1-5) buries itself in the sand with only its eyes and stinging spine showing; it is often almost impossible to see. Scooting your feet keeps you from stepping on the spine and scares the ray on ahead.

The Portuguese man-of-war is a jellyfish with fine tentacles, sometimes as much as 30 feet long. Its body sports a lovely ruffled, blue and rose balloonlike sail, 3–12 inches wide. If one of these tentacles wraps around you, the pain is excruciating. I know—one got me when I was body surfing in Hawaii. A new popular remedy suggests that meat tenderizer, sprinkled on the sting, then sprinkled with water, will ease the pain. But the best plan is to stay out of water where the animals are present. It's difficult to spot them when they're floating in the water, but on open beaches an examination of the wave-washed sands will often tell the tale, especially if the wind is blowing toward shore. The man-of-war can't control the direction of his drift, and his blue bubble-sail may wash him up on the beach with the waves. We have often seen Atlantic beaches strewn with hundreds of these creatures but have never seen them on Gulf of Mexico beaches, which may be due to happenstance.

Some sea urchins have stinging spines and it is wise to avoid them (Fig. 1-6). We have seen these round, spiny creatures camouflaged in such a way that we were strongly tempted to pick them up. They will plaster dozens of colorful shells all over themselves and it is easy for an avid shell collector to snatch them up without realizing how the shells happened to be in such a neat cluster.

Of course there are other saltwater animals that should be avoided, but it goes without saying that waters where sharks and barracuda are sighted are strictly taboo for wading. We have often spotted both cruising in close to the shallows in the Gulf, Atlantic, and Pacific surf, and close to the mangrove islands of the shallows but have had no problem with them. On several occasions as we floated among the lower Florida Keys, sharks 5 and 6 feet long hung around under our canoe, probably enjoying the shade and giving us an excellent lesson, incidentally, in the folly of dangling feet or hands in the water. Needless to say, fingers and toes could appear to be tasty tidbits. In these same areas we watched large schools of barracuda, but these were usually no more than 2 feet long. One fish collector friend tells us that he always gets out of the water as dusk nears, for there seems to be increasing feeding activity at that time.

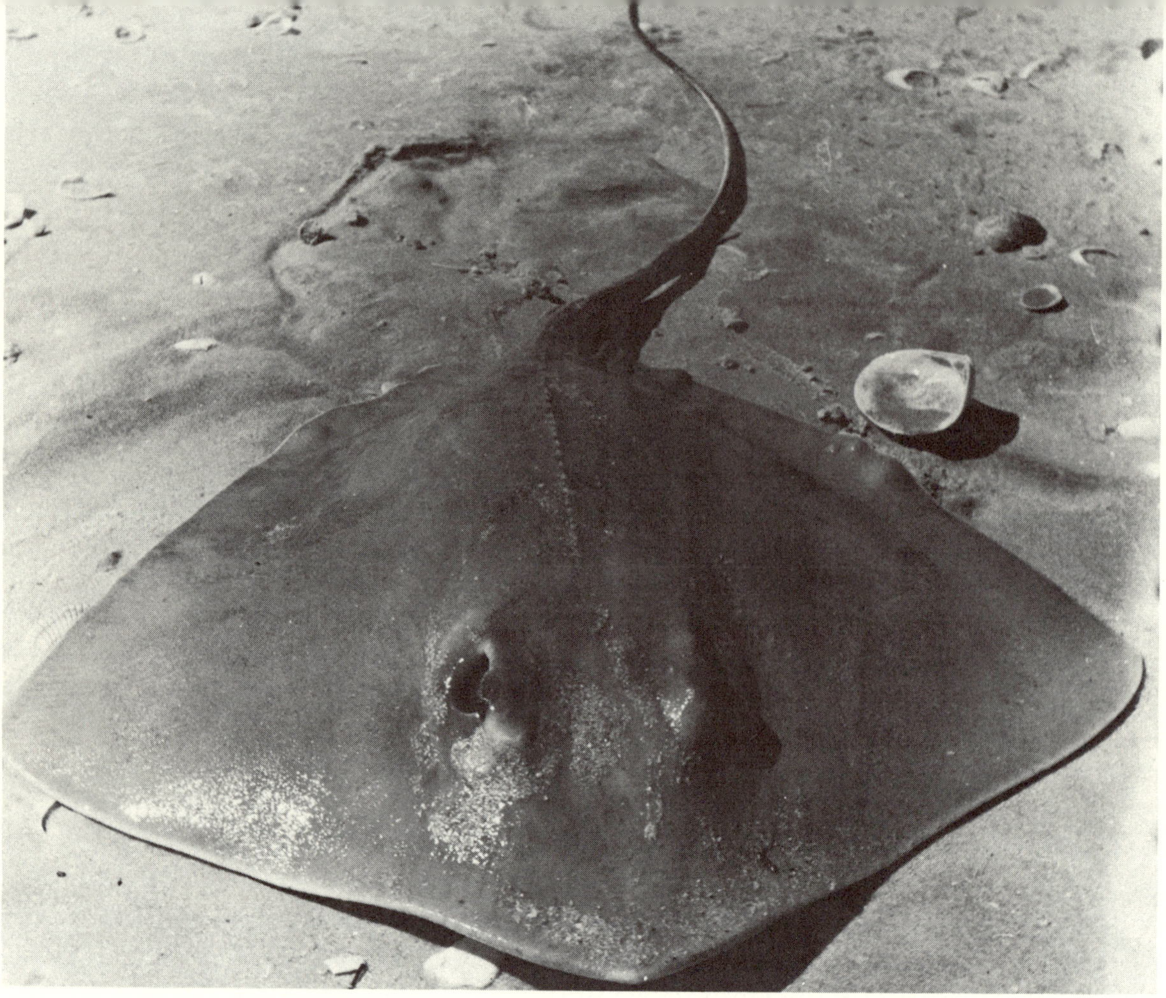

Fig. 1-5 Beware of the stingray lying in wait. He's often buried in the sand, with only his poisonous barb showing.

Fig. 1-6 Some sea urchins have poisonous spines.

Fig. 1-7   Scuba diving over reefs and in rivers is an excellent way to collect fish—but not for novices.

SCUBA AND SKIN DIVING

One of the most exciting methods of collecting aquarium fishes is diving over rocky areas or coral reefs, but this is not a technique for the amateur. It is important to learn to use your equipment correctly, whether it be complicated scuba gear or merely face mask and snorkel. Before attempting a dive in deep water or wide-open waters, a complete course with a certified instructor on the gear, in a swimming pool, is a must.

The importance of training became apparent when I learned to scuba dive in a deep cave spring in the Ozark Mountains while researching for an article on the dangers of such diving. Scuba divers had, on several occasions, died or gotten into serious trouble in that spring cave. Although I was instructed by experts, I was nevertheless constantly conscious of the dangers. These wise divers left nothing to chance, observing all the safety rules: put out a diver's flag, go with one or more buddies, take an anchored line down with you, and other essentials.

The waters of coral reefs, where some of the most colorful fish are to be found, are often only a few feet deep. With appropriate training and observance of the rules—and a lookout for predators—the diving there can be a glorious experience (Fig. 1-7).

An ordinary fine-meshed net, even a homemade one, can be used to capture fish when diving, or you may buy a marine biologist's net, which is a long rectangular plastic bag with a mesh bottom. It has a rather short handle. A longer one, such as is needed when wading, is not necessary—fish seem to be less concerned about swimmers than about boats and waders and will allow close approach, making it easy to scoop them up.

A handy collecting bucket for this method is an anchored, floating minnow bucket or an inflated inner tube with a mesh bag fastened in its center, so that you may surface and deposit the fish as you collect them.

DREDGING

We are primarily dealing with capturing fish for home aquariums and probably few amateur collectors would need to go deeper into the project than the methods described. But for those who plan a commercial business of it, the dredge, pulled behind a boat, would be a necessity, especially the smaller nets often used by shrimpers to test-dip an area before lowering their big nets. These baglike nets can be dragged behind a boat at slow speeds, then drawn up and the contents sorted occasionally.

While we are on the subject, commercial shrimpers are an excellent source for obtaining aquarium fish and other denizens of the deep. They have brought us many interesting creatures, including a brilliant yellow giant sea horse with

Fig. 1-8   One of the finest exhibits of saltwater fishes can be viewed at the Shell Factory in Fort Myers, Florida.

a "plumed" head, a small squid, and a giant black sea horse who gave birth to several hundred babies the night it arrived in the aquarium.

To sum up, any of the above methods can be successfully used in saltwater, allowing location and water condition to dictate which—happy hunting!

SUCCESSFUL SETUPS

A study of the successful operations of others is a helpful aid in knowing what to collect.

One of the finest exhibits we've seen of saltwater fishes, mostly the home aquarium type, can be viewed at the Shell Factory at Fort Myers, Florida (Fig. 1-8). Anyone planning to set up an aquarium would delight in studying the wide variety of creatures in this display. So many are represented in one place that it would be easy to decide which ones are most appealing.

There are fifty-two beautifully decorated aquariums: forty-eight are 50-gallon (200 liter) size and four are 135-gallons (540 liter) size, with many hundreds of fishes. They were set up and are maintained by Mr. and Mrs. Carl Geer, who do much of their collecting in the waters of the Florida Keys. Mr. Geer has some very decided ideas on the proper methods for collecting fishes. For one thing, he is much concerned about the practice of using drugs to stun the fish. He says that drugging not only causes the eventual death of many of the fish collected this way, but kills much of the tiny animal life in the area.

The Geers' favorite way to collect flsh is to don mask and snorkel, float the shallows over the reefs, and capture the fish in hand nets; they will sometimes use grass drags for such animals as sea horses. They consider wading dangerous: these waters harbor poisonous scorpion fish, stingrays, sea urchins, and—in water muddied by wading—there is danger from sharks and barracuda.

Geer considers damselfish and killifish to be the best suited varieties, easily adaptable to aquarium life, shipping, and so on.

Among the fishes at the Shell Factory, the anemonefish are especially fascinating. They literally wallow in the soft but deadly tentacles of the sea anemone, blissfully unhurt by the poison. We asked Mr. Geer if it's true that there is a mutual partnership between the fish and its anemone.

"There certainly is!" he told us. "The fish feeds the anemone and grooms it, and the anemone in turn protects the fish from its enemies, since the poison is deadly to most types of fishes. I've found that in an aquarium where there are, for instance, four anemones, if I drop in four pieces of food, the fish will invariably take a piece to each of the anemones—a remarkable sight." He demonstrated this and, sure enough, each anemone was carefully given a piece of food.

Any saltwater aquarium enthusiast traveling in south Florida should certainly stop by the Shell Factory to observe these lovely fishes and shop for coral, shells, and other aquarium decorations. It is particularly intriguing to see how sea fans and coral have been used at the back of the aquariums to simulate the ocean floor.

FRESHWATER NATIVES ●

Before you decide to collect from the wild, be certain you will care for all the creatures you bring home, and only take what you really need.

Even considering high water, low water, fluctuating temperatures, disease, parasites, and predators, the creatures in the lake, pond, or stream live a beautiful life—with sunshine, rain, sweet air, and water given in generous measure by the good Lord who made it all.

The determination of fishes to avoid capture is splendid, even overwhelming, in its intensity. It seems to extend far beyond the instinctive fear of being eaten to a devotion to preserve their freedom.

PREPARATION

Spring and early summer are the best times to collect. Later in the season water is usually low and, though fishes may be easier to see and capture, parasites are at their worst.

You will need small-meshed hand nets and glass minnow traps, which are preferable to wire screen because there is no damage to the fish when he attempts to escape or upon being lifted from the water (the wire ones are really pretty cruel). You'll also need heavy gauge plastic bags, half-gallon or gallon (4 liter) size; battery-driven bubbler (Fig. 1-9); Styrofoam iceboxes or, best of all, special shipping boxes, free from the tropical fish store; Styrofoam minnow pails *with lids*; and a seine. A large plastic drinking glass is nice to have for dipping and examining fishes, and a magnifying glass can help detect parasites.

To save feet from gravel bruises or cuts, wear canvas sneakers. Hat and sunglasses are necessities for many (Fig. 1-10) and a mask and snorkel are useful

Fig. 1-9 A large bucket with a battery-operated airstone will keep fish alive on the trip home.

Fig. 1-10   When collecting, go equipped with plastic bags, insect spray, and sun hat. Here Darlene collects clams from a small river.

Fig. 1-11   Seining a small stream will produce an amazing variety of creatures for the aquarium.

and fun. The sun sensitive should wear a long-sleeved shirt: even on a cloudy day, sun is doubly intense on water, and even a well-tanned hide can get a bad burn if it is unprotected.

SEINING

Plan ahead, having all holding equipment ready at the take-out point when seining.

Most seines are sold without brails—an old sailing term adapted by fishermen to mean the poles to which the net part of the seine is attached. The nets are available in many lengths. Most often a 20 footer (5 1/4 meters) is adequate, and it should not be too long to be rolled in on the brails for seining narrow channels.

Cork floats hold the top of the net at the surface and lead weights carry it down along the stream bottom. When you tie the seine net to the brails, which should be sturdy poles about 4–5 feet long, be sure the bottom edge is even with the lower ends of the brails, or fishes will escape underneath. Remember this also when "rolling in"—rolling the net over the brails to make a shorter seine.

Seining is best done with at least three people: two to pull the seine, as shown in Figure 1-11; one to go ahead, kicking up so much sediment the fishes can't see to avoid the seine. It is pulled upstream to a little cove where it can be lifted and held with the net forming a small pool. The fish are safely contained as they are selected and dipped out with a clear plastic tumbler. Before being put into containers, they can be quickly examined in the tumbler for parasites or disease. Those not wanted can be released unharmed. Dragging the seine out on a gravel bank, as is usually done, injures many of the fish and kills others.

HAND NETTING

Children are especially fond of dipping with hand nets (Fig. 1-12). Because they're enchanted with the infinite variety of underwater life, they'll have the patience to find some of the rarer creatures you might miss.

My favorite collecting method is lazy, but produces some creatures one might not otherwise encounter. Sitting in the water at the edge of the stream, lift rocks and dead leaves. You will learn much from observing the things you find there, even if you don't take them (Fig. 1-13).

Small crayfish and tiny catfish, primarily bullheads and yellow flatheads, are best found this way. After you have been there for a while, minnows and shiners will become bold enough to nibble at you; you can easily net them by holding a large hand net in one hand under the water, baited with dried shrimp or cracker crumbs. Lift it quickly: don't try to sweep it through the water—these fish are too quick and smart for that.

Searching slowly through plants along the water's edge turns up sand pickerel, blue gill, water scorpions (careful, they can really bite!) and an occasional leech. The possibilities are endless.

Using a glass minnow trap is one of the best collecting methods, involving no possibility of injury to the creatures (Figs. 1-14 through 1-17).

THE CHUM-BAG

A chum-bag can save you long hours of hunting, and brings out denizens you might never find any other way.

Tie up a nice selection of dainties, including dried shrimp, dried blood particles to add piquancy, and a drop of extract of anise for aroma, in a fine-meshed nylon stocking. Dangle it in the water. You'll attract every catfish, crayfish, turtle, minnow, raccoon, and water snake in the neighborhood. Fishes

Fig. 1-12   Melanie and Paula love dipping among the grasses and come up with some surprising finds.

Fig. 1-13   Small creatures of all kinds hide under rocks. Dale lifts a rock with one hand and grabs with the other.

Fig. 1-14   One effective way to capture small, school-type fishes is to use a minnow trap. Place a handful of crumbled crackers in the trap for bait.

Fig.1-15   Screw on the flared lid. Note that the feet, seated in the gravel, will keep the trap from washing away in the current.

Fig. 1-16 Place the trap in a creek below a narrow channel with the mouth downstream, for the fish feed in these spots — always facing upstream.

Fig. 1-17 When you lift the trap you will often find you have captured such fishes as red-bellied dace and red-sided dace, darters, and, in saltwater, gambusia and silversides.

such as cats, pickerels, and gars, who normally hide, just can't resist this luscious smorgasbord.

The chum-bag works best in freshwater, but can also be used in saltwater.

MESH TRAP

One other collecting method I might mention is useful for darters, which are normally very hard to catch. They are like tiny underwater lizards, hiding under and around rocks in rapid water. Select a place a couple of feet or less upstream from a group of darters, disturbing them as little as possible. Anchor a small-meshed onion bag with its open mouth pointing downstream, the lower edge of the mouth buried under the gravel, the top propped wide and open, using rocks or staking with sturdy sticks. As soon as the trap is in place, disturb the gravel, kicking up a great turmoil. The darters will rush upstream into the net bag. Lift the mouth of the bag carefully and remove any rocks in the bag before lifting it out of the water.

Only take a few, since darters are high-oxygen fish who need live food (brine shrimp is fine). Select the most colorful. Some are brilliantly colored, while others are quite drab. Allow plenty of room in the transporting bag.

If in doubt about the identity or habits of a creature, examine it for any signs of predaciousness, such as claspers, pincers, teeth, haptors (as on leeches) or stingers.

Take only what you can care for and transport them carefully. Respect your time, your own needs and capabilities, and especially respect the wild things, who want only to continue as they are.

2 Setting Up Your Aquarium

THE MARINE AQUARIUM ●

In discussing the setup of a saltwater aquarium, we *assume* that the beginner will want to start small. We *know* that the situation won't remain thus, for we have yet to find a fancier of saltwater fishes whose hobby does not grow and grow. So fascinating is this thing that it gets into the blood and, almost as though by magic, there appears a larger aquarium or another aquarium. Then it seems that the inhabitants have pups and more tanks appear.

Then is it reasonable for the newcomer to the project to bypass all this and just start with a very large aquarium in the first place? Perhaps that would be one answer, but we are not so certain it is the best. There are several distinct advantages to having more than one tank.

First, even though you choose the different species of fishes carefully, sooner or later, you are almost certain to get some with unsociable dispositions and it is good to have that standby tank ready to segregate them.

Second, there will come a time when a fish will be found to have some sort of illness and should be removed immediately from the community tank for treatment, to keep the disease from spreading to the other inhabitants.

Third, if you're lucky, there will be blessed events and, with all those babies swarming among all those big-mouthed adults, it's the better part of discretion to give them a home of their own. At one time we had almost five hundred baby sea horses of the giant type and over thirty dwarf youngsters in our community tank, along with their fathers; some pipefish, snails, and starfish of various kinds; hermit crabs and several other fishes of the more conventional types. Strangely, all these diverse characters co-existed beautifully until a small puffer developed a taste for a breakfast of baby sea horse, at which point another home was indicated for either the puffer or the little sea horses. In this case, as we were close to the sea, the emergency was solved by simply banishing the puffer to his original habitat. If we had not had this handy solution, that second aquarium would have been called into play. The thing that finally *did* make its use imperative was the discovery that the pipefish and other fast-moving critters were scooping up all the brine shrimp before the slow sea horses, who like to stalk their prey, were able to zero in on them.

This second aquarium was named The Stable and became strictly a horse barn, with all the colts and their fathers installed safely by themselves.

And thus, we graduated to a two-aquarium family (more on the second aquarium later in this chapter).

SPACE, SIZE, AND COST

The foregoing discussion does not establish any definite guidelines on the size or number of aquariums. Events and circumstances differ and it is necessary to play it by ear, taking into consideration many things. For instance, how much room do you have in your home to relegate to tanks? How much do you have to spend for equipment and fishes? How much time do you have to devote to the project?

An answer to the latter question is not so vital in planning, for after the initial setup, little time is required for maintenance. However, it must be a factor for consideration if the tank is to be kept in tiptop shape. The question of space and expenditure must be weighed from the first.

So, do decide *where* the aquarium is to be installed—on a counter or table, in a wall, or free-standing. What size and shape would fit that area best? With this decision made, consideration of cost is the next factor. Then shop around and get an idea of the prices of various units.

Take into consideration that complete aquarium outfits are offered by aquarium equipment dealers: the tank, hood with light, air pump, filter, decoration, and sometimes even an assortment of fishes are all figured in the unit price. This may, of course, prove to be a saving. However, it may not be as esthetically satisfying, for this makes it really someone else's project, not your own.

EXPERT ADVICE

This is not to say that you need not follow the advice of the shop manager in your selection. His knowledge is invaluable in determining the relative sizes of pump and tank; types of filter systems best for the tank you have chosen, whether under-gravel, outside, carbon, charcoal, or protein skimmer; and fishes that generally live together peacefully. Follow your dealer's advice, at least for this first project, then learn for yourself as you go along.

Most experts recommend that you start small and work up; by "small" they mention 20–30 gallon (80–120 liter) aquariums. We do not consider these small, but rather in the medium category for the beginner in home aquariums. Of course, this size does give you more room for a greater variety of fishes. Then again, children are often the instigators in this matter of collecting fish for pets, and they not only should have the smaller aquarium to tend for their first one, but would usually prefer it.

For these reasons, we have chosen to show the step-by-step setup of a 5 1/2-gallon aquarium, with the supposition that those who wish to start with a larger outfit will be able to figure the needs accordingly. Also, there are more detailed instructions for setting up larger freshwater aquariums later in this chapter, the difference being primarily the decoration: the limey shells of the saltwater tank should not be included in that of the freshwater.

AQUARIUM EQUIPMENT

First, the aquarium itself: what kind of construction? The main requisite for the marine aquarium is a tank that does *not* have an exposed metal framework, because of the corrosive action of saltwater.

There are, of course, plastic tanks. These are poured as a solid piece and do away with the necessity for a framework of any kind. However, there is a problem: plastic is softer than glass and it eventually becomes scratched and etched, losing its clarity. The ideal material, as always, remains glass.

There is the all-glass aquarium that has a complete, bonded nonmetal frame that encompasses top, bottom, and corner joints. These range from 5-gallon to 125-gallon sizes. Then there are those that have only a top and bottom frame, in one-piece design, of a black nonmetallic material. These range from 5 1/2–50 gallon (22–200 liter) sizes and do not have the distraction of a frame at the joints.

Of course, if the aquarium is to be built into the wall, the appearance of the corner joints is of no importance. The tank will be framed by the wall itself or perhaps by an additional picture-frame type molding. An inexpensive stainless-steel-framed aquarium can be used for this, if all metal which might come into contact with the corrosive saltwater is made impervious to its action with a coating of black asphaltum or other material recommended for that purpose.

One of the most beautiful of the new, free-standing aquariums is six-sided, supported by an ornamental wrought-iron base (*see* Fig. 2-6). It has a faceted, jewellike appearance and the fish can be seen from all angles. This is a great aquarium for a large area where the tank can be placed free from the walls.

The choice of sand or gravel you use in your aquarium is not merely a matter of whether you like its appearance, though this is a factor, but depends greatly on the type of filtration used.

For its beauty, and because it sets off our fishes and decorations to best advantage, we like the fine white beach sand. However, this presents a problem: we also like an under-gravel filter and very fine sand will be drawn down through the openings and not work with it, so larger gravel must be used with this type filter.

Plantings of growing greenery also make a difference in the choice of gravel, but since these are seldom included in saltwater tanks, this is not a problem, though it must be considered for freshwater. Much of the instruction for setting up freshwater tanks *does* apply to saltwater and it would be well to read that section of this chapter as well.

FILTER AND AERATION

Some fish in a small aquarium may get along quite well with only an airstone and no filter but, since this does not clean the water, it will have to be changed often. The airstone is fastened to one end of a small plastic hose which is then supplied with air by means of an electric pump. When the airstone is dropped into the aquarium, it bubbles, circulating the water and helping to dissipate carbon dioxide. We like to use a filter *and* an airstone. Why? We don't know, except that this method works well and we have found that we can keep far more fishes in a small aquarium than recommended by most experts, without casualties.

If an outside filter such as the one shown in Figure 2-10, attached to the back of the aquarium, is installed, then it is possible to use fine sea sand for the bottom of the aquarium. Whether it be sand or gravel, follow the amount recommended by the filter manufacturer, usually from 1 1/2–3 inches (4–7 1/2cm) in depth.

DECORATIVE EFFECTS

While the freshwater tank can be a beautiful forest of live greenery, the saltwater aquarium is better off with no growing plants. This does not mean that it, too, cannot be lovely, for it can provide its own wilderness—a coral forest.

All "plants" for the marine aquarium will be trees that were once made up of live creatures: coral, sea fans, sea whips, etc.; though no longer alive, they are still very attractive. There are the wide-spreading branches of the staghorn coral; the fluted fans of lettuce coral, delicate lace coral, and others. Looking for all the world like branching trees, these corals were once whole colonies of animal life.

If you find your own coral while beachcombing, boil it for a couple of hours to remove impurities before "planting" it in the aquarium. If you buy it from a dealer, it is probably pure but boil it anyway—no use taking chances.

If the aquarium is to be built into the wall, big fans of coral, sea fans, sea whips, shells, and plants can be placed back of it as well as in it, lending an illusion of more depth.

Plastic greenery to be planted in the aquarium, as well as rocks and shells, should also be thoroughly washed.

If the aquarium is to be viewed from only one side, plant the tallest items to the back, with smaller ones in front of these and to the sides, with perhaps some ledges of rock stepping off, higher at the back. Leave the center front clear of plantings, with only the clean sand and perhaps a few small shells scattered about.

Some people will wish to experiment with live plants in the marine aquarium. We must admit that we have experimented to some extent, with both good and bad results. For this reason, we have discussed the subject further in the section, Saltwater Aquarium Plants (Ch. 3).

TEMPERATURE

Tropic seas are often as warm as 78°F (26°C) and even warmer in the shallows. Fish, as a general rule—especially tropical fish—do not like too great a variation in temperature, becoming sluggish, even sick, if this occurs. For this reason the aquarium should never be placed in direct sunlight, nor should the water be allowed to get too cold. It is best to try to maintain the temperature of a tropical marine aquarium at around 72°F (22°C). Specimens whose natural habitat is colder waters can naturally stand lower temperatures without damage.

If you live in moderate or cold climates, do purchase a thermostatically controlled heater for your aquarium and set it at about 72°F (22°C). If you live in a warm climate, it is still wise to at least float an aquarium thermometer in the water and check the temperature if the house seems overly cold or hot. For tanks we maintain when we are in the southern areas of Florida, we have never needed a thermometer; we have discovered that we, like the fish, do not like too great a variation of temperature and the way we keep the house is all right with them.

SALINITY

Saltwater, be it natural seawater or artificial mixture, will evaporate, leaving the water with a stronger than normal salt content. For this reason, it is necessary to keep a check on it with a hydrometer, which indicates salinity by measuring specific gravity.

If the salinity becomes too high, either change all the water or add enough freshwater to bring it back to the desired reading, which should be specific gravity around 1.025. This should be about right for most saltwater fishes. Actually, the fish themselves will indicate to you when the water is too salty for them, rising often to the surface to take in air. If there is a need to add water to alter the salinity, do it gradually and make sure the new water is the same temperature.

pH VALUE

The usual recommended pH value (acidity or alkalinity) for water in the marine aquarium is about 8.3 and should not be allowed to vary more than 0.5 either way. However, using natural seawater and changing it occasionally, we found no need to keep a check on the pH value.

A growth of algae in the aquarium helps to correct acidity if it should occur and even adds a natural look of the wilds. It is important to be cautious, though: an overabundance of algae will not only spoil the appearance; these tiny plants, which infuse the water, could die and pollute it. If the water becomes an overall green color, you can be sure this is happening and it would be wise to change it or turn up the filtering system. At the same time, reduce the light the aquarium is getting, for light promotes the growth of algae.

A rather drastic way to tell whether the water in your aquarium is too acid is if fish begin dying for seemingly no good reason. If this happens, you will certainly need to get a pH testing kit and check the acidity. Be sure to get the kit that is made specifically for saltwater; those intended for freshwater will not do. If your kit indicates that the pH has dropped as low as 7.0, it is too acid and you will need to add either calcium carbonate or sodium carbonate to the water in an amount to bring the pH level back to about 8.3.

SETTING UP A SMALL AQUARIUM

Equipment needed to set up a small saltwater aquarium similar to the one in Figures 2-1 through 2-4 includes:

5 1/2 gallon (22 liter) aquarium
hood with light
glass cover or piece of glass for top (to prevent water from splashing on
    wiring)
air pump
under-gravel filter or outside filter with plastic connecting tubing
airstone
medium-grade gravel: colored, black, or white
plastic plants, rocks, cured coral, or shells
hydrometer (to measure salinity)
thermometer or combination heater-thermometer for cold climates

Thoroughly wash all equipment with salty water and boil the shells, rocks, and coral for an hour or two. Put the aquarium in the spot where it is to remain—it should never be moved when it is full of water.

Place the under-gravel filter in the bottom. Pour in gravel to a depth of 1 1/2–3 inches, or follow quantity recommended by the filter manufacturer.

Place the rocks in ledges toward the back and in one corner. Add the plastic plants and coral, the tallest to the rear, using the rocks to anchor them (Fig. 2-5). Bring a few of the smaller plants around the ends, leaving the front and center clear. Strew a few shells around on the sand or gravel, but not so many that it is cluttered.

Now for the water: if you are using natural seawater, this can be poured in over a sunken bowl or over your hand, to keep it from stirring up and rearranging the gravel and plants. If artificial saltwater mixture is to be used, it should be thoroughly mixed according to the manufacturer's directions, then poured into the aquarium.

Hook up the end of the filter tubing to the air pump. Plug the air pump into an electric outlet and you're in business.

We usually use an airstone as well as the filter; if this is done, the one pump can operate both filter and airstone. Install a small connecting elbow where the filter tubing connects to the pump. Slip the end of the airstone tubing on the branching end. If this connecting gadget has a control valve, so much the better; you can control the balance of air intake in both the filter and airstone.

Put the hydrometer into the aquarium, toward the back where it will be hidden by the plants. Or, if the salinity is correct, you may just leave the hydrometer in a handy place where it can be used to test the water occasionally.

Now, with the pump operating, allow the aquarium to sit for two or three days to age the water. We have found this unnecessary when using natural seawater, for it is from this same water that we get most of our fishes. But do go far out from a marina to get clean water, not polluted by oil or sewage.

You are now ready to add the fishes. We are not in agreement with other aquarists on the number of fishes an aquarium can hold. We have far surpassed the numbers recommended and have seldom lost a fish. We believe this is due to three factors: we choose fishes that get along well together, give them good aeration, and feed them well.

In the one little tank shown in Figures 2-1 through 2-4, we have simultaneously kept a half dozen kinds of crabs, a dozen sea horses, ranging in size from giant to baby, a half dozen starfish, four or five fishes, three sea anemones, several snails, and a large shell covered with live barnacles. All of these creatures were doing beautifully a month later when we released them. We feel that this is proof enough that a crowded aquarium is no detriment to the health of its inhabitants if it is properly managed. However, you must keep in mind that we were using natural seawater and changing it a couple of times a week. Also, much of the food we were giving our pets was collected right out of the saltwater bay from which they had come. We did raise brine shrimp for the little fellows, to supplement the tiny sea-life food that came in with the water. And so, the secret to our success lies in the fact that we were in a location where we could obtain the best possible water and food easily.

Fig. 2-1   A 5 1/2-gallon tank with an under-gravel filter.

Fig. 2-2   Adding coarse gravel after the under-gravel filter is in position.

Fig. 2-3   A lighted hood is a necessity.

Fig. 2-4 For sea horse trees, use either a Sea Fan, stripped of its limey coating, or a plastic tree.

THE FRESHWATER AQUARIUM ●

The essentials of establishing your aquarium are choosing a place for the tank, selecting accessories, arranging decorations, and assembling the components into a harmonious, efficiently working underwater world. Once we review specific considerations, you can set up your freshwater aquarium easily, confident you haven't made any glaring errors in either decorative or practical matters.

LOCATION

The tank will be heavy: each gallon (4 liters) of water weighs over 8 pounds (3 1/2 kilograms). The tank itself, with the base and rocks and sand, also must count in the total weight. If you use a table it must be sturdy; if it is impervious to water, so much the better. Even if the tank never leaks, you will be adding water and siphoning, and your little friends the fishes will probably do a bit of splashing of their own. Bookshelves are popular places for tanks but, unless the aquarium is small, the shelf must be reinforced; remember that weight!

The stands which are sold with tanks are the most dependable. Some are made to hold more than one tank, but even if you only plan on one, you have a shelf for equipment or decorative plants. It's best not to put the aquarium near any items that can be damaged by water. The surface of a table or shelf must

Fig. 2-5   Coral, sea fans, shells, and plastic plants work well together in a saltwater aquarium.

be level: any twist will cause leaks. All four corners of the tank must be supported evenly.

Avoid any source of heat. Radiators, air conditioners, sunny windows, and fireplaces all can play havoc with an environment you want to control yourself.

Think about accident possibilities: a friend once installed a huge tank in his gameroom, just a few inches too close to the billiard table!

EQUIPMENT AND PREPARATION

Select as large a tank as you can afford and have room for; several suitable types are shown in Figures 2-6 through 2-8. The larger the tank, the less temperature fluctuation, the more room for development of the fishes in looks, health, and habits. Also, the water in a larger tank is slower to react to any unfavorable condition, such as pollution from overabundant food or a dead fish.

Clean the tank inside and out with water, never with any kind of detergent or glass cleanser. Polish inside glass well with a dry cloth. Place the tank and its stand or table where they are to remain. Even a small tank can be cracked if it is moved with water or damp sand in it; at the very least, a joint can be strained, causing leaks.

Some sort of background should be used. Put it on first. If an under-gravel filter is to be used, it is placed in position now. Be sure to make all connections at this point. These items of equipment are well supplied with operating instructions; read them carefully, since one under-gravel filter may need a different installation procedure from another filter that looks similar. Many dealers and hobbyists prefer to use both under-gravel and outside filters, which is a good idea because the largest tank is small compared to the open conditions found in nature. A selection of filters is shown in Figures 2-9 through 2-12.

If you intend to establish a tank that will remain undisturbed for years, *do not use under-gravel filters!* No matter what the manufacturers may claim, there always comes a time when a tank will need to be dismantled and cleaned. Plants grow better with just an outside filter, but you will need to do more siphoning of the bottom to keep this setup as clean. It's a matter of choice: experiment to find what you like best.

Any heavy accessories, such as rocks or statuary, should be put in next. More than one aquarist has created a dandy starburst effect on a side glass with a rock that toppled over during cleaning, or as a result of the excavating activities of some fish or other inhabitant making dens or pits.

If you are creating a cliff at the back or ends, it can be laid up dry. If the stones are not shapes that are easy to stack, you can use an epoxy, available at your aquarium store, to stick them together.

Next add the thoroughly washed gravel. A good method for cleaning gravel is to put it in a plastic pail and run the hose to the bottom. Stir well, and leave the water running over the brim until it is clear. If your tank is large, you may have to do several batches this way. If the gravel isn't clean, the water will be cloudy and sometimes a film develops on the glass which must be scraped off.

Don't use that fine, sugarlike white sand; use a coarse aquarium gravel. The best is to be found in aquarium shops. Colored gravel is alright, if it's the proper size and will not tint the water. A good rule of thumb: gravel particles should be near the size of the letters in this book. Too large, and plants will not thrive, under-gravel filters will not work, and debris will accumulate in inaccessible spaces. Too small, and compaction quickly takes place, plants won't grow, and the bottom becomes a foul, black mess.

With an under-gravel filter the gravel must be deeper, even at the front, than you would have it otherwise. Each filter will have specific directions and pre-ferred depth will be mentioned.

In any case, the gravel will be higher at the back and sides, lower at the front. This serves a practical purpose, too: uneaten food settles to the front, where it can be seen and siphoned off easily. If only an outside filter is used, the gravel can diminish to almost nothing at the front.

Water is added next. Don't disturb the gravel any more than you must,

Fig. 2-6 One of the most attractive and practical of the new, free-standing aquariums is six-sided, supported by a wrought-iron base.

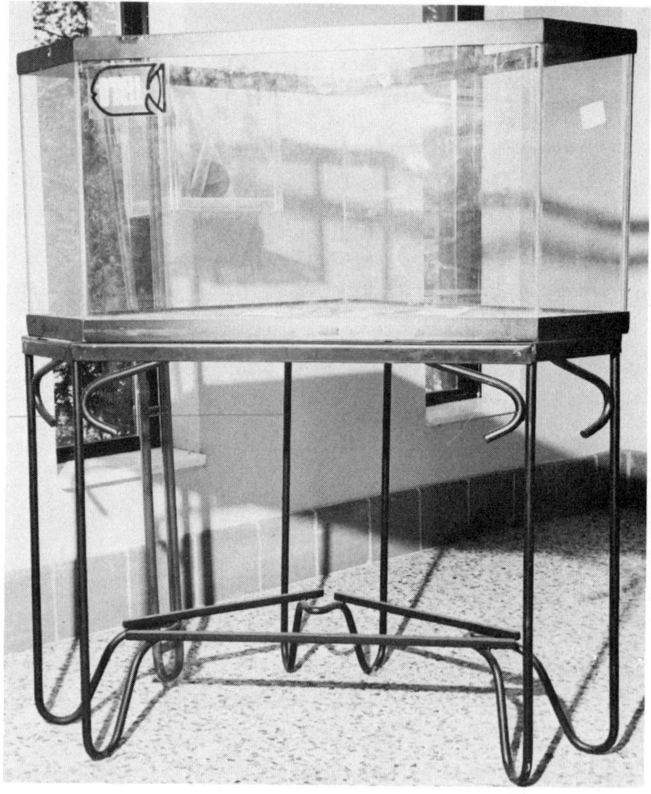

Fig. 2-7 A corner aquarium is just right for some rooms.

because even clean gravel can cloud water. Put a piece of clear plastic wrap over the entire bottom and pour the water gently on this. Fill about two-thirds of the way; you will fill it completely after the plants are in place. Add a little chlorine neutralizer before planting—plants don't care for chlorine any more than fishes do.

PLANTING

Let's hope the plants you are using are free of parasites, but if anything suspicious appears, just rinse it off. There are chemical dips designed to rid

Fig. 2-8   This aquarium has two compartments. Decorations are in the sealed dry section in the background. Story subject in this one is Little Red Riding Hood.

Fig. 2-9   These two filters are excellent for the larger aquarium.

Fig. 2-10   This filter, installed on the back of a small aquarium, is equipped with wool and charcoal.

Fig. 2-11   This type of filter is situated *inside* the aquarium.

Fig. 2-12   This small, round filter is made to go in a round fishbowl.

plants of parasites, but they may also rid you of the plants. Many times there will be leeches or other waterbugs hiding among the leaves, usually at the base near the roots, and snail-egg clusters may be on the leaves in little semiclear globs. Remove these, too. Of course any mud or dead plant tissue should be cleaned off.

Underwater plants can't be planted like terrestrial ones; holes cannot be dug in gravel with any expectation of them staying long enough to get the plant in. You will be able to install all but the larger plants by holding them with the thumb and middle finger, extending the index finger to dig a little trench and following closely with the plant. The gravel automatically closes behind, and you have put the plant in place with a single gesture. For large plants such as swords, excavate a pit, put the plant in, weigh it down with a few little stones, then shovel sand over the roots with a spoon.

For bunch plants such as ambulia and anacharis, strip the leaves off two inches of the ends and plant them close together, but not touching. These will probably have to be weighed down with stones until they take root, for they love to float to the top, just when you think it's all beginning to look so nice!

HEAT, LIGHT, AND AIR

The outside filter and heater can now be installed, and the rest of the water added. Pour water slowly onto your hand or a plate, to avoid roiling the new landscaping job. Then start the filter. The heater can be plugged in and adjusted after it has been in the water a few minutes. You won't need a heater if keeping cold-water fishes. Again, read all instructions on filter, heater, and air pump containers.

The hood can be put on, and lights turned on. The water will not be perfectly clear and your world may look a little raw and new, but there it sits, your own creation! Let the system run several days.

The hood lights, if they are not on a timer, should be turned on and off every day. Plants need their full "day" of light. Light requirements vary with individual tanks, but most often eight to twelve hours is sufficient. Never leave lights on twenty-four hours a day. This is traumatic for both fishes and plants, encourages disease, and undesirable types of algae will form.

All mechanical objects should be hidden by plants or rocks. The glaring white of the heater liner must be covered and invisible. Air lines which shine merrily and distract and destroy the illusion, have no place in decoration, necessary though they may be. For the same reason, a background is needed to hide all the filters, air lines, electric cords, and any other distracting objects.

Before you bought the air pump (Fig. 2-13), you had the dealer connect it and turn it on for you, didn't you? Good! It's always smart to make sure you won't spend your evenings listening to the obnoxious hum of a defective pump.

The air pump, like the other paraphernalia, must be silent and invisible; even very inexpensive ones should work noiselessly (well, *almost* noiselessly). Incidentally, set the pump on a soft rectangular sponge: wherever you reduce vibration, you cut down on noise.

If water gets into the pump it can ruin it. To prevent back-siphon, which could occur during a power failure, put the pump on a shelf above water level or hang it on the wall. Or if you want to use a low shelf, loop the air line leading to the pump twice (two loops) over a nail or bracket above the water level.

A TOTAL ENVIRONMENT

In creating a peaceful, clean, and altogether pleasing tank, we can and should apply the very same rules used by landscape architects and city planners. These engineers use a zone method, taking into account the type of activity and life-style that will prevail.

There will be a zone for play, one for rest, one for eating, and a sanitation system. We want most of the citizens' time to be spent at the front, so the largest open space will be there. There should be protected areas where shy fish can feel secure, and where bolder, more active ones can rest. All of us need to get away occasionally!

Sometimes an aggressive fish will select a homesite and feel so comfortable he will be relatively peaceful, while shy ones become more bold and make a better appearance, knowing shelter is near.

Even the shape of the tank is important. If the fishes you are most interested in are long, slim, fast swimmers, a long tank is the most satisfactory: they will show off to best advantage and can develop their full potential. Use tall tanks for tall fishes. Discus and angelfish need plenty of height, and will be many times more beautiful when they have a properly shaped space for their own particular needs.

Even though it doesn't offer as much surface area as we might prefer, there is a tall hexagonal tank that shows the basically round goldfish off to best advantage. It is one of the few tanks that does not demand a background. It is viewed from all sides, and should be planted with several long strands of anacharis, ambulia, or giant Sagittaria placed toward the middle. Under-gravel filters are best here, for there is no place to conceal any other kind.

Another tank we especially like is manufactured primarily for Bettas. It is long, low, and narrow. Glass or plastic partitions can be slipped into slots provided in the top edge, making square compartments for individual Bettas. This is the most attractive and practical way to exhibit a collection of these striking and dramatic fish. Without the partitions, it becomes a decorative tank, usually only 6 inches (15 1/2cm) or less deep, front to back. It is easy to fit onto a narrow shelf. The inhabitants are always close to the front and can be seen at close range. If you like taking pictures of your pets, this is the place to put them—they can't swim out of range as easily.

Don't try to establish a tank without a hood. The hood is needed for protection from invaders, dust, smoke, and any other fallout. Without the light it furnishes, your plants will not grow as well, if at all, and you won't be able to see those beautiful colors, one of the primary reasons for keeping fishes. The lights used in hoods today are especially produced to encourage plant growth and enhance the colors of fishes, plants, and decorations. Make sure to get these; the others are still available and cheaper, but the difference is remarkable.

Also, most fishes are jumpers. Even the most placid individuals will have moments when they are determined to fly like birds.

Finally, don't pull up short. Plan carefully, so that you can do it right the first time. If you find it's too expensive to have a complete 20-gallon (80 liter) setup, then buy a smaller tank that will allow you to get everything you need. Too many people buy a tank and a few dime-store guppies and wonder why their aquarium is so disappointing.

You should have a tank; hood to fit; air pump; air line; airstone; filter; a heater, unless you are keeping cold-water fishes; siphon tube for cleaning; Waterite

Fig 2-13   An air pump with branching connections can run both filter and airstone.

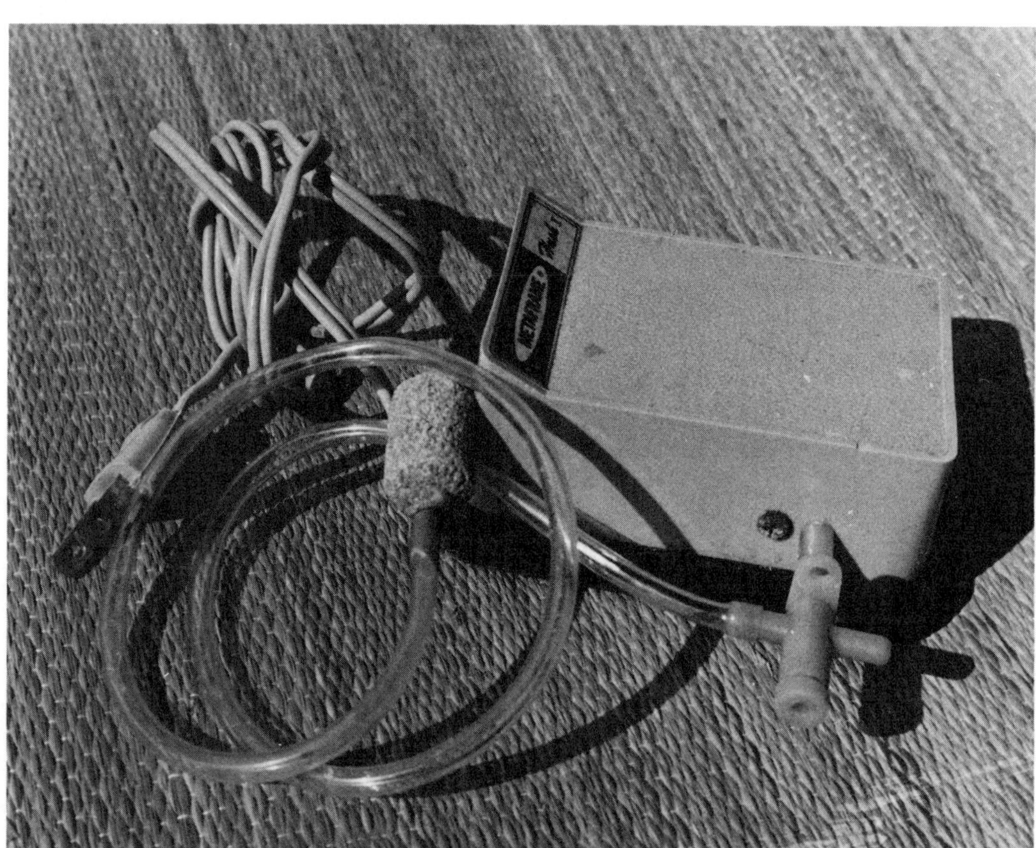

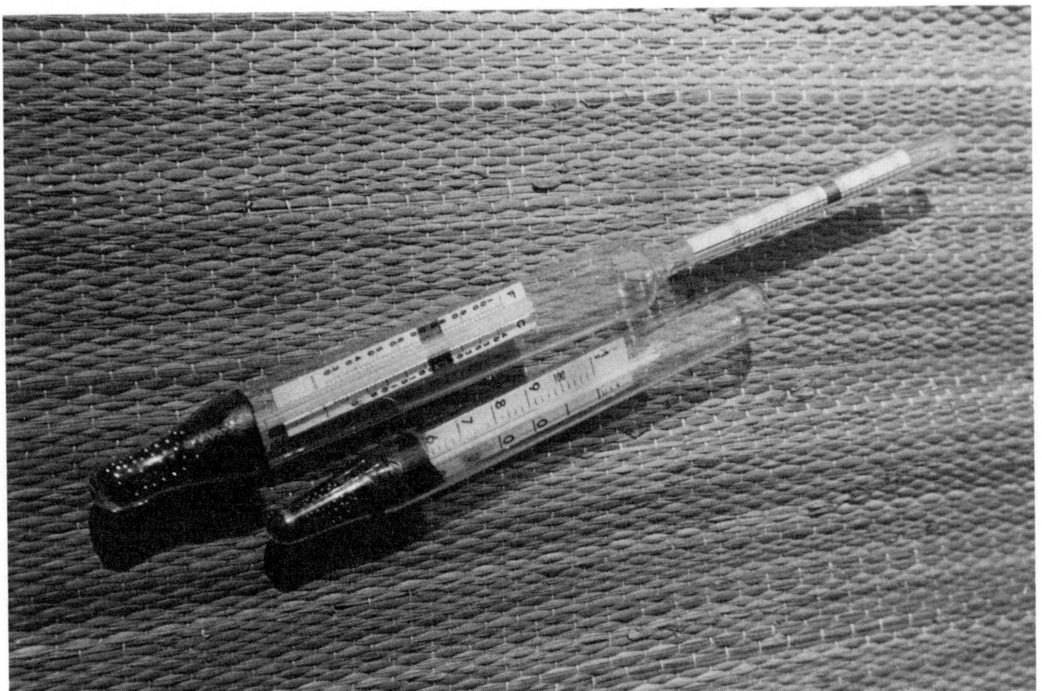

Fig. 2-14 A hydrometer to test salinity and a water thermometer are handy gadgets.

or some other brand of chlorine neutralizer; charcoal and spun wool for the filter, or whatever medium the filter you choose calls for; bulbs or fluorescent tube for the hood; sand; plants; a packet of single-edge razor blades for cleaning algae off the glass sides; a net, not too small; a pH kit and thermometer (Fig. 2-14).

No single tank, filter, pump, or whatever is *the best*. Each person will have different needs, and the fish he likes to keep will have individual requirements. It seldom pays to buy the cheapest of anything, and this is just another situation where that sad rule applies. If you can afford fancy equipment and a huge tank, wonderful! But go the whole way with whatever size you elect: do a good job with a setup you will be proud of!

ALLOW AN ADJUSTMENT PERIOD

Ideally, the system should be in operation for six or seven days before introducing the fish. If the fish simply must be put in immediately, use a chlorine-fluoride remover such as Waterite. Bring the water up to the proper temperature, and hope for the best. If it's at all possible, two trips should be made to the aquarium shop: one for the setup materials, one for the fishes.

Always adjust pH to the reading of the water the fishes are in—you can buy sodium biphosphate to acidify, sodium bicarbonate to alkalize. Follow directions on your pH test kit.

No animal should be expected to live if it is dumped directly into new surroundings without any kind of acclimation period. All fish and other creatures (frogs, snails, etc.) should be floated in their bags until the water temperature is equalized, then a little water from the tank is added to the bag every fifteen or twenty minutes. Finally, the bag is gently turned into the tank, freeing the new inhabitant. During this time be sure the bag has an air space at the top and the plastic *does not rest directly on the water surface*, sealing air away from the fish in the bag.

Keep a close watch the first few days for any disease symptoms or signs of conflict. Sometimes one fish will make an entire community miserable. Don't allow this, or the whole purpose of the tank is lost. Recalcitrant malefactors should be expelled posthaste!

A single sick fish can be removed and treated separately, but if more than one seems affected, it's better to treat the whole tank. Be especially careful to avoid chilling new fish, the prime cause of the commonest ailment, ich (*see* Ch. 9).

SPACE REQUIREMENTS

"How many fishes can I keep in my tank?" is a little like asking how high is up. Some fishes have a very high oxygen or territory requirement: examples would include sunfish and cichlids (territory); many of the marine species and darters (oxygen). Others can be almost cheek-by-jowl and live, at least after a fashion. Any of the fishes with an auxiliary breathing organ, such as Bettas, gouramis, bowfins, or gars, can be kept in more crowded conditions.

An old and accepted rule of thumb suggests 3 inches (7 1/2cm) of fish to a gallon (4 liters) of water, doubling or even tripling the fish inches if an airstone, filter, and plants are used. Count inches of fish as body inches; tails don't count. This is a good place to start, but as you learn the needs of the fishes you most want to keep, you will decide for yourself what boundaries to observe. Even the appearance of the tank has some bearing on the number of fish to place in any given aquarium: many intangible factors are in play here. If you are following the old rule and your tank looks too busy—so crowded that the effect you sought is lost—remove some of the inhabitants to see if it looks better.

Sometimes a 50-gallon (120-liter) tank with two really smashing goldfish, or three to five discus or angels, presents just the image you want—even though far below the "rule" limitations.

Another consideration is the shape of the tank. You can keep more fishes in a long, shallow shape than in a tall, narrow tank of the same capacity.

If the citizens don't grow well, hang listlessly at the surface, gasp for air, or seem especially irritable with one another, they are overcrowded. Add more aeration or greater surface, or thin out the population.

A SECOND AQUARIUM ●

The beginning fish fancier often starts his hobby with one small tank and, so fascinating is it that, like the rice pot of the fable, the project grows and grows, progressing to increasingly larger, even multiple, aquariums.

Having two or more tanks *is* an excellent idea for several reasons. Creatures that could not be included in the community tank for one reason or another can be relegated to one of their own.

For example, there are a wide variety of strange animals, such as the nudibranch, sea slug, sea hare, sea cucumber, and even the octopus, who should not be included in the community tank because of a habit of emitting a polluting "ink" or some other obnoxious behavioral patterns. And there are those whose aggressiveness makes them undesirables in a society of less aggressive fish; yet it would be a shame not to have the experience of studying these odd creatures. The second tank is the answer.

Often these strange little creatures can be found quite easily in tidal pools among the rocks at low tide. We have mentioned some of these (*see* Ch. 6, "Unusual Creatures"). We find many of these worthy of collecting, for often they are beautifully colored and altogether different from the usual connotation suggested by definitions such as *fish, crustacean, jellyfish.*

There are also such unsociable creatures as the stingray or stingaree, sea urchin, stinging anemones and live coral, and jellyfish of the poisonous varieties, all of whom should certainly be observed in an aquarium of their own.

For us, the fun of having an experimental tank is in changing its inhabitants often. When we are near a seashore it is no problem to collect these exotic animals, keep them for a short time for study and photography, then return them to their natural habitat and capture others.

A second aquarium may be needed for supposedly agreeable fishes. Some individuals, although known to be good community tank stock, will develop a quarrelsome character, while others, considered unsuited for community life, will get along quite well with their neighbors. The character of fishes, like that of humans, is often unpredictable, so determining the desirability of including them with other fishes is a matter of experimentation. Put the doubtful character into the tank with the others and keep a close watch for their reactions, removing the fish at the first sign of trouble.

For instance, starfish are known to feast on clams, prying them open with their strong arms. But, though we have always included both of these in the community tank, we have had only one single casualty: a starfish who ate a live coquina. At all other times, our starfish have calmly gone about the business of sanitation and garbage disposal, cleaning the aquarium glass and settling down on the gravel with pieces of leftover food.

Again, to prove that there are exceptions to the rules of cut-and-dried character analysis, books by experts tell us that giant sea horses will eat their offspring and should be separated from them as soon as they are born. This may be true but it has not proved so for us; among the many who have been born in our aquariums to date, none has shown any inclination toward cannibalism. The explanation of this, it seems to me, is contained in one short phrase—plenty of food. When an animal is starving it will eat most anything—indeed, humans will even eat their fellow man—but when well-fed, there is no need: it's that simple. So it stands to reason that the voracious dispositions attributed to many of the bad-guy fishes can be laid to just pure old hunger. Feed 'em properly and well and they'll most often turn into good guys.

Even so, it is still a good policy to have a second or even a third aquarium handy. A fish like a cowfish *can* pollute water and one like our little puffer, with his remarkable rate of growth, *can* develop a taste for baby sea horses. Since so many of those considered the unsociable types are some of the most interesting, it would be a shame not to have the experience of observing them.

For dedicated fishermen, there is also a decided advantage in having a second aquarium to study the actions of fishes when feeding—especially the predatory game fishes. When our lure is flicked out into ocean or stream, how can we know where those fish are lying and what sort of action will induce them to strike?

Curious, we captured and studied a variety of game fishes and were enthralled to find that each specimen had its own feeding techniques. The little bass cruised the tank slowly and when a live housefly was dropped into the water, edged toward it, cautiously, watchfully, only coming to life to slurp it in after it had moved a couple of times—proving that a lure should be worked in this manner. Observation also paid off with a small pike. A fly, dropped into the water, would cause the pike to dart forward, then freeze, lying on an angle under the fly. A movement by the fly would prompt an excited wriggle from the fish, but it was not until after three or four struggles by the fly that the pike exploded into action, striking with the speed of a snake.

After observing these feeding patterns, we were eager to put our knowledge into action on our next fishing trip, theorizing that larger fish would react the same way as small ones. Sure enough, a Rebel (minnow-shaped plug) dropped lightly into the water and left to lie for a few seconds, then moved slightly a couple of times, invariably brought results. And when we fly-fished for these predators, we flicked a black fly out into the water, gave it a slight twitch, a pause, then another twitch. Most of the time a bass, perch or bluegill would strike on the second or third movement.

When we captured a baby channel catfish, we brought it home and put it into our second aquarium—one we had set up to photograph a tadpole-to-frog metamorphosis, and the actions of a large crayfish when he shed his skin. In this tank we had built up ledges of rock for the crayfish. Upon being placed in the tank, the catfish immediately drove the crayfish from his den and established it as his own kingdom, wriggling back into it with just his nose and sensitive whiskers visible.

Right away we were aware of the difference in the feeding pattern of the catfish from that of the other predators, for a fly dropped into the water held not the slightest interest for him (though we have several times caught channel catfish on fly and spinner), so we dug up some small fishing worms and dropped one into the aquarium at the end farest from the fish. Again there was no action from the catfish. Subsequent experimentation proved the reason: old catfish demanded the tidbit served up breakfast-in-bed style! Each time we dropped the worm close to his rock, he swirled forth and nabbed it.

As a result, we now know that when fishing with live bait, a good idea is to cast as close to an old log or rock as we can get, allow the bait to sink to the bottom, and a catfish or other bottom dweller will charge out of his den and gobble it up. Just another reason for keeping a second aquarium.

It was in the second aquarium that we installed two little orange octopuses—with disastrous results! They poisoned the water to such an extent that they even killed themselves. This could have been an even greater tragedy if there were other fish with them, again proving the advisability of trying out sea life of unknown habits in a separate tank before adding them to the community aquarium.

Also, this tank (or a third) may be needed for a nursery. With certain kinds of fishes, there are sure to be blessed events. In some instances, babies left in the community tank are sure to be swallowed up by adult predators.

However, many fish owners purposely include some of the types of fishes that are prolific breeders for this very purpose: to furnish food for the other fish, with the live fry highly relished. This may go against the grain for some people. Actually, when you get right down to hard facts, I suppose this is no more inhumane than raising cattle and chickens for our own consumption. If you wish to raise live small fish for adult fish food, separate from the aquarium they are in, a second tank will serve the purpose, using such live-breeders as guppies.

MINIATURE WATER WORLD ●

There are endless ways to gratify your love of beauty and order in the arrangement of this small world. Duplicate a part of some stream or pond, indulge in some wild flight of fancy, try concentrating on colors and shapes that emphasize your fish, set a stage that tells a story, or decorate one with the aim of catching a child's fancy.

We'll call them "sets" because they are very close to being real stage sets. Every drama may be, and probably will be, enacted here: birth, growth, eating, playing, loving, fighting, and dying.

NATURAL HABITAT

One of the most popular and logical schemes is the natural set. We'll say the society for this world has been collected from a stream somewhere in the Midwest. Long, flattish rocks have been laid up around the sides and back to give the appearance of a cliff. An airstone is placed off-center front, with the air line running under and behind the cliff. A small rock can be placed in front of the airstone for concealment. The cliff will be roughly semicircular, leaving the largest space toward the front. Rather than have a sheer wall, you might want to terrace the rocks, with several levels rising from front to back, leaving a few pockets for planting.

There are no large rocks on the gravel near the front, unless they are very flat and do not detract from the general picture.

The whole idea is to give an effect, an impression, and every accessory should be carefully considered: will it add to the set, make it more intriguing, or will it merely interrupt and distract?

It's usually best to place rocks first. Some of the citizens may take to excavating, and if the rocks do not set directly on the bottom, dire consequences may result.

As soon as you are satisfied that the cliff is secure and nicely arranged, add the damp sand, two-thirds of the water, and plants. Either finish by filling the tank completely, or make the last third of the water that which was brought in with the fishes. The latter is safer for the fishes; even though it may look murky in comparison to the nice clean water of the tank, it will clear when the filter has run a couple of days.

When you collect fishes yourself, you have one great advantage: you can observe and duplicate the needs of each fish. The baby catfish were found hiding under rocks, so they'll want some good cavelike rocks to snuggle into. The same goes for crayfish: for each of these you must have at least one den. Don't put rooted plants nearby, for they will probably be dug or nudged out.

Sometimes crayfish have an urge to get to the surface, where they actually wave their pincers in the air—so an emergent piece of driftwood or a rock is important for them.

Bluegills like plant cover or driftwood shelters. Most minnows stay in riffles, so be sure aeration is good. A slight current can be supplied by a filter that has the intake siphon at one end of the tank, return at the other.

Darters hop around rocks in the swiftest flowing areas. A scattering of gravel the size of the end of your thumb, placed toward the front, keeps them feeling at home and out where you can enjoy their beguiling ways.

NOVELTY DECOR

It's fun and rewarding to create a duplicate of some especially lovely part of nature, as in the arrangement just described, but you can also try something completely new. Several novelties are shown in Figures 2-15 through 2-17.

I remember one called "Outer Space" which had a black velvety background, painted with stars and planets. White sand was sculpted like the surface of the moon and there were tall slender vertical rocks and a touch of wry wit—a bewildered-looking little green man in the middle front with what looked like a map in his hands! The fishes were generous flights of cardinal tetras, *Rasbora heteromorpha*, and glow-lite tetras—altogether a prizewinner for originality!

Your tank can be a great place to display artifacts. One friend, who wanted to show his cherished American Indian artifacts to best advantage, laid a small baked-clay bowl on its side, and strewed fine arrowheads and axheads around it. A rather poignant touch was a large, perfect spearhead driven into the sand toward the back of the tank. He had fastened a worn, broken shaft to the head with hammered lead strips. The stone head, which was rather large and heavy, was supported by two rocks concealed under the sand.

Another collector had several small stone idols—one of gray lava stone, one of golden obsidian, and another of jadite. He constructed a ruined temple and put each idol on a pedestal of cut stone. Microsagittaria sprawled around the bases, corkscrew Vallisneria wove itself in and out among the stone pillars, which were ceramic (available at your aquarium shop), and the background was made up of a rich growth of water wisteria. The effect of both of these tanks was eerie, as the silent fish wandered through what seemed to be a lost, ruined civilization.

The Hansel and Gretel tank (*see* Fig. 2-8) is actually double, with the back section left dry. A pane of glass was installed with epoxy, separating front and back, the invention of Charlotte Hopfinger.

Possibilities are unlimited, with all sorts of accessories available (Figs. 2-18 through 2-20) to create realistic or whimsical effects.

THE PEACEFUL COMMUNITY

Developing a peaceful, happy community tank is not difficult: just choose a group of very peaceful fishes or achieve a sort of armed truce where, even though the fishes are aggressive, they are so evenly matched that they manage to live with a minimum of squabbling. Each community should, of course, have similar water requirements.

We'll suggest a few combinations that we have found successful. By studying the habits and requirements of other fishes, you will be able to come up with some workable societies of your own.

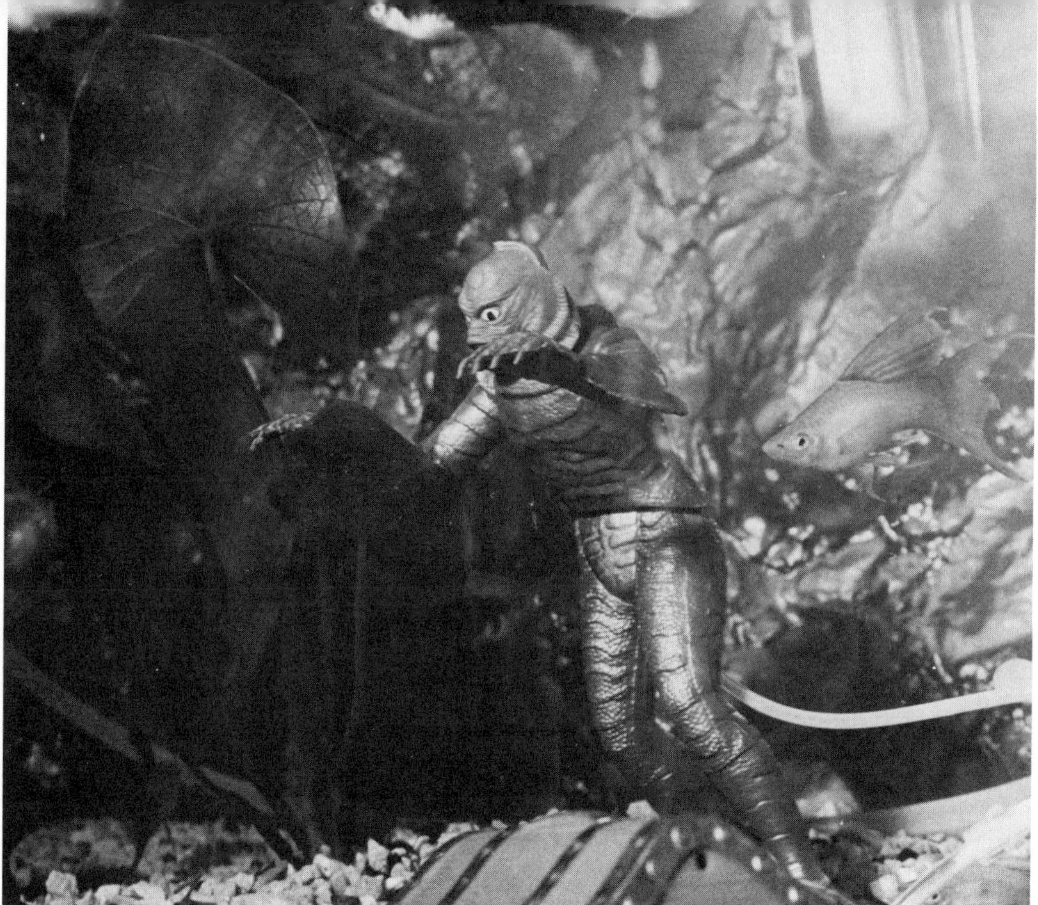

Fig. 2-15   Children love the scenes possible with the odd items to be found in aquarium shops. This scene smacks of science fiction.

The native fishes tank: sunfish, shiners, darters, little catfish, and crayfish. If there's room, and if you are not striving for a "pure" native community, you could safely keep angelfish and dwarf or pearl gouramis with these.

The very, very peaceful tank: platys, guppies, and black mollies. Green mollies aren't always peaceful.

The armed-camp tank: one male firemouth, several sunfishes, oscars, spiny eels. The eels must be introduced to the tank at the same time if more than one is to be used.

Another very peaceful tank: angelfish, pearl or dwarf gouramis, danios, Corydoras catfish.

A community requiring acid-to-neutral soft water: cardinal tetras, *Rasbora heteromorpha,* head-and-tail-light fishes, other tetras.

When buying fishes for a community setup be sure you make it clear to the salesperson so, if you are attracted to some fish that wouldn't be satisfactory, he can warn you. If he promises that all the fishes will live together in harmony and you find them shredding each other to bits, take the offenders back to the store and ask for more peaceful brutes. If the fish were sold to you as mild-mannered creatures, you should protest if they turn out otherwise.

Fig. 2-16   The skeleton with the sword in its ribs is a rather gruesome decoration, but kids like it.

Fig. 2-17   The Oriental fisherman is actually an airstone with the air bubbles issuing from his mouth.

Fig. 2-18   Aquarium shops offer thousands of items for decoration, including Oriental temples, sunken ships, and divers.

Fig. 2-19   Many natural plants are duplicated very realistically in plastic.

FORBIDDEN ELEMENTS

Most hobbyists know you can't put just anything in with fish. Some of the chief offenders would be coral or seashells in freshwater. Not only do they often have jagged edges, they will gradually dissolve, upsetting the pH balance. Shops do offer treated shells and coral, which are coated with epoxy, but the sharp edges are still there, coatings do break down, there are crevasses to harbor debris, and—if I may give a personal opinion—they look out of place in freshwater.

Some plastics are toxic: taste any ornaments before use. If the plastic is bitter or has a pronounced odor it won't do.

No detergents should be used on *any* item for the tank. Detergents are such good cleaners that a tiny trace can clean away the slime on a fish's body: fish don't get wet because the slime coating keeps them dry. If the coating is disturbed, water reaches the skin, allowing infection or disease to establish itself.

Any metallic-ore rocks, limestone, or sand made up of these, as well as *any* metal object, except lead, can cause problems.

Tobacco ashes and smoke are even more harmful to your fish than to those creating them. If you do smoke, don't breathe into a plastic bag containing fish and always wash and rinse hands well before doing any work around the tank.

Fig. 2-20   There are many self-help magazines for the fish hobbyist, and an incredible number of books!

To illustrate: my children think it's neat to let the mature angels in one of our tanks nibble their fingers—not a good practice, I admit. They demonstrated this to our friends, one of whom was a smoker. The nonsmoker tried it. Sure enough, the tame old angels nipped lovingly at her fingers. Her husband was intrigued. He touched the surface with his fingertips, just as we had done. The fish rushed to a bottom rear corner and would have no further business with any of us! They had smelled the tobacco instantly, for they never came near his fingers.

Be especially careful with any spray. Insecticides, room fresheners, hair spray, or similar products have no place in the room with the aquarium.

Don't encourage anyone to dabble in the water; the fewer foreign substances introduced, the more pure the water will be.

Stable rocks that won't dissolve are fine, but remember the sharp-edge criterion. Some fish just aren't very careful with their delicate fins and tails. Shale, slate, petrified wood, quartz, obsidian, or any gem-stone in matrix is fine, with one exception: *turquoise is poisonous.*

Concrete objects must be cured with repeated soakings through at least six changes of water. If each soaking is followed by a salt and water scrub, so much the better—use dry salt to scour, then rinse well.

There is one situation when rocks of any kind can be a mistake. If the fish you intend to accommodate are very nervous and tend to try to dash out their brains on the tank sides and obstructions, you need plenty of soft cover. Use an abundance of plants and leave out any hard-surfaced objects.

Driftwood is beautiful, but should be well cleaned every few months by scrubbing hard with a brush and warm water. It tends to darken and acidify water in a closed system. Driftwood must be completely waterlogged or it will float. You can waterlog it in a fraction of the usual soaking time by boiling for a few hours—a good cleaning method, too. Any driftwood should be scrubbed and soaked before using for the first time. If it insists on darkening the wash-water no matter how many changes you try, don't use it or save it for the diorama method of decorating—using it as part of a background outside the tank.

Many times there will be holes and crevases for plants, which is very wild in effect. I once tethered a beautiful piece in a shallow stream for a summer, after fastening on some willow moss and sagitaria. My idea was to get a really natural look. The plants "took" nicely, but upon placing them in my tank, even though there were both Gro-Lux and incandescent lights, good clean water and aeration, the plants slowly diminished in vigor and died. It's difficult to move plants from natural to artificial light. This is a good thing to remember when you buy or collect them.

Good aquarium shops have an amazing variety of decorations. Most of these are perfectly safe to use, but it's always safest to be your own expert: learn for yourself—you'll make fewer mistakes!

THE DEALER'S ROLE

It's not difficult to weed out the aquarium shops that won't be fair and helpful; indifference or ignorance is easily detected and, on occasion, a clerk or manager will be knowledgeable enough, but unable or unwilling to communicate well. If you feel your questions haven't been answered patiently and truthfully, it's a good idea to search elsewhere.

Most aquarium-shop owners and workers are kind, patient, and generous with advice.

You can ask for all kinds of help. If you find yourself stuck with more fish than you can accommodate, due to especially good growth or a large spawning, or a fish is bullying the other citizens of his tank, you might offer the surplus to the dealer. He can tell you if he doesn't want to bother with it, but chances are he can find homes for the unwanted ones. You wouldn't, of course, offer a sick or dwarfed fish to him.

For instance, we had three angels in a large tank. All was peaceful until they matured. Two of them paired off, prepared to spawn, and made life miserable for the third, a fine fat female who also was ready to spawn. The dealer kindly put her in a huge tank in his store, where she was soon bought by a hobbyist who needed a female angel which was ready to spawn!

Don't expect something for nothing—when a dealer is helpful, be sure you go to his store when you need supplies, fishes, or tanks.

③ Aquarium Plants

SALTWATER PLANTS ●

The easiest way out of the controversial subject of saltwater aquarium plants is to simply not mention them at all. But that would be cheating. We must be honest and state that on this subject we have no cut-and-dried answers. We could, of course, name a few of the "plants" that have worked for us, such as mermaid's cup, merman's shaving brush, and some various seaweeds, and let it go at that. But again, that would not be fair, for some of those we have found usable have been reported by others to be—and we quote—toxic, trashy, and a nuisance to keep planted in the sand or gravel because the actions of fish and crabs will uproot them.

It is said that saltwater aquariums are *not* miniature oceans and this is certainly true. Although it would stand to reason that plants, coral, grasses, and similar growths that occur in the area where you have collected your animal life would be quite safe to include in the aquarium, it doesn't work out that way. The thing to remember is that the closed-in world of the aquarium presents a far different situation than a wide tidal bay that stretches for miles, with the water constantly recharged from the ocean by the changing tides.

We have experimentally introduced into our tanks several different kinds of plants such as turtle grass, floating grasses of different kinds, and the red and green algaes. Though they did add greatly to the beauty of the aquariums with their delicate, intricate patterns, we invariably chickened out after a short trial and removed them, so we cannot honestly say that we gave these a good test. Since, as far as we can determine, very little has been done to find out which plants are acceptable in aquariums, it would make an interesting experimental subject.

For those who would like to try it, some of the prettiest and most decorative "plants" are the Algaes: red *Plumaria* with its fernlike branches is easy to obtain all along the Atlantic and Pacific shores; species of *Corallina*, which occur in both tropical and northern waters; *Penicillus,* or merman's shaving brush, a tree-shaped plant from 2–4 inches high, is found in all the warmer seas. We especially like the strange plant called the mermaid's cup. It is only 1–3 inches high, but quite attractive when planted close to the front of the aquarium. The only problem with this was that the fish liked to eat it and we would wind up with only bare stems. This was good, in a way, for those algae-eating fishes evidently needed it in their diet.

Other attractive decorations of the live variety which might be tried are the living corals, such as sea fans, sea plumes, and sea whips. We have not experimented at all with living coral and very little with the algaes, but intend to do so at some future time. Meanwhile, the dried skeletons of these are safe to use in saltwater aquariums and add greatly to their beauty. For sea horse trees, we use sea whips which have had the crumbly, limey outer coating rubbed off. This leaves little trees which are like hard rubber in texture and sea horses love to anchor their tails around the limbs. These can usually be purchased in shops that deal in aquarium supplies, or can sometimes be found drifted in on beaches adjacent to coral beds.

If you are not the venturesome type and do not want to take chances with the health of your fish by experimenting, it would be better to stay with the dried corals, rocks, and shells for decoration, perhaps adding some greenery in the form of plastic plants.

FRESHWATER PLANTS ●

Yet another pleasant facet of the aquarium hobby is underwater gardening (Figs. 3-1 through 3-3). Just as with fishes, the important key to success is providing the proper pH and light-hours.

Use acid-water plants with fishes requiring acid (low pH) water; alkaline-water plants with fishes preferring alkaline water. This seems to be an unnecessary statement, but most plant failures are the result of trying to grow a plant in water that's all wrong for that particular plant.

Many aquarists prefer plastic plants, which are realistic and pretty, but real plants do assist the fishes in many ways. They provide shelter for shy fishes; function as water conditioners, absorbing toxic gasses and giving off oxygen; they catch eggs or hide newborns, stimulate spawning, and keep down the growth of algae. The feeding roots of live plants keep the sand clean and sweet, and there is even a likelihood that fishes like to see growing things as well as the keeper does!

Real plants find their own way between crevasses in rocks, around ornaments, and across the sand in a natural, soft manner that cannot be imitated by artificial ones. You might be surprised to learn how much work they do for you in decorating and in maintaining a clean, healthy tank.

Fig. 3-1 A large variety of aquarium plants may be gathered in some North American streams. Here they flow out with the current.

Fig. 3-2 This selection of plants was found in a single stream.

54 *The Complete Home Aquarium Handbook*

Never buy a plant that doesn't look perfectly healthy. If plants are brown, bruised, crumpled, or losing their leaves they are already too far gone to reclaim. The best time to buy plants is as soon as your dealer unpacks a new shipment. Ask him to call you when they are delivered, so you will have better chances of success.

A casual visit to the aquarium store may prove disappointing, plantwise, for the selection may be old and picked over. If you are especially interested in a specific plant, ask about it; the dealer may order it, or at least keep you in mind if it should arrive in a future shipment.

Plants must have good light, which is best supplied by the new Gro-Lux fluorescent tubes, or a combination of fluorescent and incandescent bulbs. They also must have several hours of darkness in each twenty-four hour period. A good starting place would be to allow eight to ten hours of light daily. This would be a minimum; if they don't grow well you will need more hours of light unless your light source has unusually high wattage. The depth of water also makes a difference; more light reaches plants in shallow aquariums where the light source is closer. Experimentation will tell you what plan to follow.

Fig. 3-3   It is fun to collect your own lovely plants.

AMAZON SWORD PLANT

Echinodorus sp.

One of the best-loved of all aquarium plants, the Amazon sword plant presents many forms. The one most often seen is the long-leaved "centerpiece" that dominates the aquarium. There are lace-leaved forms, medium-sized types, ripple-leaved versions, and the very small pygmies and miniatures, which form a fine groundcover only 2–4 inches high. The largest ones, depending upon water, food, and light, may be anywhere from 2 feet (60 cm) to 8 inches (21 cm), with the smaller types stair-stepping down from there.

This plant will grow well in a clean sand medium if there are enough fishes present for fertilizer, but shows its best progress in a rooting medium of potting soil covered with gravel, either in a pot or planted directly in the bottom sand. Great care must be used when adding soil to the tank bottom; none of the fishes that might disturb the bottom should be present, and no bottom filter can be used.

Amazons do not need strong light and will promptly decay if algae is permitted to grow on their leaves. pH should be near neutral. The sword is a fine plant for tall, slow-moving fishes.

Plant a sword with the crown (juncture of leaves and roots) exposed, making sure all roots are covered. Too deep or too shallow planting will ensure failure. Remove all brown leaves as they appear. If brown, rotted spots appear toward the middle of the leaves, best discard the plant; it's likely that it's diseased.

EEL GRASS

Vallisneria sp.

Several varieties of *Vallisneria* are available, from the large (2 feet or a little more) giant val, to the 8–10 inch (21–26cm) plant so often seen in aquariums all over the country. It's a very graceful, grasslike plant whose leaves may be straight or, as in the corkscrew variety, nicely twisted into a spiral.

One of the most adaptable of plants, the vals like plenty of light and propagate so willingly they must be thinned every few months. The pH factor should be neutral to slightly alkaline.

Don't plant just a few, hoping they will fill in the space around them: they seem to need one another's company for best growth. Plant a dozen or so, 1–2 inches (2 1/2–5cm) apart, and they'll take right off. They do *not* grow well in the company of *Cryptocoryne* varieties.

WATER FERN

Ceratopteris thalictroides

Ceratopteris thalictroides, a nice mouthful in anybody's language, is a plant that enjoys the company of guppies, Bettas, gouramis, and any other fish that wants a neutral-to-alkaline environment. Young goldfish look especially pretty against this background: they may take an occasional nip for snacks, but it grows so rapidly no damage is done.

The plant is light green with rounded, compound leaves which grow as a rich clump for a time, developing baby plantlets on the notches of the leaves that reach the surface. When this happens the old plant ceases its root function, deteriorates, and must be replaced with one of the young ones. Left floating, it gives shade and protection to small fishes and grows fairly well, but is not as long-lived as when the roots are planted.

To ask for the plant, say *"ser' a top' ter us thal ik troy' des,"* or "water sprite," probably its most popular name.

FOUR-LEAF CLOVER

Marsilea sp.

Also sold as water shamrocks, the four-leaf clover plant is one of the most interesting aquarium additions. Not commonly seen, it has been receiving more interest recently.

It's a fern found in the shallow waters of the United States, having a very wide range (west to east, and south), but is not easily found, for it is not plentiful anywhere.

Most often cultivated in soil-gravel mixtures in greenhouses receiving natural light, it may be an ungainly long-stemmed thing with a four-leafed umbrella effect at the top. But in an old, well-established aquarium, with neutral-to-acid water, a transformation takes place: all new growth becomes progressively shorter until an emerald green mat is formed by the tough, stringy runners.

The stronger the light, the larger the leaves and the longer the stems will be. With a medium artificial light, charming thickets develop—taller at the back of the tank, where the sand is higher, sprawling forward into the shallower sand. The fern works its way between rock crevasses, where it may be an inch (2 1/2 cm) or even less in height. The leaves are round and shiny with a convex shape.

WATER WISTERIA

Synnema triflorum

Although it is relatively new to most aquarists, wisteria is similar to water sprite, though not related.

It grows into a lush, bushlike plant, branching out from the main stem. Though it is not as long-lived as the swords or *Cryptocorynes,* it could be considered a semipermanent plant, needing trimming frequently. It roots readily from cuttings, prefers neutral-to-slightly-acid water and subdued light.

BUNCH PLANTS

Elodea, fanwort, ambulia, *Ludwigia*

These plants can be treated as one, for they have similar requirements. Sold in bunches as cuttings, they must be separated into single strands, trimmed of brown tissue and the lower leaves, and planted separately, though close together.

They all like strong light, ten to fourteen hours daily, and will disintegrate without it.

Cryptocoryne sp.

Like the swords, *cryptocoryne* (say *crip' toe core' een*) comes in a good variety of sizes, all of them fine for the aquarium. They tend to adjust their mature size to the tank size—very considerate of them.

They are planted and cared for like the swords, except they like the water a little more acid, around pH 6.8 or a little less. They make good companion plants to four-leaf clover.

They propagate, again like the swords, by runners, and soon form pretty clumps if they are happy. Oftimes, they'll even find their way down through stone cliff arrangements to appear below the parent plant, creating effects not possible any other way.

This plant does well in subdued light, but will grow in stronger light if algae is kept off the leaves. It should be planted with the crown exactly at the surface.

DUCKWEED

Lemna minor

Duckweed is a common plant found all over the United States floating on the surface of still ponds and lakes. It is composed of one to three tiny leaves, with a single root. The tiny plants form widespreading masses, often completely covering a pond.

Since it is seldom sold in shops, you may get a starter sample of it when it rides in with other pond-raised plants or gather it yourself; be sure to look it over for parasites.

Its only real value is as a food for fishes who love plants. Using it may save more treasured aquarium plants from damage, especially when goldfish are being kept.

CRYSTALWORT

Riccia

Riccia (say *rik' ki a*) is pretty, growing into roundish masses at the surface or just below the surface of ponds and lakes. It can be used like duckweed, and is a fine cover for tiny fishes.

Both plants need lots of light.

DWARF MADAGASCAR LILY

Nymphea sp.

Often sold in variety stores as an "underwater banana plant," the bunch of long fingerlike tubers is the seed body of a small-flowered water lily.

Plant it with the "bananas" half covered. Roots will form (hopefully: it's a bit touchy) and round, water-lily-type leaves begin to form on short stems. If it's happy, it makes a cluster of these leaves, which gradually grow longer stems, finally reaching the surface. It often stays in the leaf-cluster stage for months, which is pretty and interesting because of the strange "bananas."

4 Maintenance

A good general maintenance program should include a weekly or biweekly siphoning off the bottom of about 10 to 15 percent of the water, and replacement with water treated for chlorine, or aged water. This is water allowed to set in glass or plastic containers for several days while chlorine dissipates naturally. Any water added should be at the same temperature and of the same pH as that in the tank. This is called "topping off."

An indispensable tool is the hand-operated Squeeze-bulb Vac (Metaframe also makes a battery-operated version, Aqua-Vac). It is a long, rigid plastic tube device with a rubber bulb which, when squeezed, picks up gravel, swirls it around, sucks out sediment, and returns the water to the tank through a fabric bag, straining out the dirt. The idea here is to return the aged water to the aquarium, but I disagree with this premise; water at the bottom is loaded with undesirable substances dissolved in the water, yet heavy enough that they stay at lower depths. They should be removed entirely. This can be easily done by removing the cloth bag and inserting a length of flexible plastic filter tubing. Thus the water is carried out into a pail or, if conditions permit, out a nearby door or into the sink.

This device works so well that our largest tank, set up over ten years ago, has never needed to be dismantled for cleaning. A reminder: be sure to pick up and clean gravel all over the bottom, letting it fall back into place as it is rinsed clean.

A more modern gravel cleaner is on the market now, powered by the pump used with the tank setup, but I still prefer my own.

With each topping off, the filter—if it is not an under-gravel model—should be cleaned and the filtering medium changed. If the tank is sparsely populated and not overfed, the topping off and filter cleaning can be done only once or twice a month. Watch water clarity and filter: you'll soon learn how often to clean. *Clear water isn't always clean;* if it looks clear but has a yellow tinge, there is a high level of dissolved substances present, and you may suffer deaths in the tank.

Power filters with the pump mounted above or below, on the filter itself, will show a diminished flow when the medium is dirty. They just won't work at peak efficiency when they get too dirty, which is fine: it's time to clean. Don't let this chore slide.

The glass front and sides should be kept clean—wash the outside surfaces with water and a little white vinegar. Then polish with a dry cloth. Inside glass is scraped with a single-edge razor blade to remove algae and scum. There are other cleaning devices to be had, but a razor blade does the best job.

About every month, check the pH balance and correct it if necessary. A very inexpensive pH kit, which will last for years, can be bought at aquarium shops. Complete instructions come with each product. Any pH change should be accomplished very gradually—take a day or two to make even a slight change.

Keep all light tubes and bulbs clean. Fluorescent tubes diminish in efficiency after about a year. Replace them in eighteen months to two years if plants seem to be losing vigor, or if they look dimmer than they should.

If the hood isn't fitted with a glass or plastic protective plate over the light tube or bulbs, you should add one. Put a piece of glass on top of the tank under the hood to keep condensation off the electrical fittings and bulbs, and clean it frequently. Many of the newer tanks have special rails to hold the glass.

There just isn't much work involved in keeping a clean, healthy tank if these few chores are done faithfully.

5 Live Foods

The key to keeping certain kinds of fishes and having them spawn is live food. A few fishes refuse to live without it, many will subsist on dry and frozen foods without showing their best colors or alacrity, and only a few will produce more of their kind.

If you want to do right by your collection, make the feeding of some kinds of live food a part of your maintenance program. You will be lavishly rewarded with lively, brightly colored fishes, bent on showing you how beautiful and long-lived they can be.

The dear Lord has given mankind an endless supply of intriguing creatures to study. With your microscope or magnifying glass you will see beautiful, graceful creatures in infusorian cultures, or watch engaging little brine shrimp hatch and row themselves about on their backs. In freshwater ponds you can observe hair snakes, who don't really develop by spontaneous generation from horsetail hairs, they just look that way! You'll see algae cells or water bears (*Hysibius* sp.). Yes, they really do resemble teddy bears.

Collecting live foods gives us just one more reason to get out where all nature waits to entertain, bringing forth some new adventure or some new jewel of beauty for our inspection.

Something always turns up. We once found a darling little newly hatched soft-shell turtle (*Trionx ferox*). It was only about the size of a half-dollar, with a soft, flexible brown shell marked with dark polka dots. At home in the tank of domestics, he made it the first order of business to leave V-shaped notches in the tails of even the fastest-moving fishes. When returned to its stream, it thanked me by leaving a matching notch in my finger. Sometimes knowledge comes hard!

APHIDS

In early spring and summer, aphids—which are actually plant lice—gather in congested masses on the growing tips and buds of plants. They may be red, brown, black, or green. These naked-looking, soft-bodied little bugs are dearly loved by fish and terrarium inhabitants.

Gathering only in a garden where you are sure there is no insecticide present, pluck off the infested leaves, buds, or tips. Switch them in the aquarium water, or bend the plant parts into a container of water and rinse them off to be carried to the fish.

Look for aphids on any soft, new plant parts.

BRINE SHRIMP

It would be great if someone invented the perfect method for hatching and raising brine shrimp (Fig. 5-1) to adult size, for this live food is very important to the health of baby fish and sea horses. So far, all the systems we have tried present some problems: some of the eggs fail to hatch; when feeding the newly hatched shrimp to fish, we find that it is almost impossible to keep at least a few

Fig. 5-1   Dry brine shrimp eggs, when placed in a saltwater mixture, will hatch in about twenty-four hours.

Fig. 5-2 The cone-shaped hatching bag sold in many aquarium shops is excellent for hatching brine shrimp.

of the empty egg cases from getting into the aquarium. Actually, we have not been able to see that these egg cases have in any way hurt our fish, but when reading instructions on hatching and feeding shrimp, in other publications, we find dire warnings that these empty cases could clog gill openings, or something of the sort, so we try to avoid including them as we strain the shrimp.

We have experimented with many different kinds of hatching containers and will discuss the ones we think best. One of these is a plastic bag in the shape of a cone, sold at many aquarium shops (Fig. 5-2). These bags are made of heavy, clear plastic and one advantage of using them is that they hang on the wall out of the way.

Fill the bag with water, mix with artificial sea salt made especially for this purpose, sprinkle the dry shrimp eggs into it, and install an airstone. The best temperature for hatching is around 75°F. With good luck, the eggs should begin to hatch in about twenty-four hours. When you see a reddish fog in the water it's the baby shrimp.

The advantage of the cone-shaped container is that, when the airstone is removed, the shrimp will settle to the bottom and most of the empty egg cases

Fig. 5-3   A makeshift brine shrimp hatching container can be made by cutting the top from a water container.

will float on top, making it easier to siphon the shrimp into another container with a hose. Or if the cone is equipped with a hose at the bottom, as some of them are, just drain off as many shrimp as needed. For either method, the shrimp should then be strained through a small piece of fine cloth and added to the aquarium by simply rinsing the cloth in the aquairum. Then the hatching water can be returned to the cone and the airstone reactivated.

Almost as good a method is that of using quart, half-gallon, or gallon jars and following the same procedure, dropping an airstone into each jar to keep the water moving. It is a good idea to keep several jars going at once, in several stages of development. As the shrimp in one are used up, start another jar, so that there will be a constant source of food.

One hatching container we have used with fair success is a two-gallon plastic water container with the top cut out (Fig. 5-3). The advantage here lies in the fact that this container has a spigot near the bottom; after the eggs have hatched and the empty egg cases have floated to the top, the shrimp can be drawn off through the spigot. Strain them through a piece of cloth, as previously described, add them to the aquarium by rinsing the cloth in it, then return the strained water to the hatching tank.

Though newly hatched brine shrimp are needed for tiny baby fish and sea horses, adult brine shrimp are great food for adult dwarf sea horses and larger fish. To raise brine shrimp to adult size requires a different method than merely hatching them, for they must have algae for food.

It is then necessary to promote a growth of algae in the shrimp container by exposing it to sunlight. The more sunlight the better: for this reason, use a wide glass pan, such as a baking pan. Add the sea salt mixture—suggested proportions come with the dry shrimp eggs—place the pan in sunlight, allow algae to develop on the sides and bottom, then add the eggs. With this method an airstone is not needed, for wide exposure to air provides enough oxygen. This system can also be used to hatch and keep baby brine shrimp. When you are ready to collect either baby or adult shrimp for feeding, cover one end of the pan to darken it. The shrimp will go to the lighted end and can be collected with a suction hose or an oven baster.

If algae fails to develop in the pan, as is sometimes the case in winter when there is little sunshine, add some pieces of lettuce to promote its growth.

Brine shrimp are among the finest of all foods for most small and very young fishes. Even though raising them can be a bother, it is well worth the trouble to have healthy fish.

MOSQUITO LARVAE

Culex sp.

Bettas always come to mind when I think of mosquito larvae as a fish food, for they love it so—flooding with color after snapping up each one, seeming to flush with righteous satisfaction at having rid the world of one more mosquito.

Many fishes love larvae. It is a fine food for any fish with a large enough mouth, but has caused fishes with more ambition than sense to strangle.

Several precautions should be mentioned. *Culex* larvae are subject to a disease that looks like a fungus, causing sickness and even death in fishes, particularly their hereditary nemesis, the Betta. Look the larvae over: healthy ones are clean, smooth, and brownish; their movements are crisp, quick, and alert. Sicklings are white or very pale, swollen looking, slow moving, often showing a fluffy funguslike appearance about the head and body. Don't feed these to any fish if even a *small* percentage of them don't look right. *Throw them out.*

If your culture or collected larvae is accompanied by other insect larvae, look for any strong-jawed specimens and use them only if you are sure they are harmless.

Bloodworms, recognized by their red color and S-shaped swimming postures, are one type that I personally just don't trust. They often are capable of chewing up a fish even after being swallowed.

You can collect *Culex* larvae in any stagnant pool of water. Tin cans in the city dump are usually loaded if they are holding any water at all.

It's also easy to attract the adults to your own pail of water, there to lay their eggs in little black rafts the size and shape of a grain of rice.

To make the water more attractive to mosquitoes and to develop food for the larvae, crack an egg just slightly and place it in the water. The nutrients, slowly seeping out, gradually contribute to the welfare of the young. This doesn't offend the neighbor on the other side of the fence as much either. It's not terribly rotten smelling, but I wouldn't publicize my activities too much, all the same. Being declared a public nuisance would be embarrassing. Place the *Culex* nursery somewhere out of the wind and sun.

Soon the water surface will be crowded with larvae, hanging head down, their tail snorkels at the surface, for they are air breathers. They snap their bodies to the bottom at any disturbance or to feed, grazing the bottom like cows.

Net them out, rinse well, and watch your happy fishes gorge.

The larvae can be stored for weeks in a covered, well-marked container in the refrigerator. This slows their metamorphosis into adults.

DAPHNIA

Cladocera family

Daphnia may be found in quiet ponds, often in such numbers that one sweep of a large, deep, fine-meshed net may bring in as much as you have room to store. Don't overcrowd, or you'll have a nice Jambalayade Dead Daphnia. Add a big chunk of ice to the insulated foam container to make them last longer. You'll also be able to transport more this way.

Daphnia are often called the perfect live food, but since there is no perfect live food, this is a slight exaggeration. Certainly they are one of the better ones. As with any food, don't overdo, because the chitinous shell is laxative and too much might kill your fish.

You can find red, green, or brownish-gray ones forming a large cloud in the water. Live-food specialists like the red best, saying they are more nutritious. There are variations in form, but all resemble little round-bodied fleas.

Green water can be cleaned up by introducing a large serving of daphnia, after first removing the fish. Replace said fish as soon as the water has cleared. What a nifty surprise they encounter upon their return—a gourmet buffet!

Since daphnia consume oxygen, adding too many at once could cause your fish to be smothered; to repeat, overfeeding of any food, no matter how good, is not wise.

Water fleas (a very descriptive name) are most numerous in spring, in the kind of water you least like to wade in—near city dumps or below cattle-feeding pens—so plan to have a net with a nice long handle.

If you're not careful, parasites can ride in with daphnia, so always examine each feeding in a shallow white pan or bowl, and collar any suspicious-looking strangers.

It should be mentioned here that there is a likelihood of internal parasites and disease spores and virus occuring in any live foods, excepting brine shrimp, so the use of live food or raw fish involves a measure of risk. One friend, a fish pathologist, has told me he won't give any live food to his fish.

Again, we weigh the advantages and disadvantages, and come to our own decisions.

FRESHWATER SHRIMP

Gammarus sp.

Strongly resembling a sow-bug or pill-bug, *Gammarus* is a fine citizen, contributing its bit toward cleaning up organic matter that might otherwise foul the tank, protecting its own eggs and newly hatched young, and generally minding its own business. They swim backwards, on their backs.

Found in small, shallow areas of freshwater streams, they can be considered a good fish food, but my first and only attempt at using them left me with a guilty feeling. As the first shrimp fell through the water, young were dislodged from its brood-sac and the mother was frantically trying to regather her little ones as she sank. They were all eaten before they reached the bottom, but I remember returning the rest of the captive shrimp to their home stream.

Learning that they mate and stay together for long periods, perhaps for life, strengthened my sympathy. Lots of other foods are more easily available, anyway.

One hobbyist uses them, not as fish food, but as janitors in fry tanks. They are interesting to watch, swimming with nonchalant ease on their backs, mating, and working happily away on the bottom and sides of the tank.

FRUIT FLIES

Drosophila melanogaster

A wingless variety of fruit flies (including gnats, drunkards, and vinegar gnats) is available from research laboratory suppliers and live-food companies. The flies were developed from the winged variety as a convenience for the people who do research on genetics and the factors influencing growth.

Most of us have had enough casual experience with them to know what they like to eat—old tomatoes, overripe fruit of all kinds, bananas in particular.

These flies make a very good fish food but keep the container, a half-gallon or gallon (4 liter) wide-mouth jar, screened. Some individuals make monkeys of their trusting captors by developing wings.

They are easy to keep—whatever temperature suits you will do—but never allow sun to shine on the container. Start a new culture every week or so.

Collect and feed with a dampened finger or net.

INFUSORIA

Infusoria is the first food of the smaller types of newly hatched egglayers. Consisting of one-celled plant and animal life, it occurs naturally in any body of water, including aquariums, but not usually in sufficient numbers to nourish a spawn of young fish.

It can be cultured very easily by using a half-gallon (2 liters) or so of aquarium water, adding crushed dried lettuce, dried aquarium plants, egg yolk which has been cooked, dried, and powdered, or infusoria tablets bought at the aquarium store. Kept in bright light at a temperature of 74°–85°F (23°–30°C), it will become cloudy gray in a couple of days, and will be usable as long as it does not begin to smell rotten.

It is fed to newly hatched fishes as soon as they begin to swim and look for food. Adding it before this time is unnecessary and could foul the water.

You will be able to detect dust-fine moving specks, usually some type of protozoa. But most of the creatures can be seen only with a good hand lens or a low-power microscope. Beware! It's easy to lose hours just watching and categorizing all the fascinating lifeforms gliding through the water, staggering to think a whole world of life is to be found in a single drop of water!

MEALWORMS

Tenebrio sp.

Mealworms are larvae of the black beetle (*Tenebrio molitor* or *T. obscuris*). For larger fishes, salamanders, newts, frogs and turtles, mealworms are good, clean, easy-to-raise food. Just keep them in a half empty oatmeal box, where they will have a wonderful time.

They feed constantly at temperatures of 50°–100°F; one can place an ear to the box and hear the munching going on in a steady, tiny rumble.

To supply moisture, add an occasional slice of apple. When it's dry, replace with a fresh one.

Mealworms retain their form for several months, then pupate and become black beetles. With little encouragement the beetles lay eggs which become baby mealworms, and so on and on. They will not migrate to other pantry cereals as long as their oatmeal supply is adequate.

WHITE WORMS

Enchytraeus albidus
Dendrobaena subrubicunda

Of the many kinds of white worms, there is only one that is hardy enough to be kept by hobbyists—*Enchytraeus albidus. Dendrobaena subrubicunda* has a habit of appearing in red worm (earthworm) cultures, thriving for a short time, then disappearing. For this reason they can't be relied upon; the main reason for including them here is so that you will know, if your white worm culture suddenly goes out of business, there's a strong chance you didn't have the proper species in the first place.

E. albidus will produce a good steady population if kept in a wooden box (about 6 inches [15 cm] deep, 18 by 12 inches [45 by 30 cm] wide) of compost soil with a glass cover resting directly on the soil. Keep damp, but not soggy, at 40°–65°F (5°–16°C), feeding every few days with bread soaked in milk, cooked oatmeal, or Pablum. Never use anything with salt, sugar, or pepper in it. The small amount of salt and sugar in bread is harmless, but salted crackers, for instance, would not be good. Scrape out a shallow trench, place the food and worm culture in, then cover over with a very little soil (maybe a quarter of an inch). A little experimenting will show you how much and how often to feed.

To use the worms, lift back the food and take out a few clusters of worms. Either rinse in a cup of water or lay them on a paper in strong light. When they leave the soil and gather in a tight, clean ball, drop them to the fish. Most fish love them, but don't feed white worms more than three times a week—they are very rich, so alternate with other live and dry foods.

Occasionally little roundish insects will move in with the worms, but they will do no harm and are also good fish food.

6 Saltwater Creatures

FISHES ●

ANEMONEFISH

Tomato Clown: *Amphiprion ephiprion*
Maroon Clown: *A. sebae*

Of all the marine fishes, with the exception of the sea horse, the little clown-fish are our favorites. I expect this is due primarily to the remarkable relationship they have to their pals, the sea anemones (color Fig. 15). Here exists a close partnership in which the fish feed and groom the anemones, and the anemones, which are poisonous to most fish, protect their little friends from predators.

Some scientists try to explain away this phenomenon as accidental, rationalizing that there is no purpose behind the actions of these creatures. We have watched them too often to accept this, for the dedication displayed between them is far too apparent in all their actions to be coincidental.

There is not the slightest doubt in our minds that the fish *do* purposely feed the anemones. Scientists will tell us that the fish is hiding the food for later use, but this does not stand to reason, for eventually the fish would learn that the food disappears and they can never recover it.

We have watched this act with awe. In an aquarium in which there were four large, beautiful flowerlike anemones, four pieces of fish were dropped to the sand. Immediately the fish grabbed up the pieces and carried them to the anemones, carefully placing them into the maw of each, then "standing back" to watch and see that the anemone did not reject the food. When one piece was pushed out by the anemone, the fish would pick it up and carry it to another, repeating the process until the food was retained.

The fish are then repaid for this devotion. They use the anemone for protection from their enemies. When threatened by a large fish predator, the clown-fish will excitedly rush to its anemone friend and snuggle down among the tentacles that are deadly to other fishes. This happened often as we were photographing anemonefish. The flash of our strobe would send them frantically burrowing into their friends' protective tentacles.

There are several kinds of clownfish, ranging in color from pale yellow, brown, and maroon, to scarlet. Most have bands of black and white. These are found primarily in the waters of Africa and the East Indies. These fish are egg-layers. Several people have reported successfully spawning them, but as far as we can determine, there is no record of these babies having been raised to adulthood.

We can highly recommend anemonefish for aquariums—with the inclusion of sea anemones. However, it would be best to have only these two kinds of creatures in the tank.

The anemones will eat pieces of cut fish and shrimp and even small balls of ground meat. The anemonefish are also easy to keep, eating smaller pieces of the same foods.

SALTWATER ANGELFISH

Queen Angelfish: *Angelichthys ciliaris*
Blue Angelfish: *A. isabelita*

Among saltwater angelfish, two of the most beautiful are the queen angel and the blue angel. Many fish change color, and even shape, during the various stages of their lives and this is certainly true of the angelfish. For example, the young of the queen angel and the blue angel are so much alike that identification cannot always be certain. However, as they grow older, the distinguishing spot or "crown" on the head of the queen angelfish appears (color Figs. 2 and 5).

The queen angel is known to be a rather querulous sort of character when placed in a tank with other fish, even of its own species. Considering this fact, it might be well to pause for thought before purchasing one for a community tank. However, there are exceptions to every rule and this certainly holds true with live creatures; though there are apparent characteristics in the different species of fishes, there often occurs that rare one who is an individualist. So occasionally you may be fortunate enough to find a queen angelfish who is agreeable to togetherness. It is a matter of trial and error.

Captured when adult, these two fish—though beautiful and highly desirable for their lovely colors—would be too large (1 1/2–2 feet) for the average home aquarium. But if aquired while young, they will grow slowly.

The color of these fish varies greatly during growth, but is generally bright blue with shades of brilliant yellow. A black spot on the forehead, usually surrounded by a ring of blue, identifies the queen, who might otherwise be mistaken for a blue angel whose colors, though similar, are not as bright.

Fig. 6-1   Blenny (*C. saburrae*) in his shell home.

Although pugnacious in defending their territory, these fish do well in captivity and seem to become attached to those who care for them.

The queen and blue angels are not the only saltwater angelfish adaptable to aquarium life: there are many others, ranging in size from 3 inches (7 1/2cm) to about 2 feet (60cm).

All angels do well when fed live brine shrimp but can become accustomed to white worms, small earthworms, and frozen shrimp. Natural foods include crabs, barnacles, and other invertebrates.

BLENNY

Florida Blenny: *Chasmodes saburrae*
Sailfin Blenny: *Emblemaria pandionis*

Blennies are small, predatory fish identified by their fins, which stretch from the head to the tail in an unbroken fan. The colors are generally splotched shades of gray, but a few may have touches of red, yellow, and blue.

Blennies in southern waters are seldom over 3 inches long. They can be found in tidal pools, hiding under rocks, or in old empty shells in saltwater bays (Fig. 6-1).

A blenny makes an excellent aquarium pet and, when given a den of some sort, will establish a monarchy in the best king-of-the-castle tradition, guarding it viciously from all comers.

Last winter we scooped up a large, empty horse conch shell in a dip net and brought it home, primarily to observe the live barnacles encrusted all over the exterior, only to find after placing it in the aquarium that it was the abode of a little blenny. The fish would lie in his doorway peering out, dashing forth only to gulp up food. But in a very short time it was so tame it would eat from our fingers, lying in wait in the entrance of the shell, giving eager little wriggles as our fingers with the bits of food entered the water, then rather daintily nipping off the bite.

We think every salt-water aquarium should have a resident blenny. Acquiring one should be easy for anyone who has access to a saltwater bay, for almost every large shell that we have taken from the shallows this year has been the home of either a blenny or a toadfish. And do bring along the little guy's home.

BOXFISH

Burrfish: *Chilomycterus schoepfi*
Spiny Boxfish: *C. antennatus*
Web Burrfish: *C. antillarum*

The burrfish or boxfish, which is closely related to the puffer, is a serene though stickery character who can be found in the shallow bays of most tropical seas (color Fig. 6). It is so slow-moving that it provides great sport for scuba or skin-diving photographers, watching the diver interestedly and only moving a short distance away. In fact, several times we have scooped these fish up in our small dip nets while floating the grass flats in our canoe in the Pine Island Sound area. Because of the large size (10–12 inches long), we kept these fish in an aquarium by themselves and released them in a few days; so we cannot report from experience on their adaptability to community tanks. We hope to obtain a small 3–4 inch (7 1/2–10cm) specimen and study its reaction to multiple dwelling.

The boxy, burr-covered, light-colored body of the *C. schoepfi* has swirling, wavelike fine stripes of dark blue and yellow. The most beautiful markings are the round, yellow-circled black spots on the back and lower pectoral fins. The eyes, as in all boxfish and puffers, are a lovely glowing bluegreen.

The *antennatus* has a reddish-pink body dotted with black. The fins and tail are a delicate bluegreen, as are the eyes.

The web burrfish, *antillarum,* has spots that strongly resemble armor plate.

These fish, like most saltwater, bottom-dwelling fishes, will eat almost any kind of bait food. Living in its natural habitat on small shrimp, it uses its powerful teeth to crush the rather thin casings of the tubeworms to get at the meat.

Like the puffer, the burrfish can blow himself up into a fat ball when aroused. You will often find these puffed up, dried carcasses in shops, even made into lamps.

BUTTERFLY FISH

Copperband: *Chelmon rostratus*
Common Butterfly: *Chaetodon ocellatus*
Four-eye: *Chaetodon capistratus*

Like the angelfish, the multicolored butterfly fish, which grows to about 6 inches (over 15 1/2cm), is found in the Western Atlantic tropics (West Indies, Panama, Bermuda, Hawaii, Florida Keys). It is not an easy fish to capture, and not inexpensive to purchase, thus making it quite a prize for the aquarium (color Figs. 7 and 14). Since coral reefs are the habitat of this fish, a scuba or skin diver who has access to such a reef is in luck and may, with patience and persistence, manage to collect one.

We have viewed with longing the many bright and beautiful fishes when floating over reefs of the Pennycamp Underseas Gardens in the Florida keys. Glass-bottomed boats or our Aquascope reveal the coral gardens in all their miraculous beauty, and the many gorgeous fishes make them a living rainbow.

Alas, at this park the fish, as well as the coral, are protected and collecting is prohibited. This is good, of course; before the prohibition was put into effect, commercial dealers and casual collectors had almost demolished the lovely coral—even blasting it to obtain the great growths—and several species of fishes were rapidly being wiped out in the process.

There are many kinds of butterfly fish, all of them beautiful. Our favorite is the copperband butterfly, with its silvery-white and brilliant yellow-orange stripes. It can be identified both by its color and by its long nose and black eye-like spot on the upper part of its body near the rear fin. *Chelmon rostratus* is one of the long-nosed butterfly fish and, in our opinion, one of the most beautiful of them all.

The mouths of all butterflys are quite small and they should be offered tiny bits of food: fresh shrimp, cut fish, and small glass shrimp. When they are first captured, they may require live food, for this is their natural diet. Live adult brine shrimp will fill the bill and they will become gradually accustomed to taking other foods.

CLINGFISH

Gobiesocidae

The only Latin name we could find for the clingfish is the family name, *Gobiesocidae*. We are certain there must be several species, but no matter: if we found a longer name than that, it would overpower the one little clingfish we have owned, who was only about an inch long (2 1/2cm) and so flat it looked like an integral part of whatever it was clinging to.

Our fish was a baby, but since clingfish are relatives of the little blenny, they are quite small as adults, with a 6-inch (15 1/2cm) fish considered a monster. Because of their small size and because they are inoffensive little critters, these fish can be included nicely in the aquarium.

They are, as the name implies, clingers. A sucking disk on the underside makes it possible for them to cling to most anything—the glass of the aquarium, a shell, a plant, your finger. We decided our little clinger, Stickums, was a night-feeder, for it seldom moved about during the day.

Although generally of blotchy shades of light to very dark grays, some species of clingfish have touches of green, blue, and yellow, especially on the under-side—which is usually what you see as they cling to the aquarium glass. Little Stickums had a delicate pink belly, but since he was only a baby, this may have been due to juvenile coloring.

These fish, like their relatives the blennies, will eat most any kind of cut fish or shrimp. We decided that Stickums must eat the algae that had collected on aquarium rocks.

Clingfish are, of course, bottom dwellers and can often be captured in a fine-meshed dip net or seine among grasses. Or they may be found clinging to shells or rocks, though they are difficult to see because of their flat bodies and small size.

Since we found so little information in our research on this fish, we are not at all certain of the extent of their habitat, but can only say that we have found them in shallow waters of the Gulf of Mexico.

COWFISH

Lactophrys quadricornis
L. cornutus

The colorful little cowfish, like the sea horse, wears its skeleton on the out-side. Or to be more exact, it has a boxy shell that is made up of six-sided plates, fitted together like mosaic; the fins and tail emerge from holes in this shell like the rudder and oars of a boat.

The cowfish is found in the tropical Atlantic from the Carolinas to Brazil. If one is occasionally found north of its usual habitat, it is thought to be due to its slow, sluggish movements which allow it to be carried by the swift-moving Gulf Stream.

A comical-looking little fish is the cowfish, with its humped back, tucked-in face, and bony "eyebrows" that remind one of a cow's horns. It makes a docile and interesting pet for the saltwater aquarium. However, we have read that some cowfish exude a poison that affects other fish, and even themselves, when in a closed system like that of the aquarium. We cannot state this for a fact, for we had no trouble with the cowfish we kept in our community tank, but perhaps that was due to the fact that the only one we had for any length of time was quite small.

Colors of the different species of cowfish vary. The *quadricornis* generally has a light body with pastel shades of blue, yellow, and green in broken stripes. The *cornutus* is a pinkish red, with blue dots scattered indiscriminately over it. The young may vary even more in coloring, often with more brilliant hues.

The mouths of these fish are quite small and this should be taken into consideration when preparing food for them. Since they are partly herbivorous, it is wise to occasionally cut up tiny bits of lettuce or spinach for them, as well as experimenting with other types of the usual aquarium foods, to find out what an individual cowfish will accept.

Fig. 6-2   Cowfish: *Lactophrys quadricornis*. Its bony "eyebrows" resemble a cow's horns.

DACYLLUS

Three-spot: *D. trimaculatus*
Three-stripe: *D. aruanus*

The little *Dacyllus* with their unusual shapes and markings should, by all means, be included in the marine aquarium. Both *trimaculatus* and *aruanus* have round, flattened bodies and large fans of fins. Both are great little fellows for the home aquarium since they seldom reach a length of more than 3 inches (7 1/2cm).

As a general rule, these are not difficult fish to feed. They will eat dry food, frozen brine shrimp, and bits of fish. Since they enjoy playing hide and seek, it is a good idea to include shells, coral, rocks, or artificial plants in their abode.

The three-spot is unusual among fishes, in that it has a very dark, almost black, body with a gleaming white spot on its back near the head, and another on each side.

The three-stripe has the same short body, but its marking are made up of vertical silver and black bars.

Dacyllus of one species or another can be found over coral reefs, particularly in tropical Indo-Pacific waters, the Red Sea, and even in Australia.

FLOUNDER

Starry: *Paralichthys stellatus*
Peacock: *Bothus lunatus*

There are several species of flounder and flatfish: all seem to do well in captivity, though some of them may grow too large to house comfortably in a small aquarium. We have often dipped up small, 1–2 inch (2 1/2–5cm) flounder in our nets while floating in the grass flats of saltwater bays and installed them in an aquarium for observation. And we have also caught fairly small flounder on hook and line, while fishing in the Pacific Ocean with live bait or pieces of shrimp.

One problem with the inclusion of these flat little fish in the aquarium is their shyness. Our little spotted flounder, Polka Dots, would disappear for days at a time and then reappear, furiously ruffling himself along the bottom of the tank, chasing fairy shrimp. Such tendencies to hide make the flounder not particularly desirable for the aquarium. Polka Dots caused no community problems, however, and it was always a happy surprise when he did come flouncing forth.

The main interest offered by the flounder is his unusual figure. Here is a fish who swims on his side and, as he grows older, one eye moves over with the other, so that both are on one side of his head. In spite of the fact that you won't see him very often, perhaps his odd looks will make him enough of a rarity to merit his inclusion. He eats most anything other bottom dwellers eat.

Most types of flounder are not particularly colorful, but do have interesting markings—especially the peacock flounder. This fish, abundant in the Pacific from California to Alaska and west to Asia, has a pattern of scattered circles, very much like that of the tail of the peacock.

Flounder will do nicely on worms of all kinds and shrimp. Since its food in the wilds includes several kinds of crustaceans, these should be included if it is possible to obtain them.

GOBY

Saltwater Neon Goby: *Elacatinus oceanops*

The goby is a versatile little coral fish, adaptable to both salt and freshwater as well as the in-between, brackish type.

The neon goby has, as its name implies, a strikingly bright blue stripe running horizontally along its side: it seems to light up with neon brillance as the light catches it. This stripe is even more highly accentuated by the black stripes that run parallel to it on each side.

The range of this goby is the Hawaiian and Easter Islands; they are found also along the Florida coast. It is an egglayer and will sometimes breed in captivity if a compatible pair can be matched up, though it is difficult to raise the fry. The main trouble seems to be that, due to their tiny size, the babies must feed on microscopic food—at least at first—and this is not so easy to supply. This microscopic animal life may be present if there is algae in the tank. Then, as the babies grow larger, they should be given newly hatched brine shrimp.

We have read that although these little fish get along well in a community tank, it is best to have only a compatible pair of them, for a third often promotes trouble. However, we have seen whole schools of neon gobies swimming happily together, their lights flashing like the exploding darts of sparklers, so we suspect that, like many species of fish, there are exceptions to the rule.

If these fish are to be adapted from saltwater to fresh, or vice versa, it should be done by gradual conversion through a brackish state.

GRUNT

Porkfish: *Anisotremus virginicus*
Bluestripe Grunt: *Haemulon scirurus*

The porkfish is a colorful fish of the grunt family which ranges from the West Indies to Florida. There is very little to identify the porkfish in relation to its shape, except that its forehead is rather humped and the mouth set low. But with its fine, bright, yellow and blue horizontal stripes and the wider black and yellow bars which run on a diagonal across the eye and behind the gills, it can usually be identified without too much trouble (Fig. 6-3). As you can imagine,

Fig. 6-3   Striped grunt and sergeant major (*Abudefduf marginatus*).

its coloring makes it an attractive addition to the home aquarium. Add to this the fact that the porkfish can often be caught on line and hook, and that it adapts nicely to confinement, and you have a desirable sort of fish.

This fish will attain a weight of 1–2 pounds (1/2–1 kg) but can be kept small when captured as a youngster. It is a night-feeder, so it will lie quietly during most of the day but will not necessarily hide as many night-feeders do.

The porkfish will do well on most types of saltwater aquarium foods but prefers shrimp and small fishes.

The bluestripe grunt is another fish that has bright blue and yellow stripes running the length of its body. The body, which attains a greater length than that of the porkfish, is also slimmer. Its top fins, extending in an unbroken line along its back, and its tail are black. Unlike the porkfish, the mouth is quite large, making it possible for it to take larger pieces of food. This fish too is found in Florida and the West Indies.

JAWFISH

Yellowhead: *Opistognathus aurifrons*
Pacific Jawfish: *O. rhomaleus*

Jawfish are remarkable in that they seem to have the odd habit of standing erect on their tails—when they are not lurking, with just their heads out, in holes in the sand.

The many species of jawfish display diverse characteristics. All dig burrows, but some species—when disturbed while out of their burrows—will dash in headfirst while others will back in tail first. One thing they all have in common is that the male incubates the eggs in his mouth: it is a strange sight to see one of the fish lying with its head out of its hole, partly opened mouth full of large, pearly eggs. We have watched their antics with amazement. How do the fish manage to eat during the incubation time? We do know that they will lay the eggs down on the sand in order to burrow out of their hole when it has become partly filled with sand, then take up the eggs again, so perhaps they do this when feeding; or it is possible that they, like the toadfish, do not eat at all during this period.

We have never owned one of these fish and cannot draw on personal experience, but we have been told by several people who have experimented with them that they never had a successful hatching of eggs, though the father seemed devoted to the care of his potential offspring.

The yellowhead jawfish has a long, slender body of pearly white with a creamy yellow head and has fins extending almost the length of its body to the rounded tail.

The Pacific species is spotted with a thicker body and larger head. It, too, has fins the entire length of its body, but much larger, the most distinctive identification mark being a large black spot, among the smaller polka dots of the fin, near the head.

The natural food of this fish includes zoo plankton. If it is possible, feed it tiny live food, but try to adapt it to other food by feeding small bits of cut fish, shrimp, and frozen brine shrimp.

LIONFISH

Large Zebra: *Peterois antennata*
Small Zebra: *P. Volitans*

There are many species of lionfish occurring along the Atlantic coast and in the Indo Pacific. The two shown in Figures 6-4 and 6-5, which run from 5–12 inches (13–30 cm) long are some of the most attractive for aquariums (color Figs. 10 and 18). But when dealing with lionfish—also called scorpionfish—remember that the spines of the beautiful creatures are deadly poisonous, not only to other fish but to humans as well! The presence of lionfish, stingrays, moray eels, and some of the sea urchins is reason enough why wading in marine waters, or thrusting your hands into holes in the rocks, can be tricky business: all of these can inflict serious wounds. It stands to reason that none of these should be included in aquariums within reach of children, and any adult who takes care of the aquarium should be warned of the dangers when these are present.

With precautions taken, lionfish, with their brilliant, plumed beauty, make excellent aquarium pets. However, make it a point not to include small fishes, for even those able to avoid the poisonous spines will disappear into the big mouths of the lionfish. These fish prefer live food but will get along nicely on shredded or chopped shrimp and frozen adult brine shrimp. Most lionfish are live-bearers but we have not heard of them giving birth in captivity. Here is an experiment that might prove rewarding. Just imagine an aquarium full of baby lionfish!

This is a regular peacock of a fish who displays his magnificent featherlike fins like a real egotist, changing to a wide variety of colors according to his changes of moods. At one time he will appear almost white, at another he will be suffused with a half dozen brilliant colors. A strikingly beautiful fish!

MOORISH IDOL

Zanclus canescens
Z. heniochus

This is a great little fish for the aquarium since it seldom exceeds 8 inches (20 1/2 cm) in length. When captured small, like most other fishes, it can be kept small. Like the butterfly fish, it is a reef fish and not easy for the collector to come by, since not all of us have the opportunity to dive over coral reefs. It occurs mostly in the Indo Pacific. Its scarcity, as well as its beauty, makes the Moorish idol a much desired, though rather expensive, fish.

This fish looks very much like the freshwater angelfish, except that its mouth, which is quite small, protrudes in a pout; and there is a horn above the eye rather like that of the cowfish. The body color is yellow, with two dark bands, one running from the forepart of the very long dorsal fin along the body and through the eye, and the other stripe beginning at the rear of the dorsal and ending at the anal fin. The tail is partly black but bordered by yellow. There are also stripes of blue running close to the dark ones.

An extremely attractive fish is the Moorish idol and a great addition to the aquarium. It gets along well with the other fish, as a general rule, but sometimes suffers attacks by them on its long, tempting dorsal fin, which is often so long that it extends beyond the body.

Feed this fish very small pieces of shrimp, bits of lean beef, and adult brine shrimp. Also encourage algae to grow in the aquarium and if it is not present, add bits of lettuce.

Fig. 6-4   Lionfish: *P. antennata*.

Fig. 6-5   Lionfish: *P. volitans*.

Pipefish

Northern Pipefish: *Syngnathus fucus*
Gulf Pipefish: *S. scovelli*

The pipefish, an elongated relative of the sea horse, is so like this animal—with its horselike head and armor-plated body—that instructions as to capturing, keeping, and feeding the sea horse can be followed for the pipefish (see Fig. 6–19).

The northern pipefish is found in waters from Nova Scotia south almost to Florida. The Gulf version, which is generally smaller, inhabits all the grass flats and estuaries of the Gulf of Mexico and is easily captured by dragging a seine or dip net among the grasses.

Sea horses and pipefish get along well together in a tank. The pipefishes, lacking the prehensile tails of their relatives, perch among the branches of the sea horse tree like long, straight sticks. The only problem with keeping these two kinds of animals together is that the pipefish move with more speed and can easily outdistance the slower sea horse in the dash for grub, gobbling it up while the sea horse is still myopically zeroing in on the quarry.

It has been our experience that pipefish, like sea horses, must be fed live food—preferably small grass shrimp or glass shrimp if the animal is a large one, or adult brine shrimp if it is the smaller species or a baby. Like the sea horse, it is the male of these creatures who carrys the eggs in a brood pouch, giving "birth" to the youngsters when they have developed to free-swimmers.

SALTWATER PERCH

Sand Perch: *Diplectrum formosum*

We are thoroughly confused about the name of this fish, for we have heard the same critter called by four or five different titles, and will probably get some static from readers on our classification. Nevertheless, we are going to stick to our guns, for the natives where we occasionally catch the fish call them by this name and that's good enough for us—they have to be called *something!*

This is a pretty little fish, and when captured small will be a good aquarium resident (Fig. 6-6). It is a long, rather slender fish with a rounded body very much like the wrasse, but with a shallow notch in its tail. Stripes, running horizontally along the light-colored body, vary through blue, reddish brown, and even green and yellow.

This fish is a hearty eater and will scoop up large quantities of whatever kind of food is dropped into its tank. It can be found in most temperate and tropical waters, and will bite on small bits of shrimp on small hooks. If the fish is not injured by the hook—we have found that it seldom is—this seems to be the best way to capture it.

Fig. 6-6   Sand perch: *Diplectrum formosum.*

PUFFER

Northern Puffer: *Spheroides maculatus*
Southern Puffer: *S. spengleri*

This odd little fish—most are from 3–5 inches (7 1/2–13cm) long—has unique protection from his enemies: the simple process of puffing himself up with air or water to a size so large that the predator can't swallow him (Fig. 6-7).

The puffer has one special beauty feature that, in addition to this strange characteristic, makes him a good acquisition for the aquarium: his eyes, which are the iridescent pinks, blues, and greens of precious opals. Body colors vary with the species. The northern puffer has a cream and green speckled body, shading to white on the belly. The southern puffer is generally the same color, but with less definite markings. The body is round, with a head that tapers to a snoutlike nose.

This fish is a voracious eater, usually feeding on crustaceons and mollusks, but it will eat almost any kind of bait fish if it is small enough, as well as cut shrimp, fish, and live shrimp. In fact, it was his appetite that managed to get our little puffer, Voracious, banished from the aquarium back to the bay where we had found him.

Fig. 6-7   Puffer: *Spheroides spengleri.*

Voracious was quite small when we captured him in a hand net among the grasses, and we were pleased to find that he got along beautifully with the other fishes in the community aquarium. The only problem was that with his speed he was able to scoop up large numbers of brine shrimp before the slow-moving sea horses could get them.

But then came disillusionment. The puffer grew quickly and when he was about 1 1/2 inches long, we began missing baby sea horses. We were puzzled until old Voracious was caught in the dastardly deed of gulping down one of the tiny horses. In one swoop I snatched him up, rescued the little sea horse, and immediately pronounced sentence on the criminal—banishment!

The best plan when including puffers, as well as other predators in the community tank, is to make sure to have only fish of similar size.

REMORA

Remora *remora*

We once had a remora for a pet and found it quite easy to keep—for the short time we had it. The fish had been attached to a large redfish Ray caught while fishing among the Gulf islands. As he drew the red into the canoe, the strange

Fig. 1   Spadefish: *Chaetodipterus faber*. This handsome group cruises through its coral forest.

Fig. 2   The Townsend or queen angels are some of the most brilliantly colored of fishes.

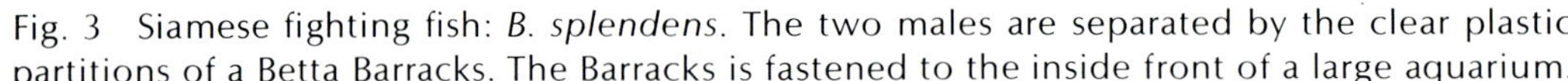

Fig. 3   Siamese fighting fish: *B. splendens*. The two males are separated by the clear plastic partitions of a Betta Barracks. The Barracks is fastened to the inside front of a large aquarium.

Fig. 4   This prize-winning goldfish pair caress and kiss one another most of the time.

Fig. 5   A blue angelfish and sergeant major share this aquarium.

Fig. 6 Burrfish: *Chilomycterus schoepfi*. This fish always cruises slowly along the bottom of the shallows and is easily captured.

Fig. 7 Long-nosed copperband butterfly fish: *C. rostratus*. This is one of the loveliest of the reef fishes.

Fig. 8   The brilliant ribbon eel is an interesting addition to the aquarium.

Fig. 9   Achilles tang: *A. achilles*. With its near-black and scarlet coloring, this surgeonfish is a showy pet for the aquarium.

Fig. 10   Large lionfish: *P. antennata*. Looking like a gorgeous butterfly, he nevertheless sports barbs that are deadly to humans and other fishes.

Fig. 11   Citation, the giant sea horse who gave birth to 500 babies.

Fig. 12 Royal Gramma: *G. loreto*. A startingly unique fish, its front half is a deep rose-mauve, shading to the rear through blue to yellow.

Fig. 13 A large, brightly colored hermit crab in his mobile home, a whelk shell.

Fig. 14   Butterfly fish: *C. ocellatus*. A little jewel of a fish.

Fig. 15   A contented group of clownfish: *A. ephiprion*. These anemonefish are never far from their friends, the anemones. The fish enjoy wallowing among the tentacles even when no danger threatens.

Fig. 16   Angelfish: *P. scalare*. This is one of Darlene's beloved old angelfish. There are pretty four-leaf clover plants in the background.

Fig. 17   Green moray eel; the morays look more menacing than they really are because they must keep their mouths open to breathe.

Fig. 18   Dwarf scorpion fish or lionfish: *Pelerous volitans*. Very alert and responsive, they spread their fins and rush to the front of the tank at the sound and sight of a set of keys, jangled to get their attention.

little fish dropped from it. Wanting to study it more closely, we plopped it into a bucket of water with an aerator and took it home to install in the aquarium. Knowing the remoras like bits of fresh fish, we kept some frozen and fed it cut pieces, and it seemed to do quite well on them.

Though these fish are called shark suckers or shark remoras because of the suction pad on top of their heads, they are not parasites at all. They use the suction merely as a means of clinging onto the underside of a larger fish, riding along in order to be present when the big predator makes a kill, at which time the remora hops off and scoops up the leftovers.

Also, remoras do not necessarily relegate their attentions to sharks alone, but will hitch rides impartially on almost any large fish, and even on skin divers. Our remora, lacking a host fish on whom to hitch a ride, used as a substitute the aquarium walls, the aerator tube, and even our hands when we cleaned the aquarium.

These fish are found in most warm seas but it is not easy to capture one except as we did, by bringing in one that has attached itself to a larger fish.

We only kept our remora a short time, for it was over 10 inches (25 1/2cm) long and we felt that the small aquarium we had at the time did not provide sufficient room for it to move about freely. We have read that the fish can attain a length of about 3 feet (90cm). However, we believe that a small remora, though not a showy color, being a shiny blue-gray, would make an amusing and unusual acquisition for an aquarium, and we will be on the lookout for one as we fish.

One good way to obtain one of these fish, as well as many others such as sea horses, is to contact commercial netters. They are certain to bring in large numbers in their nets and might be willing to save the specimen fish in a bucket of water. We have obtained several prizes this way.

ROYAL GRAMMA

Gramma loreto

This beautifully colored 4-inch-long (10cm) fish should certainly be included in the aquarium, for it is one of the most brilliantly hued of all. The long, slender body shades from purple at the front through rose to yellow at the tail; there is usually a black streak running on the diagonal from the eye to a spot of the same color on the fore part of the upper fin (color Fig. 12).

This prize of the aquarium fish world can sometimes be found hiding under rocks and ledges in Bermuda, Bahama, and Venezuelan waters. It will take live food, especially adult brine shrimp and small fish; with patience, it might be persuaded to eat some frozen shrimp. Like the jawfish, it has the odd characteristic of hanging head up in the water, when it is not hiding in holes in the rocks.

SAILOR'S CHOICE

Haemulon parrae

This small fish with its fine blue and yellow stripes, and others of the same family which are found in most of the warm seas, will adapt nicely to aquarium life. But again, as with all fast-moving predatory fishes, they should not be included in the same aquarium with slower-moving creatures such as sea horses. Because of their speed, they'll scoop up all the food before more deliberate creatures can move in. Also watch out for the relative sizes of any community tank fish inhabitants, for one of your favorite small fish may become merely a juicy bite for a hungry sailor's choice.

This fish, when captured small, will remain a good size for most aquariums and can be fed the usual aquarium food. Like most marine fishes it prefers live food, such as live glass or grass shrimp, but will also eat cut pieces of frozen shrimp and fish.

One way we have found to obtain these fish is simply with hook and line. A small hook baited with a bit of worm or shrimp will often do the job; if the fish is carefully removed it will usually not be injured. It is wise to wet your hands before removing it in order not to rub off the slime that is so necessary to the fish for protection against diseases and parasites.

SEA ROBIN

Prionotus carolinus
P. tribulus

This fish, with its winglike pectoral fins and crawdad-like "feet" is quite an addition to the aquarium, especially if one could be so lucky as to obtain a southern sea robin, with its brilliant rainbow colors. Like the toadfish, he is a bottom dweller and will be found lying on the sand, often hiding under clumps of grass or among rocks. The largest of the species may reach 3 feet in length and sea robins of one kind or another can be found all along the American Atlantic coastal waters and in the Gulf.

This fish is easy to keep as it will eat most any of the usual aquarium foods, such as cut fish or shrimp, live shrimp, and worms.

Our first view of a sea robin was quite a startling experience. We had anchored our canoe in an inlet in Florida's Pine Island Sound and were fishing the 6–8 foot holes, when I caught the remarkable fish. It was about a foot long and as I brought it in, it fell off the hook and into the bottom of the canoe. Instead of flopping around, as any self-respecting fish should do, it raised itself up on its front feet (flipperlike fins) and began walking toward me, clacking its mouth in loud smacks. Its scaled body flashed half a dozen bright colors and patterns.

Curious to know who on earth the critter was, we installed it in a bucket of water and, stopping the first commercial fisherman who happened near, asked him if he could identify it for us.

"I've fished these waters, man and boy, for fifty years," he told us. "And I ain't never seen *nothin'* like that thing before!"

We later identified it from books as a southern sea robin, but this species is surely not plentiful. Our subsequent experiences have been comparable to that of the commercial fisherman—we have never seen another sea robin of this kind. We were not even able to find its Latin name, and have wished since that we had taken pictures of it to show to some of our fish biologist friends for more accurate identification.

SERGEANT MAJOR

Abudefduf saxatilis
A. marginatus

These coral reef fish, which usually do not attain a length of more than 8 inches, are found in the coral waters of Florida and south. Coloring is generally yellow on the back, shading to a bluegreen on the sides and to almost white on the underside. The six vertical dark bands, forked tail, and slightly rounded fins make identification fairly easy (*see* Fig. 6-3 and color section, Fig. 5).

This is an excellent fish for the aquarium and will do well when included in schools. Sergeant majors will eat most anything the average saltwater fish will eat—lean beef, pieces of fish and shrimp, clams and other shellfish, and frozen brine shrimp—making them an easy fish to care for. Do encourage algae to grow in the aquarium by exposing it to sunlight occasionally, but if this does not occur, feed the fish bits of lettuce or spinach now and then.

SPADEFISH

Chaetodipterus faber

The spadefish can be found in waters ranging from the West Indies to Cape Cod and can grow quite large. We have seen spadefish which were as wide as a large dishpan, weighing as much as 6 pounds. However, if captured young and kept as pets, they will usually remain a reasonable size for the aquarium.

The spadefish is often called an angelfish because of its round, flattened shape and curved dorsal fin. It is a relative, but can be identified by the silver and black body. The black stripes alternate in size and length, running across the body. They lend it a zebra-like appearance, with some of the stripes completely circling the body (color Fig. 1).

Invertebrates are the chief food source for this fish, which has strong crushing jaws. A good way to capture it is by skin-diving, especially in rocky channels where shellfish are to be found.

These fish swim in schools, which makes them easier to capture than the loners. Since they like togetherness, it is good to have as many as three or four in your school to keep them happy.

SURGEONFISH

Achilles Tang: *Acanthurus achilles*
Shoulder Tang: *A. olivaceous*
Blue Tang: *A. coeruleus*

The beautiful tropical Achilles tang whose range, like most members of this family, is the waters of Micronesia, Polynesia, and the Hawaiian Islands, is a prize of the fish world. This family includes the surgeonfish and the doctorfish, deriving their names from the jackknife-like "blades" on their undersides. This blade is hinged near the tail of the fish and fits into a groove in the body, dropping down with the opened blade forward in Jack the Ripper style when the fish is threatened. It is well to be wary when handling the fish for it can inflict a severe wound.

Fig. 6-8   Shoulder tang: *A. olivaceous.*

Fig. 6-9   Lipstick tang: *Naso literatus.*

The Achilles tang, like others of its family, has a flattened, oval body, with the small, pouty mouth set low on a rounded face; the upper and lower fins sweep in unbroken lines all along the body (Figs. 6-8 and 6-9). Though growing to a length of 10–12 inches, this fish is quite a showy specimen if it can be accommodated in your aquarium. The body shades from an almost midnight blue to maroon and there are bright scarlet, heartshaped markings on its sides, with a band of the same color on the tail (color Fig. 9). Other markings of light blue and white are on the face.

The mouth of this fish is quite small and it will require small bits of food. Its chief food consists of algae. This should be encouraged to grow in the aquarium; if it is not present, spinach and small bits of lettuce should be offered.

This applies also to the shoulder tang—an attractive but less colorful fish of a mauve to gray shade—and to the blue tang—a silvery blue fish with darker blue fins and tail.

TOADFISH

Gulf Toadfish: *Opsanus beta*

There are many species of toadfish—perhaps as many as forty—found in temperate as well as tropical seas. We consider the vicious-looking Gulf of Mexico toady one of the best fish obtainable for the saltwater aquarium. He is so ugly with his big whiskered head, his huge toothy grin, and wide, round wing fins which spread threateningly at the least provocation, that he always receives a great deal of attention from those who view him in an aquarium. Added to this is the fact that he lurks, troll-like, under a rock ledge or in the opening of a shell with his mouth partly open, glaring at all comers as though he would like to take a bite out of them—as he probably would, given the chance.

We have found these little fish viciously guarding their eggs, which were plastered on the inside of large, aged horse conch or whelk shells (see Ch. 6, A Colony of Animal Life). When we bring them in to install in our aquarium, we always bring along their home if it happens to be a shell.

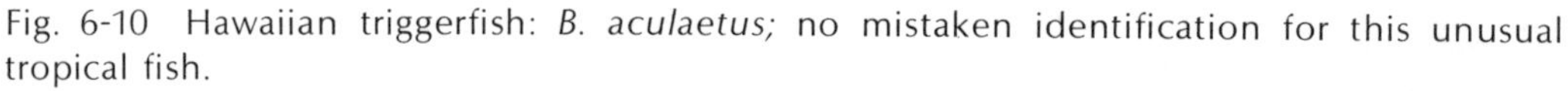

Fig. 6-10 Hawaiian triggerfish: *B. aculaetus;* no mistaken identification for this unusual tropical fish.

We have read that these fish attain a length of about a foot, but those we have captured were invariably about 4–5 inches long. They are quite easy to keep, for they will eat almost any kind of cut fish, shrimp, and live glass shrimp—except when they are brooding eggs. Then they will not eat at all, until the babies are on their own.

We have grown very attached to our toadies. Hasn't it been said that a mother will love her ugliest child best?

TRIGGERFISH

Hawaiian: *Balistapus aculaetus*
Queen: *Balistes vetula*

There are many species of triggerfish but, since all cannot be discussed in one book, we have chosen the two easiest to obtain: the Hawaiian triggerfish and the queen triggerfish.

There is never any problem with the identification of this little fish, who bears the weighty Hawaiian name of Humu-Humu-Nuku-Nuku-A-Puaa, for its pugnacious looks, big head, and dark stripes which run down on a diagonal toward the tail from about the middle of the body. The body, which can reach a length of 12 inches, is yellow, lightening toward the underside to almost white. A dark stripe runs directly down from the eye and another deep orange one is carried from the edge of the mouth back to the gill, giving the fish the appearance of having a large mouth (Fig. 6-10). Often there are also blue and red stripes bordering the dark ones that run toward the tail.

The spine, which gives the fish its name, is located in front of the dorsal fin. It is not known to be a weapon, but merely a tool which the fish uses to balance himself when resting against plants or rocks.

This fish can be temperamental in its feeding habits, but will generally become accustomed to eating the usual aquarium foods. It is a good idea, though, to add lettuce to the aquarium occasionally if it has not developed a sufficient growth of algae.

The Humu-Humu-Nuku-Nuku-A-Puaa, though generally thought of as a citizen of Hawaii, can be found in areas other then the Hawaiian Islands: Melanesia, Micronesia, West African waters and the East Indies.

The queen triggerfish, which is common in Florida waters with a scattering of them further north, is another beautiful fish for the aquarium, though tending to run larger than the Hawaiian species. An adult can reach a length of about 16 inches, but like most fish will not grow too alarmingly if captured young and kept in an aquarium.

The body of the queen is yellow-orange but it is one of those chameleon-like fishes that changes hues with its moods. Bright blue lines run around the mouth

Fig. 6-11   Wrasse (*D. megalepis*) and Maroon Clown.

Fig. 6-12   Squirrel fish: *Holocentrus xantherythrus*.

and across the face. The large fans of fins begin back of mid-body and reach to the tail in an unbroken sweep. The eye is surrounded with thread-sized lines that give the fish the coy look of a girl with extra-long lashes.

As with the Hawaiian triggerfish, the queen does not always take to life in a community tank and may have to be separated from the other inhabitants. It is wise to include it in an aquarium that can be easily watched for a time, to determine the characteristics of the individual fish.

WRASSE

Yellowtail: *Coris gaimardi*
Dwarf: *Doratonatus megalepis*

The wrasses are, as a general rule, shallow water tropicals, but a few can be found in temperate waters. Since there are hundreds of species of wrasses, and obviously it would be impossible to discuss them all, we have chosen to feature the two we are best acquainted with.

In the first place, let us hasten to say that we do not recommend the inclusion of most wrasses in the aquarium, even though many of them are beautifully colored. With their barracuda-like teeth, they are likely to rip up their fellow residents. And with their obnoxious dispositions, even if several of one species are put together in a tank of their own, there may be trouble. However, this may not be true of all wrasses, for we have read reports from some aquarists that their experience with the yellowtail—a fish that averages about 8 inches long in the wilds—has proven him to be a peaceful fellow. And this is a very pretty fish. It has a long, round, maroon body with black-circled white bands across the back and its rounded tail is a bright yellow.

Wrasses range in size from about 3 inches to 10 feet, and in color all through the rainbow. They are day-feeders; at night, several species rest by lounging on the sand on their sides.

Dwarf wrasses are best for the average aquarium: for one thing, they seldom grow to more than 3 inches; for another, some of them are quite brilliantly colored. For example, the *Doratonatus megalepis*, which can be found from the West Indies to the lower Florida waters, is a bright green (Fig. 6-11).

Wrasses can be captured around rocks, to which crabs and barnacles are attached, for their natural foods consist of these, as well as prawns and mussels and any other crustaceons and mollusks that their teeth can crush. Scuba and skin divers often capture these little fish with the clear plastic dip nets, but it is not easy because they will hide in holes in the rocks.

Aquarium wrasses can be fed pieces of fish and shrimp and the other animal life mentioned above, or you can include these creatures alive in the aquarium and let the fish shop for their own food.

THE UNCOMMON CREATURES ●

For many people the decision to keep aquarium fishes results merely in a trip to an aquarium shop, the purchase of the needed equipment and fishes, and the thing has been accomplished. We feel that these people are missing the real fun of the project, for unusual animal life is often not to be found in this prosaic manner, but in a bring-em-back-alive safari to ocean, lake, pond, or creek.

This is not to say that we do not buy many of our fish from shops. If we are not to make journeys to distant lands for them, this is the only way many of the beautiful, exotic-colored specimens can be found. As an example, most everyone would like to own a brilliant yellow, black, and white butterfly fish, the *Chelmon rostratus;* but for a citizen of North America to attain this fellow would require a trip to the waters of the Indo Pacific.

Even though some of the most gorgeous of the aquarium fishes must be bought from aquarium dealers, other fascinating types can be collected from your native waters, wherever you might live. Understandably, these are often more highly treasured than the purchased ones because you have had the excitement of the chase. And too, many of these are more in the animal than fish category and, naturally, reveal more individual characteristics than fish.

Examples of animal life often not considered for aquariums are the hermit crab and starfish for saltwater; for freshwater, the crawdad or crayfish and tadpole. These are all quite easily captured, as described in the appropriate sections in Chapter 1.

The four mentioned are only a very few of the interesting creatures that can be collected from the wilds. From saltwater you might want to collect sea horses, pipefish, barnacles, anemones, live coral, shellfish of all kinds, octopuses, nudibranches, sea hares, and so on.

From freshwater ponds, lakes, and creeks come the tadpole, with its exciting metamorphosis from a blob with a tail to a handsome frog; the crawdad, who will constantly be constructing dens; water scorpions, who look like praying mantises; salamanders, who at one period in their lives must live out of water on a high island in the aquarium or a raft.

It is these remarkable little creatures with their diverse characters that make the work of keeping an aquarium worthwhile. However, often one of these animals will not be adaptable for some reason or other; the beauty of it is that, if this happens, it is an easy matter to release the critter back into its natural habitat. Such a character was the giant waterbug, Mr. J. Horrible Bug, who—though exceptionally interesting, due to the fact that he carried a bee-comblike cluster of eggs on his back—bit the hand that fed him (or rather, the hand that was cleaning the aquarium). He was banished, along with his offspring who were tiny replicas of himself, back into the spring stream from which he was captured.

Even if some of these animals are not to become permanent residents of the aquarium, their stay will provide memorable experiences and, incidentally, real-life studies in marine and freshwater biology.

SEA URCHIN

Strongylocentrotus drobachiensis

The sea urchin, although a hands-off kind of critter due to the poisonous spines some of them sport, can be included for variety in the marine aquarium. Their colors vary, according to the species and the area in which they are found, covering many shades of red, purple, and even green (see Fig. 1-6).

Most sea urchins live around rocky areas or on the sandy bottoms of shallows. On the upper Gulf of Mexico coast, in St. Joseph's Bay, there are reddish-purple urchins literally covering the sands of the shallows. These fellows have a strange camouflage that may prevent their detection unless one knows what to look for: simply a pile of small shells! Yes, the urchin plasters empty shells of all sorts all over himself and lugs them around as a very effective camouflage coat. Seeing the pile of beautiful little shells, the unwary shell collector may rush to pick them up. And strangely, even though there are many aged and eroded shells lying about, those chosen by the urchins *are* invariably pretty: so much so that we are strongly inclined to believe those urchins have an artistic sense of beauty.

We have had sea urchins in our aquariums at various times, but not for long periods, so cannot state positively that they do not cause trouble. We can only say that ours got along quite peacefully with the other fish and animals, consuming chunks of clam meat and cut fish in the same manner as the starfish, settling down over them and "absorbing" them into their maws.

SHRIMP

Banded Coral Shrimp: *Stenopus hispidus*

While one does not ordinarily think of shrimp as inhabitants of the marine aquarium—except as food for the other critters—they can be quite interesting and attractive. Especially novel is the banded coral shrimp, which is striped a bright red and white, looking like peppermint stick candy. This shrimp is usually no more than 3 inches long, but we saw some at the public aquarium at The Shell Factory in Ft. Myers, Florida, that must have measured at least 5–6 inches; so bright and strange were they they they brought forth exclamations of surprise from all visitors.

Then there are the little glass shrimp (or grass shrimp or fairy shrimp) which can be collected from the grasses of most tropical saltwater bays. Though not colorful like the coral shrimp, these can afford variety for the aquarium and are easily kept, eating all the ordinary aquarium foods. These shrimp do afford an interesting study in biology, for they carry their eggs along the lower part of their bodies, constantly fanning them with their many rows of legs or tentacles until they hatch. Even then, the parents are reluctant to give up their offspring to the cold cruel world; for some time, as the babies attempt to escape, they'll snatch them back and tuck them firmly in among the others.

As mentioned in the section on foods for aquarium fishes, this is one method of feeding the smaller inhabitants. Just capture a number of egg-carrying glass shrimp and include them in the aquarium; as the young develop, they furnish food for the other fishes.

CRABS

There are several kinds of crabs that are excellent additions to the saltwater aquarium, for they are the sanitation engineers of the tank. They are quite interesting to watch as well, though some, such as the spider crab, can be a nipping nuisance to the other fish unless they are quite small.

We especially like hermit crabs because of their fascinating habit of changing homes. Having no shell of their own, they don the empty shells of other critters for protection from their enemies (color Fig. 13).

The first hermit crab to be installed in our aquarium came in quite by accident and turned out to be an avid home swapper. That made him a treasured acquisition, for we had no idea when we left the aquarium what guise Rover would take when we returned.

Our experience with Rover began when we found a lovely moon snail shell, brought it home, laid it on a white sand dollar, and placed it on a table as a decoration. To our surprise, the supposedly empty moon shell got up and scuttled off the sand dollar and across the table. An examination revealed that it contained a small hermit crab.

Still selfishly wanting the shell for myself, I put the crab in my aquarium. Searching through the shell collection, I chose four shells of various kinds, comparable in size to that of the moon shell, and placed them in the aquarium in a row.

We settled down to watch the results. Sure enough, Rover, who constantly traveled along the sand in search of bits of food, came upon the treasure trove of houses almost immediately and excitedly began home-shopping. He would feel the shells carefully all over with his sensitive clawed hands and then reach far into the openings, examining the interior. Finally, after ten or twenty minutes of this meticulous scrutiny, the cautious home-swapper settled on a small whelk shell. With a rush that was almost too fast to see, he scurried from the moon shell and backed into the whelk. The swiftness of the operation is, of course, a necessity to keep the soft, vulnerable body from being snatched up by a hungry predator.

Rover's propensity for house-swapping was only one of the idiosyncrasies that made him an amusing pet: his constant and furious activity was another. He was never still. Hermits are scavengers, eating anything that doesn't move.

OCTOPUS

Octopus vulgaris

Our single experience with the inclusion of octopuses in the aquarium was a dismal failure. We had been told by other aquarium fish hobbyists that it was difficult to keep these creatures alive in captivity, but when an unusual swirling tide brought dozens of little bright orange octopuses to the beach on Florida's Sanibel Island, along with a great drift of shells, we couldn't resist trying the little eight-legged animals in the aquarium.

We installed two of them in a bucket of water with a battery operated airstone for the trip home, then set them up in a well-filtered, well-aerated aquarium.

Two days later they were dead and we have not the slightest idea why. These were the only sea creatures, in all our years of experience, that we failed to keep alive. They had plenty of food—small fish and shrimp—and the water of the tank seemed clean, as they had not thrown out ink. We even added additional air-stones when we noticed that the bright orange color of the octopuses was changing. This is a sure indication of trouble with many fishes, though some-times the bright flush in an octopus means excitement.

When there seemed no improvement, we tried changing all the water but nothing helped. Later research has led us to believe that octopuses are toxic, even to themselves, in a closed system; though we have known of some being kept successfully in quite large containers. Of course, we are not ruling out the possibility that since we found these on the beach they may have been out of the water too long to survive.

One point that needs to be stressed, in case you plan to keep octopuses for pets, is that they should be kept in covered tanks—or you may wake up some morning to find that they have taken a moonlight stroll on the floor.

Other people have related experiences with their attempts to keep octopuses that were comparable to ours. During one trip to the Florida Keys to collect aquarium critters, we met Dr. Edgar Lotspeich and his wife, who were also col-lecting. They told us of their attempts to raise baby octopuses from eggs. The remarkable thing was that the eggs hatched at all in the aquarium (we've tried hatching some out, and failed at that, too), but Dr. Lotspeich said that the eggs he had were almost ready to hatch when he got them. At any rate, the eggs hatched; then, when the babies were two and three days old, they began to die. These were plucky little fellows who, even a short time after hatching, sent out ink when they were disturbed and it's possible that they simply poisoned them-selves. However, Dr. Lotspeich got some excellent pictures of the series of these little fellows from developing egg to free-swimming animal.

We still plan to try to keep octopuses in an aquarium, if the opportunity again presents itself, but only if we have a very large tank. Also we would want to study the successful experiments of others more extensively for advice.

SEA HORSES

Giant: *Hippocampus hudsonius*
Dwarf: *H. zosterae*

Everyone who keeps aquarium fishes has his favorites among the inhabitants of the tanks. For us, without exception among the saltwater fishes, it is the sea horse.

There is something about this little creature that intrigues mightily (color Fig. 11). Here is a fish so very different from the generally accepted definition of "fish" as to be totally unrecognizable as such (Fig. 6-13). There is his alligator-like armored body, with the monkey-like tail that grips onto plants and coral; the horse-like head, with its turreted eyes that can move independently of each other; and, in the male, a brood-pouch very much like that of a kangaroo. Added to these idiosyncrasies is the fact that he swims upright, thus making him especially unique among fishes.

The skeleton of the sea horse appears to be worn on the outside of its body, but in actuality the alligator-like armor is made up of a series of bony plates which overlap in a covering. The sea horse also has an internal skeleton resembling that of other fishes, and it propels itself through the water with tiny, almost transparent, fans of fins.

Sea horses are found primarily in warm seas but a few specimens inhabit North American waters as far north as Cape Cod. They can be purchased by mail, but be sure to order from a reputable dealer and be prepared to take care of your horses when they arrive. They will be shipped in a container of saltwater and oxygen. Then they will, like other fishes, require an aerated, filtered tank (aquarium or fish bowl) with ocean water or water to which a special sea salt has been added. (See Ch. 2, "Setting Up a Saltwater Aquarium," for further hints.)

Our first experience with sea horses was a tragic one. In the first place, we ignorantly ordered the horses in November, a time of the year far too cold for them to be shipped north to Missouri. The dealer, who should have known better, sent them through regular parcel post, though we had given instructions for them to be sent by air and had made arrangements for the airport to call us to pick them up as soon as they arrived. As a result of this fiasco in shipping, the little things lay in the mailbox in 40° weather for probably two hours. When we finally got them established in the aquarium, it was obvious from their actions that the trip had been disastrous.

That night a pregnant male gave birth to immature babies and died in the process. During the next day all the others were gone.

It is apparent then that if the horses are to be shipped to temperate or northern states, it had better be in the summer. Of course the ideal way to obtain the horses or, in fact, any other tropical fishes is to purchase them from an aquarium fish shop in your area or get them when you are on a trip south and keep them warm in a container furnished with saltwater and oxygen or with a battery-driven airstone. There is more about these handy gadgets in Chapter 2.

Remember too that these horses need an amazingly large amount of food and it is necessary to be prepared with the live groceries—brine shrimp for dwarf sea horses and grass shrimp or glass shrimp for the larger giant sea horses.

Attempts have been made to adapt sea horses to living entirely on frozen brine shrimp and dry food, but most have failed. However, we have had reports from friends that they have succeeded in the project and they will point out certain horses that are currently living without live food. But these experiments have not been of long-term duration and we are eager to know the results after several months' time. The person who can make it possible to keep sea horses

Fig. 6-13 When sea horses become amorous, holding hands (tails) and lovingly nuzzling each other, it is certain a wedding is scheduled for the near future.

Fig. 6-14   The male sea horse gives birth; this one is very pregnant.

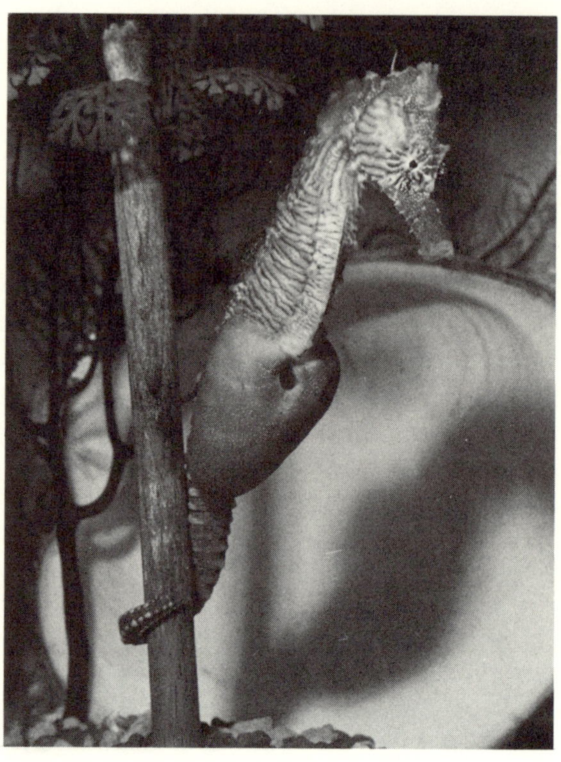

Fig. 6-15   This male's pouch is beginning to dilate.

Fig. 6-16   This tired father gave birth to over five hundred colts. The water and tree are full of babies.

Fig. 6-17   Our dwarf sea horse, Ralph, is in the process of giving birth to his thirty-three babies.

Fig. 6-18   A good comparison of the sizes of the dwarf and giant sea horses.

Fig. 6-19   A tree full of pipefish and sea horses.

without raising live food will make a great contribution for saltwater fish fanciers.

Until some smart soul does give us a foolproof, non-live food, the best method of feeding sea horses is still live brine shrimp: newly hatched for babies, adult for adult dwarfs. The giant type horse needs the 1/2-inch glass shrimp, which can be gathered among the grasses of saltwater bays with a fine-meshed net or purchased from some aquarium shops. (See Chapter 5 for more detail.)

You can, if you live near southern seashores, capture ample food in an hour or so to last a goodly number of sea horses for a week. Simply float the shallow waters of grass flat bays in a small boat and dip up clumps of the grass in fine-meshed nets, sorting through it and dropping the proper-sized shrimp into a bucket of water. Or you may wade and seine them from the grasses. And the time is well-used; it gets you into that beautiful outdoors and anything that does that is worth the time. Often, while getting our canoe ready to go out after shrimp, Ray is asked if he is going fishing and he will answer, "Well—not this morning. Have to go out to the north forty and harvest some fodder for the horses." Actually, as we dip among the grasses for the shrimp, we usually come up with several sea horses, some pipefish, and starfish in the process, for this is their natural habitat.

A few of the "dos" in keeping sea horses for pets: do keep them in a filtered, aerated container; plant a sea horse tree or sea whip, plastic plant of the ferny type, or other object suitable for them to hitch themselves to; and be sure the greedy little guys have plenty of live food. Of course, as with any other saltwater fishes, make sure the water is the proper salinity, testing it with a hydrometer (see Ch. 2). Remember that the evaporation of the water increases salinity; it will eventually become too salty and have to be changed or freshwater added.

"Don'ts" on keeping sea horses: don't put them in aquariums in which fast-moving predators have been included, for these will deplete the food supply before the slower-moving horses can feed. Don't allow the temperature to drop below 60°F or rise much above 90°F. The ideal temperature for sea horses is about 80°F.

We have read that giant sea horses will not breed in captivity and that even when a pregnant one gives birth, after being captured in the wilds and installed in an aquarium, the babies cannot be raised to adulthood. We cannot dispute this, but we have observed our giant sea horses making love, their tails wrapped around each other, and faces rubbing in touchingly tender caresses. Also, babies born in our tanks have survived for at least a month (Figs 6-14 through 6-19). We were not able to carry on the experiment for longer than that. Much as we would have liked to observe them for longer periods, we travel too much to permit it, and our aquarium critters must eventually be turned over to others or released back into their natural habitat.

In this matter of survival, it is likely that the main reason for casualties is lack of the proper food—or enough of it—for it stands to reason that with proper diet these creatures should breed and survive in captivity. Those of you who decide to include giant sea horses in your aquarium could do an important service to other saltwater fish fanciers if your experiments are the ones that prove that statement to be correct.

STARFISH

Brittle Starfish: *Ophiothrix spiculata*
Common Starfish: *Asteriidae echinaster*

Another creature who does well in a saltwater aquarium is the starfish. These are easily obtained while dredging, or floating and drifting the grass flats of saltwater bays, dipping into the grasses with long-handled dip nets. In the bays

Fig. 6-20   The common starfish: *A. echinaster.*

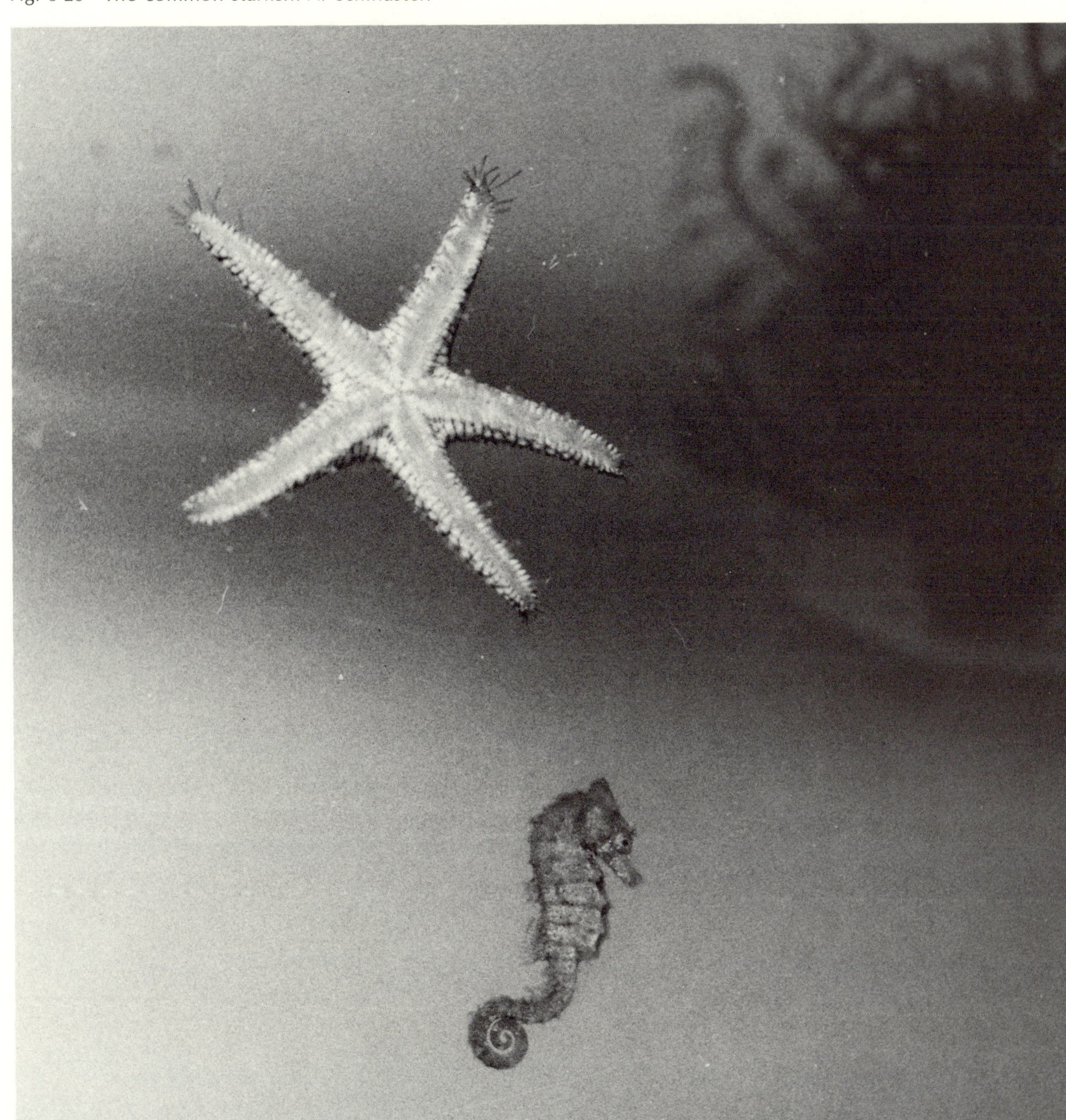

Fig. 6-21   The brittle starfish: *O. spiculata.*

of the Gulf, one netful of grass will usually contain several common stars of sizes from 1/2 inch to more than 3 inches (Fig. 6-20). Often in that same net there will be a spidery brittle star or two (Fig. 6-21).

The brittle stars require careful handling; they have a tendency to lose an arm if picked up by it, although it will eventually grow back. Once in the aquarium, they happily (like the common star) go about the business of live-in housekeeping. They will even wash the windows, slowly working their way up and down the glass walls as well as consuming any bits of leftover food that are on the bottom of the aquarium.

There are many kinds of starfish of the temperate and tropical zone classes, including the basket star which has so many branching arms that it resembles a clump of grass and is quite difficult to spot. Others, such as the sunflower star, can have as many as twenty arms. The starfish range in color from brown through shades of red, with some types black or creamy white, and there are some species who reach a size of 3 feet! Most are egglayers with a metamorphosis from free-swimming larvae.

The stars are voracious predators which, in the wilds, wrap their arms around shellfish, such as clams, force the shell apart with the suction of their arms, then dine on the luckless inhabitants. However, our starfish seem quite content to feast on whatever kinds of meat we drop into the tank, be it bits of shrimp, fish, clam, or hamburger. So well do they flourish that we have never had one die in the aquarium, though we have kept them for months.

We think that such creatures as the starfish and sea horse add tremendously to the interest of an aquarium, for they are so unlike the accepted image of "fish"; their actions, too, are very different. And as far as we have been able to determine, especially when dealing with starfish, there are simply no real problems with bad dispositions or even with diseases. The only casualty we have had that could be blamed on a starfish was the death of one coquina, and we strongly suspect that the coquina was not really a good aquarium citizen in the first place.

EELS

Moray: *Muraenidae*
Conger: *Congridae*
Ribbon: *Rhinomuraena*

Eels are not the easiest of aquarium fish to capture, and when installed in a tank they are often hard to see because of their habit of hiding under rocks or down in the sand; but they do lend interest to a tank and some kinds have gorgeous coloring.

There are so many species of this creature that we will only speak of a few that we are personally acquainted with, though many remarks could apply as well to most kinds.

The conger attains a huge size in the wilds, but when captured young can usually be kept aquarium-length—if you have a rather large aquarium. This applies as well to the moray and ribbon eels. The adult spotted moray is somewhat smaller than the 6-foot green moray, attaining a length of about 3 feet and the ribbons can grow to a length a little short of this (Figs. 6-22, 6-23, and color Figs. 8 and 17).

There are those people to whom such marine life as eels and octopuses are repulsive. They would not want them in their home aquarium, preferring the more conventional fishes, but these creatures are, after all, an integral part of marine life. Even though you may not want them as permanent residents, do try keeping them for a period of time for observation and study.

Eels prefer live food but will become accustomed to eating pieces of shrimp and fish. A friend of ours likes to hand-feed his eels, using a long tube on which he skewers pieces of food. He lowers it to the eels, who viciously tear the food off.

Eels as well as octopuses should live in covered tanks, for they are roamers and might run away from home. We knew of one moray who squeezed himself through the small overflow pipe of his tank and was found the next day strolling along the floor.

Eels are egglayers but the spawning habits of many species are still not at all well known. They occur in practically all the waters of the world, fresh as well as saltwater. The green and spotted morays are in tropical oceans, though the spotted eel is occasionally found as far north as New Jersey.

ANEMONES

There are such a wide variety of anemones—"the flowers of the sea"—that it would be impossible to discuss more than a small number here. They occur, in one form or another, in all warm seas.

The anemones, though looking exactly like blossoming plants, are sea animals (Figs. 6-24 and 6-25). They have a single polyp for a base, with many white or colored petallike tentacles radiating from it, and are quite showy in the marine aquarium. Colors range through the entire spectrum of hues.

Anemones can be purchased at many marine aquarium shops (though they are rather expensive) or can be found fastened to rocks, often on the underside of ledges, old shells, or even embedded in the sand in shallow water along the beaches.

Care must be taken not to injure these delicate creatures, for they must be dug up with a spade when buried in the sand, or pried from their tenacious hold when on rocks. The best manner of collecting is to bring in both the anemone and the rock to which it is attached, if possible.

It is best to keep the anemone in an aerated bucket until it can be placed in the aquarium if a long period of time is to elapse, though they will live for short periods without aeration. For those who collect their own aquarium critters, the best purchase you could make is a battery-driven air pump complete with an airstone to aerate the collecting bucket.

When the anemone is dropped into the aquarium, it will look lifeless at first, but in a short time the tentacles will open into a flower and begin searching the surroundings for food.

Feeding the anemones is a simple matter (Fig. 6-26). Merely drop small pieces of fish, frozen or fresh shrimp, or hamburger down among the tentacles. It will either accept your offering by drawing it down into its gullet or, if not hungry at the moment, reject it by pushing it aside with the tentacles.

Fig. 6-22   Moray eel: *Muraenidae* species.
Fig. 6-23   The moray eel lies in wait for careless fingers and toes.

Fig. 6-24   Anemones and anemonefish (clowns) have a close partnership. The fish feed the anemones and then use the tentacles — which are poisonous to most other fishes — for protection from predators.

One of the anemones we found in the shallows of a Gulf bay was a lovely rose shade, another a pure white, and still another a creamy yellow with trimmings of delicate green (color Fig. 15). All of these, as well as some reddish-brown ones, thrived in our aquarium as did some tiny ones from 1/8–1/4 inch in size, which were introduced into the aquarium by accident on rocks or shells.

Use caution when handling anemones. Always remember that the anemone's natural feeding habit is to sting its victim into submission and, unless you want to become its victim, handle with care! Some are poisonous to the touch and

Fig. 6-25   Another type of anemone. Baby clownfish are hiding among its tentacles.

others can emit a fine jet of water that will shoot up with surprising force—if this gets into the eyes, it can cause severe pain.

When introducing anemones into the aquarium, be sure to give them some rocks or shells on which to attach themselves. Often you will find that your choice of a base does not suit the finicky critters and they will "walk" from one end of the aquarium to the other in an effort to find more comfortable lodgings.

Anemones can be found in sizes from 1/8 inch across to 4 feet and should be chosen according to the size of the aquarium. One of the most beautiful aquariums we have ever seen was peopled with only a huge, two-foot anemone and a school of brilliant tomato clown anemonefish. Strangely, this type of fish can simply wallow among the tentacles of the anemone without the slightest harm when other fish would be stung to death. This is an amazing partnership, the anemonefish taking refuge among the tentacles of their pals when danger threatens; in turn, the fish groom and feed their host. As we mentioned earlier, when we discussed those fish, we have seen one of them drop a piece of shrimp into an anemone's center, stand back and watch for a moment, and if the food is rejected, the fish will pick it up and feed another anemone until one of those in his aquarium accepts it. And so it is obvious that, for the marine aquarium, at least one anemone and a few anemonefish are a must.

Fig. 6-26   Carl Geer sometimes feeds his anemones by hand, placing pieces of fish in their maws.

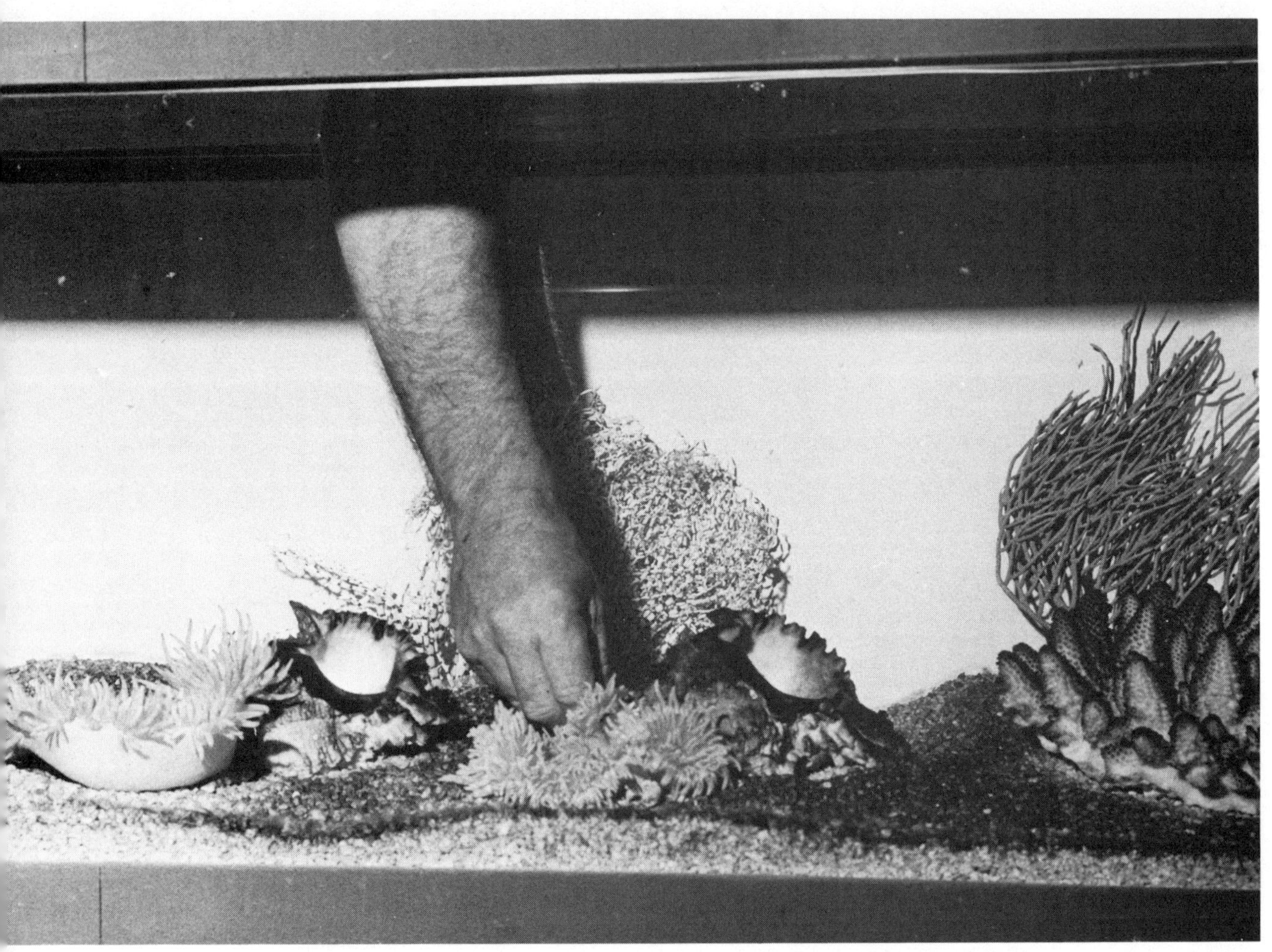

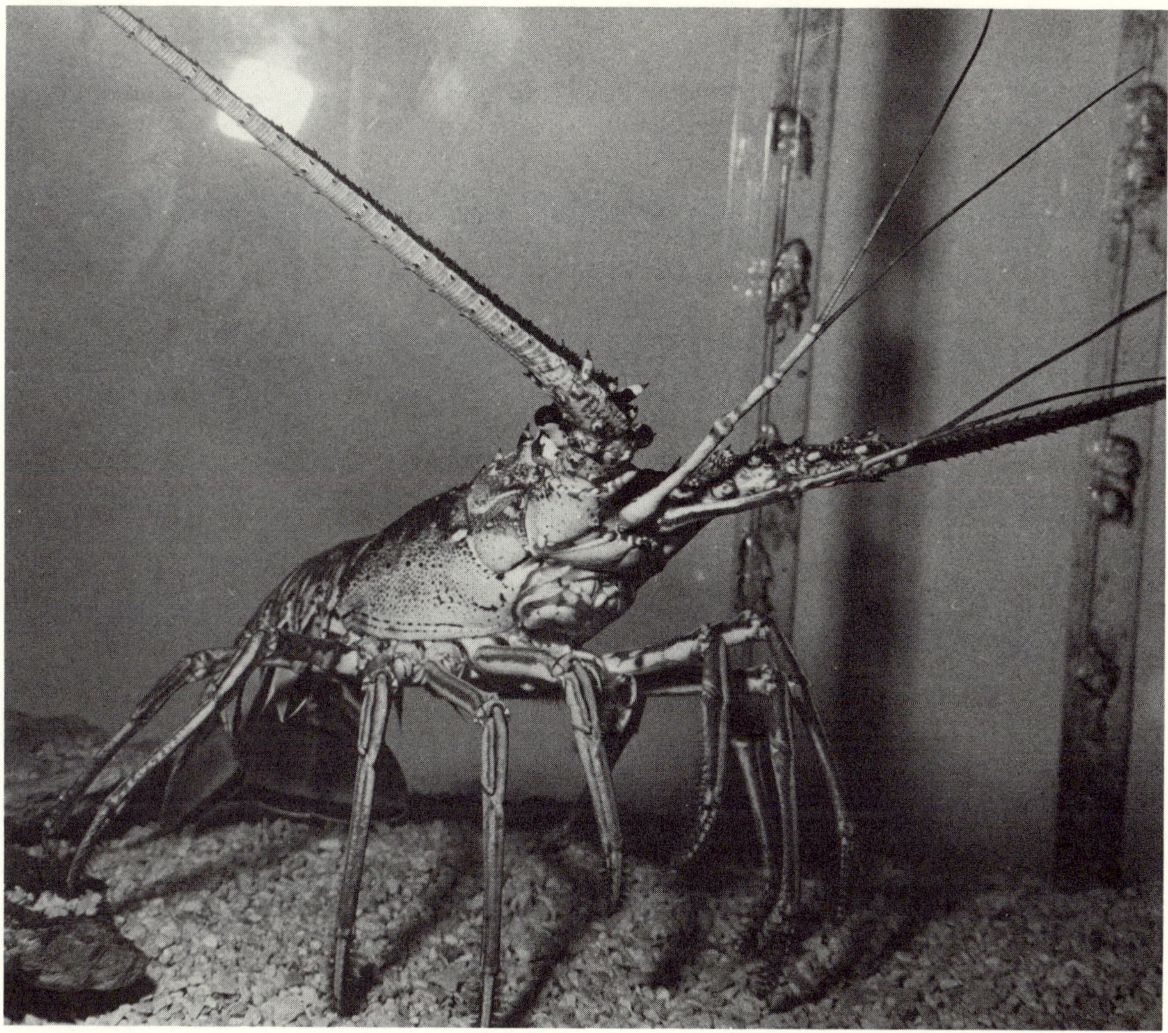

Fig. 6-27   The Florida lobster is an interesting creature, but will quickly outgrow all but the largest aquariums.

A COLONY OF ANIMAL LIFE ●

Don't overlook the fact that an old, empty shell can turn out to be the home of an amazing colony of creatures, among the most exciting of all your aquarium additions.

We had, for years, passed up old, barnacle-covered shells as unsuitable for collecting. One day, upon spotting a blenny hiding in a large horse conch shell, we brought it, along with its home, back with us and placed it in the aquarium (see Fig. 6-1). To our surprise, that shell literally came to life and was found to be the host of a dozen or so different species of marine life.

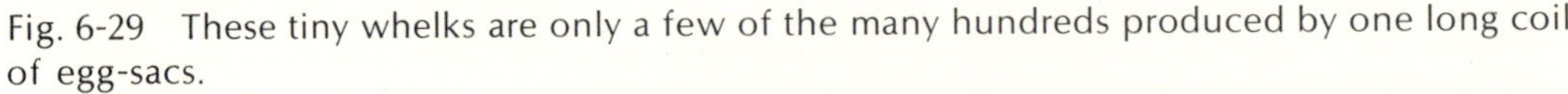

Fig. 6-28   The whelk egg-sacs in this coil are beginning to open and release tiny whelks.

Fig. 6-29   These tiny whelks are only a few of the many hundreds produced by one long coil of egg-sacs.

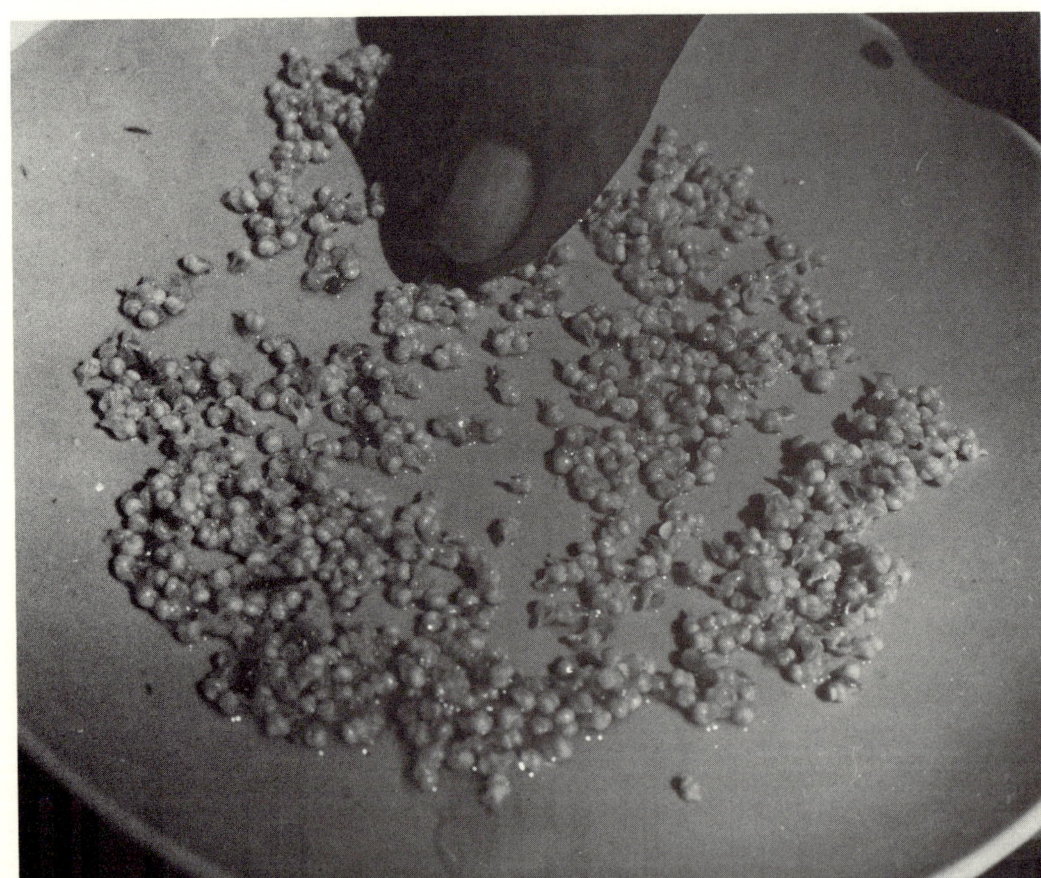

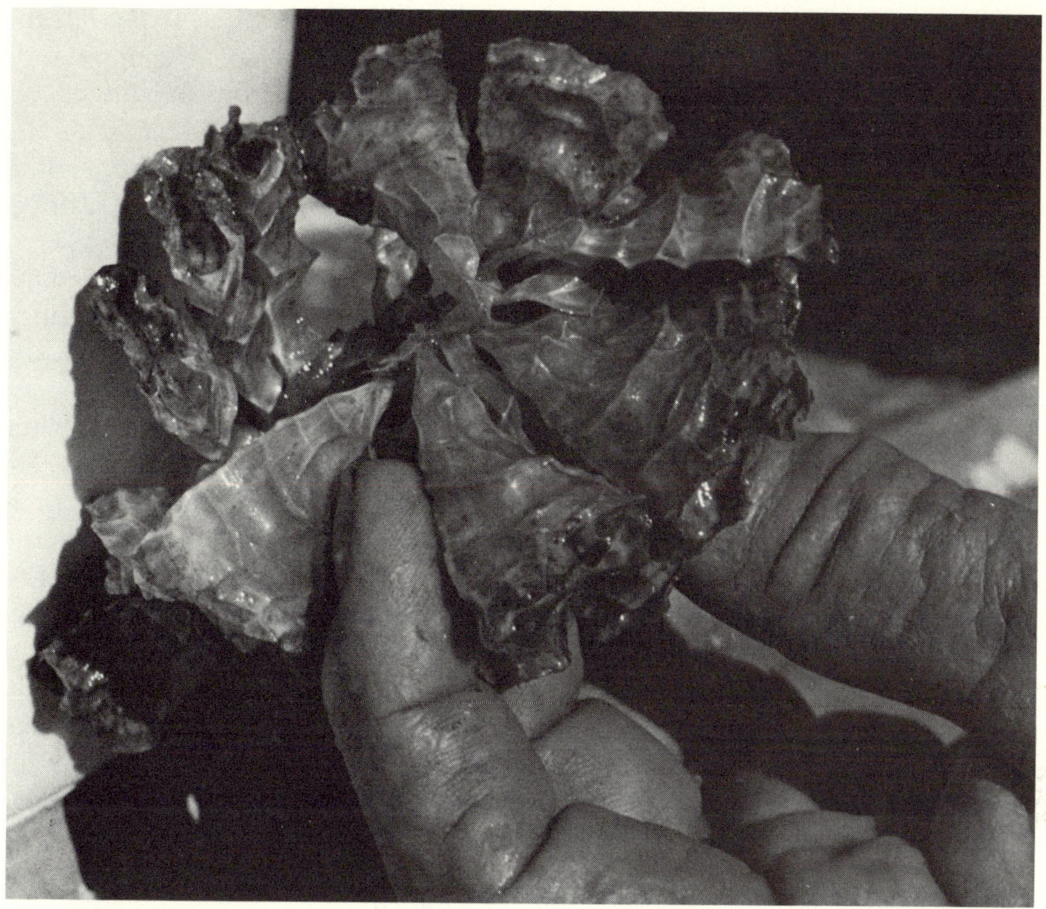

Fig. 6-30   The horse conch egg-sacks are in a large round cluster.

Fig. 6-31   Crown conch egg-sacs are found as round disks cemented to old shells, logs, or rocks.

There was first the pugnacious little blenny who continued to live in the shell, guarding it like a king his castle. This fish was only about 2 1/2 inches long and it immediately became a pet, eating bits of shrimp from our fingers.

The second dweller we discovered was Nippy, a red crab who had taken up residence in a partly opened, empty oyster shell, which had attached itself to the side of the large conch. The crab would scuttle forth to clean up leftover shrimp that the fish missed, but always returned to his oyster-shell cave.

There was also a large, white cluster of horse conch egg cases attached to the shell, with the tiny conches visible through the casings. And all over the conch were barnacles. They came to life as soon as we placed the shell in the aquarium and busily began sweeping the water with their delicate fans.

Several slipper shells, plastered to the side of the larger shell, which we thought were empty, soon opened slightly and small, white antenna emerged, testing the new surroundings. Several snails, which had appeared as dead as the slipper snails, came to life and took up their housecleaning job on both the conch and the aquarium glass. Two of these small snails had "planted" camouflaging grass on their backs and went about their business looking like walking plants.

Probably the most surprising revelation came when we discovered that the outside of the shell was the base for several sea anemones. The small, flowerlike anemones, in red, yellow, and purple hues, were as pretty as blossoms! To our delight, these opened up soon after we put the shell into the aquarium and put on a show for us.

The nice thing about this experience with the aged shell and its colony of wildlife is that all these creatures seemed perfectly at home as aquarium residents and all lived and flourished for the couple of weeks they remained in the tank. We hated to consign them back to the bay, but eventually the aquarium was needed for more experiments.

This introduction of the old conch and its many residents was one of the most exciting of our experiments and we hope others will try it. Keep a magnifying glass handy in order to closely observe the marine life on the shell, for many of the creatures are so very small. We wonder what a microscope would have revealed on that shell! As it was, some of the tiniest of the sea anemones and other creatures could only be fully appreciated by viewing through the magnifying glass.

FISH EGGS

An uncommon aquarium addition, often overlooked and yet quite easily obtained, is the many eggs of the water creatures. The astounding variety of designs these eggs take is fascinating in its own right; if they can be hatched in captivity, collecting them is even more worthwhile.

The eggs of our toadfish provide an example. He was discovered in an aged conch shell and when placed in an aquarium, along with his shell, was found to have bright yellow eggs plastered all over the inside of the shell. We were careful in transferring the fish and his home, but we need not have worried—*nothing* would have dislodged this dedicated little fish, who constantly fanned the eggs with her fins and tail, even as we moved the shell.

The study of these eggs as they developed into big-headed, big-eyed, pink babies was something we would not have missed. For days, each of these babies was still attached to its egg and getting sustenance from it. They swayed in the water currents as the toady continued to fan them. And the remarkable thing was that during all these days of developing the parent fish never left the eggs for a moment—even refusing to eat, though we dropped the food into the shell. She would simply pick it up and carry it to the opening and spit it out.

Shellfish eggs are quite easy to find, for almost every old empty shell has at least one type of eggs fastened to it. Some kinds might be quite small, but the whelk and conch egg cases are large white clusters, easy to spot. These are shown in Figures 6-28 through 6-31, showing the long coil of eggs laid by the whelk as compared to the round cluster laid by the conch and tulip snail. All of these have distinctive forms, which make them easy to recognize. However, there are many others that, when hatched, turn out to be a surprise. There was a big cluster of eggs that hatched out dragonlike little creatures that we subsequently found to be mountain boomers, a type of freshwater lizard that is a land-water creature. And there was the morning after we had put a jellylike clump of eggs into the aquarium that we found the thing swarming with tadpoles. And there was the waterbug who carried his eggs around on his back. These eggs were still carried for several days after they were hatched out into perfect replicas of the parent, often falling off and being tucked back into the comb by the parent.

Fish eggs will not always hatch, for if they are not close to maturation, they may require some quality lacking in the aquarium or in our care of them. For instance, we found a small, orange octopus washed up on shore in a pile of shells. A large pen shell near him contained pearly, tear-shaped octopus eggs, so we assumed that these were his eggs. The partially opened shell, with the eggs plastered in it, was placed in an aquarium along with the octopus, but the octopus refused to clean and tend the eggs. When it died after a couple of days, the eggs failed to develop, even though we suspended an airstone in the shell in the hope that this would approximate the cleaning action of the parent. We decided that very likely these were not, after all, the eggs of the octopus we had captured and that it was not about to tend someone else's kids. Quite a disappointment, but a worthwhile experiment in marine biology.

A cluster of horse conch eggs or a long spiral of whelk egg-sacs, when held up to the light will often reveal baby shellfish that are almost fully developed. Include these in the aquarium and watch the show as they emerge. We found a long coil of whelk egg cases which had washed up on the beach. Not really having much hope for them, as it seemed likely they had been out of water too long to live, we placed them in a bucket of water in the canoe. When we lifted the bucket from the canoe a few hours later, there were baby whelks all over the place, crawling up the sides of the bucket and swarming over the egg cases.

In your saltwater aquarium, include a few glass shrimp that are carrying eggs on their undersides. You will find that they are constantly ruffling their many feelers or legs, fanning the eggs. Like the waterbug, even when the babies hatch and start to fall off the parent's body, she will hurriedly snatch them up and tuck them back on. Eventually they will escape and will furnish food for larger creatures, proving her wisdom in not allowing her offspring to escape to the wide world of the aquarium too soon. These little shrimp are especially good food for baby sea horses and other small predators.

Watch for eggs of water creatures on rocks, old shells, grasses, and even floating free in the water, some of them near the surface. Though we have pictured some of these eggs for identification, we think it is a great deal of fun to come upon some we cannot recognize, and wait eagerly for the hatching.

7 Freshwater Creatures

FISHES ●

GOLDFISH

Carassius auratus

Centuries ago the Chinese, those people who love to develop life-forms to extreme idealistic degrees and do it so well, were responsible for bringing into being those regal little jewels that drift gracefully through tanks, bowls, and pools all over the world.

The goldfish: toy and prestige symbol of courtesans and kings, it has now become a strange paradox. The fine ones are difficult to find and expensive to buy; the ordinary ones are the staple ware of aquarium shops and dime stores at less than half-a-dollar each.

Even more than the guppy, goldfish are the most ill-treated creatures in all fishdom. Housed and fed inadequately, they will still live and display their beauty, even for those ignorant or uncaring of their true requirements.

When one has seen the robust color and size attained by properly kept goldfish, one realizes again we have three options: good, better, and best, best being represented by the most dignified, exotic fish available—the very last word in status pets. Like all cats and some well-bred dogs, these fish give the clear impression of allowing the keeper to tend their needs, as obeisance due any regent.

Now let's discuss the means of claiming for ourselves the full potential of this beauty from the Orient.

Goldfish require more room than most other fish, the usual suggestion being a gallon of water for each 2 inches of body length (excluding the tail). For truly well-developed specimens, double or triple this (the gallons, not the inches!) and bear in mind the water surface is more important than actual gallon content. A wide, low-profile tank is always best, for they need plenty of oxygen, best supplied in a tank of this shape. Aeration and filtration are always advisable, and temperature should stay between 65°F and 75°F. Many homes are often warmer, but warm water holds less oxygen and encourages disease, so it's wise to try for this temperature range.

For best results, a preponderance of live and frozen food should be given. These fish will live for years on dry foods alone, but the difference is remarkable in the ones on a wide-variety diet. Goldfish pellets, flake food, and shrimp pellets all have their value and should be included. Goldfish are heavy eaters and should be offered all they want two or three times a day, but watch closely to see that they are eating, not just spitting it out. Never feed "a little extra"—see that they clean up every feeding in less than ten minutes. Experience will teach just how much to feed. If there's time, hand-feeding is a good idea; the keeper can determine that all the fish are getting enough, and no food falls unnoticed to the bottom. When feeding whole angleworms this is a good idea, for a live angleworm can hide in the gravel to make quite a mess when it dies. For smaller customers, worms can be chopped. This sounds like a horrid job, but it is much easier if the worms are first frozen on a piece of cardboard, which then becomes your chopping-block. It's best to rinse all worms once before feeding.

Most of the popular forms of goldfish are far removed in shape from the original carplike fish, which had a very practical, long fish-type body. All but the comet and common wakins have short, humped, rounded bodies, with corresponding distortions inside, where stomach, air-bladder, intestines, and all other ogans must scrunch up together (Figs. 7-1 and 7-2). If a goldfish gulps down too much dry food, it will swell inside the stomach, crowding the other organs and causing swim-bladder trouble, constipation, and other disorders.

Green stuff is enjoyed and can be supplied by dry foods made for plant-loving fish, chopped lettuce, boiled chopped spinach—one of the best, for it deteriorates slowly—and various water plants on which they sometimes snack.

The most common problems, constipation, swim-bladder disorder, and fin congestion, are associated directly or indirectly with poor feeding or dirty water.

For general maintenance, follow the usual procedures of frequent topping-off, always siphoning off old water from the bottom, careful feeding, proper temperature, and adequate room.

Choosing a goldfish is a matter of highly individual preference, since there is a shape, type, and color for every taste. The color should be clear and bright, as should the eyes. Never buy any fish with cloudy eyes and don't buy from a tank where other fishes look ill. A split fin will probably heal and shouldn't cause too much concern if all other healthy signs are present. Red streaks in fins or tail mean trouble, as does a ragged, whitish look at the edges. If the fins or tail are not spread and the top fin (dorsal) erect, pass on to another tank. All fins must be carried well, with an "under full sail" look to them. The body should have a well-fed appearance, never hollow around the spine or stomach. If gills

Fig. 7-1 Common goldfish: C. *auratus*.
Fig. 7-2 Short-bodied goldfish.

Fig. 7-3   Red-cap oranda.

stick out at an awkward angle, or are red and swollen, that's not the fish for your collection. In short, all the fish in the tank you select from should be clean, alert, and uninjured. Any deviations from this simple rule will probably mean trouble for the underwater Eden you hope to contrive, and there is nothing decorative about animals in poor health.

One unexpected complication may arise in highly bred fish, veiltails and orandas (Fig. 7-3) in particular. At Charlotte Hopfinger's home, we admired one of the most spectacular veiltails we had ever seen, a pure white of almost extravagant perfection. She sighed with resignation, "It would be a champion, if it weren't a roller! Every time there is the least bit of stress, over and over she goes!" We drew nearer. Sure enough, at our approach, the lovely creature began a head-over-heels demonstration of a fish with the nervous quimsies. Fear in most animals communicates readily; as we watched, some of the others in the tank began the same disoriented actions. No matter how good the fish, it can't be shown if the deportment is poor.

Fig. 7-4   Pearl-scale, oranda, and celestial.

For the aquarium, where conditions will be closely monitored, all the types are appropriate. The more extreme the deviation from the original form, the more care will be necessary. Celestials, water bubble-eyes, telescope eyes—any of the highly developed eye types—must be kept in a tank free of sharp objects: no rocks, artificial plants with points, or craggy ornaments should be present. Although the fish usually are able to heal a punctured eye-bubble, it's risky. Types with modified eyes or fins, which swim slowly, would be at a disadvantage in a pool, vulnerable to predators, and the carefully cultivated features of lion heads, veiltails and black moors (Fig. 7-5) would be wasted and unnoticed.

Most hardy are the ones closest to the original. Wakins, the plain, carp-shaped goldfish is pretty and undemanding (see Fig. 7-1).

Comets come next, with a streamlined body shape, long pointed fins, alert manner, and speedy, bright movements. This form, said to be the only type developed in America, should be streamlined in all particulars; the body is long and not humped, the tail three-quarters or more the length of the body and forked, the forks coming to a point. Dorsal is high and erect; all fins are long and pointed. The eyes are normal.

Black moors (Fig. 7-5) offer nice contrast, the best ones being coal black, with no bronze or gold apparent. They can offer quite a surprise: old ones may "decolor," changing to gold or calico! Any moor showing gold or bronze while young will turn a deep bronze, or approach the much-sought-after chocolate coloring—not an unattractive color phase, but considered undesirable in show fish. The eyes protrude. There are both fantail and veiltail forms.

One very old English book on goldfish suggests keeping one or two moors with other goldfish as a sort of barometer. Their coloring shows slime and fungus diseases before they would be detected on other colors. We personally enjoy them for the drama a black fish introduces. We saw a striking tank decorated all in red: red gravel and background, red and green artificial plants, a bubbler in the form of a little Chinese fisherman slightly off-center, and the only fish were about a dozen fine black Chinese moors (see Fig. 2-17). Imaginative and decorative!

Fig. 7-5   Black moors.

Fig. 7-6   Webtail veiltails.

Readily available and hardy, a good show-type fantail has a divided tail, which is about half the body length, shallowly forked with points rounded. Body depth should be three-fifths of body length, with all fins slightly rounded. Its eyes are normal.

In the beautiful and very popular veiltail, look for a body that is rounded, with the depth—vertical measurement from top of back to bottom of stomach—two-thirds the length of the body. The dorsal fin should be high and spread, not lopping over or crimped. The tail must be completely double; that is, divided into two tails, not joined, even near the base. This is called a webtail (Fig. 7-6), which is pretty, and perfectly alright for a pet, but not for show. The tail should be at least three-fourths the length of the body, squared off, not forked, with no distortions. All fins should be long and veillike, but sturdy, never ragged, with a smoothly rounded shape and no points. Eyes are normal, not protruding.

Lionheads are more highly developed yet—considered by some to be grossly distorted, by others to be lovely. In the exaggerated head development, a "bramble," raspberry-like growth appears as the fish matures, completely enveloping the head. Older fish often slough off some of this growth, which can impede gill function and hide the eyes. There is no trace of a dorsal fin, and the tail is not long, but divided. The body depth should be approximately three-fifths of the length, with all fins rounded. Needless to say, this is not one of the faster swimming fishes! Normal eyes.

One of my personal favorites is the Oranda (Fig. 7-3), which is reasonably hardy for such a highly refined animal. Depending upon the type, the bramble may be confined to the area between the eyes, making a stylish topknot, or it can cover the entire head. The body depth should be two-thirds the length, with a fully divided tail possessing a shallow fork (three-eighths or less). The tail should be at least three-fourths as long as the body, hopefully longer. There is a fine high dorsal, and the other fins are correspondingly long, coming to a nice crisp point. Eyes are normal.

Another version either deplored or admired, depending on one's own sense of beauty (or justice!) is the celestial. First seen in sacred temple pools in the Orient and jealously guarded from the exploitation of outsiders, according to legend the eyes of the celestial (Fig. 7-4) are forever and unceasingly turned toward Heaven, the sockets bulging below. They tend to bump into each other a lot, as would anybody whose eyes can only stare upward, and feeding is a bit of a problem. There is no dorsal. Be sure you will use extra precautions if you intend to keep this one, not known for its hardiness.

Similar to the celestial is the water bubble-eye, which sports large, jiggling bags of fluid under the eyes. All precautions must pertain here, needless to say.

Most of the forms mentioned here are seen in all the colors and patterns found in goldfish.

There are many scale-types not described here: pearl-scale, with raised, pearl-like scales (Fig. 7-4); malt-scale; clear scale; and albino versions of these, probably the least hardy of all.

To learn what a fine goldfish should be, go to exhibitions, contact hobbyists, and choose the ones most appealing to you.

If you buy from a dealer who keeps a clean store with many well-cared-for tanks, you will have a greater chance of success, and you may be lucky enough to find one you can trust for accurate advice. But in the main, be your own expert; learn all you can about the types you think are most interesting—be choosy, particular, and discriminating. After all, you respect your time and effort and want maximum results, with the finest, most lovely tank or tanks that can be developed. We are not discussing a bouquet of cut flowers or some other temporary decoration. Goldfish live for years under ordinary care, and as long as twenty-five years with extraordinary care, so let's make it worthwhile!

Sexing goldfish can be done when the fish are mature, at about ten to twenty-four months, depending on food, temperature, and water conditions. Also, maturity varies a great deal from one type to another, the commons and comets being most precocious.

The famous "breeding tubercules" are a fairly reliable indicator: males develop small white bumps on the gill covers and leading ray of the dorsal and pectoral fins when ready to spawn. Occasionally females show this trait, but not often. The male will attempt to drive other fish, bumping their sides, nudging at their bellies, and showing general aggressiveness. Young males tend to be smaller than females the same age.

Females will, of course, have a heavier body when full of eggs and often are lopsided, with one side of the belly a little more bulgy than the other. As her readiness approaches, the vent area will enlarge and protrude slightly.

In older pairs that have previously spawned there is often a loving, caressing attitude that becomes more urgent just before spawning (color Fig. 4). An old mated pair is a very pretty sight, never far apart, always touching, obviously enjoying petting one another, acting like a serenely well-married couple.

The most orderly and productive method is to separate the two by partition-ing the tank, which should be at least twenty or thirty gallon size. A glass or Plexiglas partition is best. Rubber or plastic fittings are sold that will help keep the glass in place, or you can use ordinary 1/2-inch rubber tubing, split along one side and slipped onto the glass. Without fittings, you can prop the glass in place, but there should be a minimum of hard, lumpy objects, and the sharp edges of the glass should be inaccessible or fins and noses might be harmed. Sandpaper or even an emery board may be used to smooth sharp glass edges.

Controversy rages among experts concerning gravel. Some insist that gravel harbors bacteria and mulm, and damages long fins and tails. Others are just as sure the gravel does more good than harm, trapping mulm, keeping it from constantly being stirred through the water and, of course, there must be gravel if a subsand filter is wanted. "You pays your money and takes your chances." I do lean toward the gravel advocates. Even daily siphoning won't keep a bare tank free of debris, most of which stays partially suspended.

The fish are fed as much as they want several times a day, live food predomi-nating. Temperature can be from 65°–75°F; usually no heater is needed.

Give the tank a full day of light, turning off lights at night. pH is not especially important: somewhere in the middle range.

When the female is obviously very ripe and both show great interest in getting together, remove the partition early one morning, turn on the lights or open the drapes. Add the spawning mops, which can be water hyacinths, bundles of floating plants, or best and most practical from all aspects, a couple of white or green nylon spawning mops. Buy them, or make them from bundles of nylon yarn, fastened to corks or pieces of wood. They should hang down into the water about 7–8 inches, and be of a full, generous width.

After a preliminary introduction period, the male will begin to drive the female, chasing and butting at her. This may continue for several hours or a day or so. She should have places of refuge for rest if he is too tiring and insistent.

Finally they will plunge into a spawning mop, releasing eggs and milt. The eggs stick to anything they touch and expand as soon as they are in the water.

You must be on hand to remove the mops or the parents as soon as egglaying ceases, for goldfish fancy freshly laid eggs, as do so many other egglaying fishes.

Since the eggs have a very high oxygen requirement, spread the mops in large shallow plastic, glass, or enamel basins, or—and this is preferable—place in a well-aerated shallow tank. Water should have been prepared beforehand, and be the same temperature as that in the spawning tank. Whatever container is used, it should be free of any sediment.

Depending upon temperature, eggs will hatch in three to five days. Ideal temperature is 70°–75°F (22°–24°C), no higher, too warm an environment causes premature hatching with inferior, weak young.

The yolk sacs will nourish the hatchlings for one and one-half days, but newly hatched brine shrimp must be at hand when the fry begin swimming

Fig. 7-7 Young goldfish from a single spawning showing variations in color, finnage, and body shape.

around looking for food. Feed them frequently, keeping the tiny bellies orange and round with brine shrimp, but use careful judgment: too much food will cause oxygen to be depleted and unused shrimp will die and pollute the water. Too little, and there will be starvation and stunted fish.

Until they're a month old, the fry are very touchy about any change in water or being moved; if you must move them for any reason, use extreme care with a clear plastic or glass cup, never a net.

A sponge filter is very useful at this time; it filters the water without endangering even the smallest fry, or you might remove the cover of a small inside filter, use a top layer of fine charcoal in it *over* the glass wool, and run it at a gentle rate (see Fig. 2-11). There should be aeration, but never so violent as to exhaust the young.

Depending on variety, the bronze color will begin at about four or five weeks to give way to orange, white, calico, or whatever the mature color will be. No matter how pure the background of the parents, there will be quite a variation in all characteristics: finnage, body shape, and color will be different from one individual to another, with only a percentage reflecting the preferred conformity to type (Fig. 7-7). Do not try to raise all the young unless you have adequate space. Better to raise a few very fine fish than risk losing them all due to overcrowding, or stunt the lot. Only a percentage of the young will be well-developed representatives of their type, so concentrate on these.

RED RASBORA

Rasbora heteromorpha

For color, life, and dash, it's the snappy-looking little red rasboras. The overall color is silver, overlaid with a bright, translucent coral, with a distinctive black triangle worn proudly at either side. Small, 1 3/4 inches long, peaceful, alert— *R. heteromorpha* moves around the tank gracefully and quickly, never nervous or jerky—an altogether excellent little fish.

Though they will live well up to five years and show good color and activity in the average neutral pH tank, they will be at their best in a more acid condition, say 6.0 or a little below, with the softest water available. Large schools of these little gems always make the best display, and they show to best advantage when accompanied by neon tetras, head-and-tail-light tetras and similar fishes.

Clean rainwater, filtered over a layer of peat, filter wool, and charcoal, a temperature of 76°–78°F, a few *cryptocoryne* plants, and a diet of white worms, daphnia, and brine shrimp, and your friend *R. heteromorpha* may even spawn for you.

If spawning is desired, separating males and females for a time, while giving a good conditioning regimen of live and frozen foods, is always beneficial. Males are determined by the more pointed, forward-angled lower point of the black

Fig. 7-8   Fire eel, one of the spiny eels.

triangle, and more intense reddish streak along the back immediately before the tail. The lower point of the females' black triangle is less distinct, and does not come forward to a point.

After a long and peaceful courtship, the female glues her eggs on the underside of a leaf. There is no parental care of the spawn, so the pair may be removed, the young being fed as any other small egglayer fry.

SPINY EELS

Mastacembelidae Sp.

In recent years, some very interesting fishes have been imported. They are generally called spiny eels, but they are not technically eels. They were given the name "spiny" because of the spines that are found at the front of the dorsal.

Although there is a variety of colors and types, behavior is basically the same. Most of the day is spent with the middle or rear half hidden in the sand or behind a rock. The head is posed at an alert angle, hoping for unwary prey. These are very voracious fish. While not a menace to any neighbor too large to fit into their mouths, they will snap up any fish small enough, no matter how expensive!

These fellows often become very tame. With patience they can be coaxed to eat from one's fingers and, although they should be started on live foods, they can be taught to eat particles of shrimp or meat.

Their swimming movement is beautiful and full of grace.

If you plan to keep more than one, buy them all at the same time. Don't plan to add others later, as the established one will drive the new ones mercilessly.

The tank *absolutely* must be covered. In the small crevasses between heater and hood, fit pieces of vinyl screen. Occasionally eels decide to go exploring, and they can squirm through very small spaces.

In a large tank, eels will reach a length of at least 14 inches.

One of the most attractive is the fire eel (Fig. 7-8). It is chocolate with vivid red-orange markings: an outstanding beauty.

The best temperature is 78°–80°F (26°–27°C). If the water is allowed to build up mineral content, the eel shows its discomfort by investigating every possible means of escape. Siphoning and replacing of water should be done every three or four weeks, at least.

If all needs are met, eels will live a long time.

CICHLIDS

It isn't possible for me to say of any one fish family, "this is my favorite," but this one rates right up there at the top.

The cichlids (say *sick'lids*) are very intelligent and long-lived—five to ten years. Their spawning habits are highly developed, with fierce devotion shown to the little ones. The sight of a small fish-parent who will fight anything, no matter how large, to protect its young is very moving.

Cichlids come from Asia, tropical America, and a few are to be found in parts of Texas.

They are, in the main, aggressive fellows. They are usually best kept in a tank of their own, but some can be community members if their neighbors are large enough.

Most of them are dedicated to digging pits in the sand and never seem quite content with the furniture arrangement, changing it constantly. Some will even boost small rocks from one place to another. Plants get torn up during all this activity. Plastic ones, well anchored with stones, improve appearances and give cover and resting areas for the less active ones. For this reason, a rock cave or a flower pot on its side is very useful. If the hole in the pot is of a size they might try to squeeze through, smooth and enlarge it to prevent injury. Sometimes they become so excited they don't employ good safety rules!

The majority of their waking moments are taken up with thoughts of spawning. They are forever digging pits, staking out brood territories, and trying to find some willing partner. There should be more females than males. If any one fish seems to be taking more punishment than it returns, remove it, for some individuals seem, like some humans, to get more than their share of bullying.

The best method of getting a well-matched pair is to let them form partnerships of their own choosing. If you don't have the room for this, select a well-fed pair and put them in a partitioned tank of at least 10 gallon (40 liter) size, where they can see one another and get acquainted. They aren't easy to sex; males tend to have more color and pointed anal and dorsal fins, while females may show more fullness in the stomach.

There is good reason for this gradual introduction. One may be ready to spawn before the other, and the reluctant one might be killed by its impatient partner.

When they both show great interest in meeting, and the female is rounded and ripe-looking, try allowing them together. Watch closely. If each seems to be holding his own, even though there is considerable squabbling, chances are good of a pairing. They will clasp jaws and tug furiously, time and again. There will be much repeated kissing and chasing—altogether an athletic courtship. The most important thing to watch for is that both are participating. If one retreats, looking for refuge, and shows no interest in the festivities, replace the partition and try again later or substitute a different fish.

Let's say all goes swimmingly. The pair is in a clean, large aquarium, with plenty of prospective spawning sites—caves, flowerpots—and about 2 inches of clean sand. The angels and discus like a piece of slate or marble, leaned against a side glass, but most others prefer the aforementioned items. The temperature is 80°–82°F (28°–30°C); pH 6.7–7.0. If you are observant, you will see the spawning tubes, which appear a day or so previous to egglaying. The female has a more blunt, broad tube, the male's being more pointed. After meticulously cleaning the inside or outside of a flowerpot, the female begins to glue the semitransparent eggs to the cleaned area. The male follows closely, spraying milt over each batch. This will continue for two or more hours, with several hundred eggs being deposited.

You must now decide whether to raise the fry yourself or leave the eggs with the parents. Some risk is involved with the natural method; one or both parents may eat the eggs or young. As is common with alert, aggressive animals, they are nervous, and a real or imagined menace may cause them to eat their offspring to save them from a more terrible fate! If this happens, one parent may dispatch the other, either through grief or revenge.

Raising cichlids by hand is done by all the large fish farms. It is more certain, and they have the staff and equipment. You can do it, but it takes a little work and care. The eggs and their pot or slate are put into another 10-gallon (40 liter) tank, in which the water temperature and pH are similar. A fungicide is added, and an airstone is placed so that a gentle stream of air passes over the eggs. Every effort must be made to ensure the nursery is clean.

In about four to four and a half days, the eggs begin to quiver; they are developing! A few days more, and the little glass slivers that are fish begin to swim. Now they are offered newly hatched brine shrimp, sifted daphnia, and a little finely powdered dry food. Don't overload the water with food, but see to it that the glass slivers all have round, orange tummies at all times. Development from this point on is rapid and feeding should be frequent.

Watching a fond couple of cichlids raise their babes is so absorbing and intricate that no one should miss it. The parents keep on cleaning at the mass of eggs. When the tails develop, they bite each egg from its place and start a long

Fig. 7-9   Mated pair of *P. scalare*, showing sexual differences. Male *(left)* shows less curve from ventral to anal area; female *(right)* has a distinct belly curve.

ritual of moving their progeny from one carefully guarded sand pit to another, picking them up in their mouths, spitting them into the new location.

Some authorities speculate that the purpose of this is to offer a moving target, never staying in one place very long. Others believe this is the only way the parents can be sure every baby has a really good scrubbing, for each single one gets this mouthing, chewing treatment in its trip to the new brood site.

At night the parents usually return to one particular pit and hover over their brood like hens!

On occasion one parent, usually the male, will decide to do all the work himself. He will drive the female away, not allowing her anywhere near the young. If this happens, remove her: she will either make him so nervous he eats the eggs or kills her, or she might just decide to dine on young cichlid herself.

Throughout the brood period the adults must be fed. They have no trouble telling a luscious daphnia or shrimp pellet from one of their beloved offspring. As soon as the little ones can swim, they are ready for small live food, as mentioned before.

The whole family looks so lovely together it is hard to remember: don't let them become overcrowded. As you remove some or all of the fry, observe the reactions of the adults. One may blame the other for the disappearance of the young and take such offense as to consider strong punitive measures.

We might say of the cichlids: they may be headaches, but they are never boring!

Pterophyllum scalare
P. eimekei
P. altum

There are several species of freshwater angels, but the one most commonly seen is *P. scalare* (Fig. 7-9 and color Fig. 16). They all have basically the same requirements and habits.

Considered by many to be the single most desirable fish, the angel is regal in appearance: tall, laterally compressed, with broad, flaring tail and the manner and bearing of a monarch. Intensive selective breeding has produced a wide variety of colors and finnages. There are veiltail versions of the original, and the color ranges from silver marked with black (*P. scalare, P. eimekei*) or brown (*P. altum*) to a pale moonlight yellow; there is a lace-patterned black over silver, a half black, half silver, and a solid, velvety black.

The short-tailed silver—the natural, unimproved variety—is most hardy. Because of the hardiness, extra alertness, and intelligence, he is my personal favorite. The more highly bred varieties become delicate as the degree of refinement progresses, but all are relatively easy to keep.

A temperature of 75°–80°F (24°–28°C), pH of 6.8 to neutral, a 10-gallon or over (40 liter) tank which is well-planted, and twelve hours of light daily will

Fig. 7-10   Male angelfish.

Fig. 7-11   Female angelfish.

make them very happy, especially if they have all the frozen and fresh brine shrimp, dry flake food, and angleworms they can eat.

Angels are considered shy fish, and so they are with strangers. But they soon become accustomed to their keeper and respond with all the demonstrative affection of a dog or cat, coming close to the front, quivering with excitement, showing every evidence of joy at the approach of a familiar face. I kid you not—they do learn to recognize people and, unless strangers are frequent, they will hide at the approach of one.

The most foolproof way to pair angels is to raise a group together and, observing closely, remove the pairs as they are apparent. A mature pair can be detected more by behavior than appearance (Figs. 7-10 and 7-11): the female has a markedly broader stomach and may seem to show a more rounded belly above the anal fin, with more of an angle between the belly and the juncture of the fin, whereas the male has less fullness at the belly, which tends to have a straighter outline from the ventral area of the chest to the beginning of the anal fin (see Fig. 7-9). They will lock jaws, seem to be bickering among themselves, and will prefer to stay close together, driving others away.

A proven female can be introduced to a known mature male, and often this works very well, but the best way is the natural way.

Temperature should be 80°F (25°C). A good selection of plants should be used, with a nice-sized Amazon sword plant included. Commercial breeders spawn thousands of angels in bare tanks with a strip of slate to receive the eggs, and there is no reason to condemn this practice; it works efficiently. The planting is suggested assuming you will want the tank to be attractive. Also, rarely, one or the other is scrappy and the less feisty one may need cover.

Every case is different—even the same pair will deviate from the norm when it comes to spawning. Most often the procedure goes thusly: after a courtship that features play-fights and jaw-locking with a little tug-o'-war thrown in, a long, opaque, diagonal surface such as a sword plant leaf or strip of slate (about 8 by 3 inches [21 by 8cm]) will be selected, and both fish will clean it of algae with their mouths, taking several hours to do so. The spawning tube of the female, which is blunter than that of the male and extends in a backward direction, will emerge; she will begin to place the adhesive eggs in precise rows on the clean surface. The male's tube appears, more pointed and slanting forward, and he follows her closely, fertilizing the eggs. They may work for two or more hours, taking time off to chase any intruders away, and lay several hundred eggs.

When the eggs are laid, you must decide whether to rear the young yourself, which is a little more trouble but safer, or to allow the parents to care for the eggs and young, which is more dangerous for they may eat them.

To raise the young yourself, remove the leaf or slate strip and place it in an unplanted, clean 10-gallon (40 liter) aquarium of the same temperature and pH. Add enough Methylene Blue to the water to tint it light to medium blue, and prop the eggs diagonally and facing the bottom of the tank, so that the bubbles

Fig. 7-12   The male preparing to move the last of the babes to another sword plant leaf. Over a hundred have already been moved. Leaf has been reused several times, shows fraying.

of an airstone can very gently flow over them. The eggs will begin to quiver on the second day, and by the third will start falling off the strip, to lie on the bottom of the tank, in an ever-increasing mass of vibrating little glass slivers. Do not disturb them; in a few more days they will attempt to swim. When they are free-swimming, offer *infusoria,* and raise as you would any other cichlid. If they need *infusoria* at all, it will only be for the first two days; be sure to offer newly hatched brine shrimp on the second day.

To raise the young naturally, leave them with their parents; if all goes well, they will give you a wonderful demonstration of family devotion, sharing in the cleaning and protection of the eggs and babes. The eggs are constantly fanned and mouthed by the parents, who take turns intently cleaning, cleaning. When the eggs first begin to develop, one or both parents will decide to move them, regluing them to another leaf (Fig. 7-12). This moving from place to places goes on until the fry are swimming in a little cloud. It's touching to see the parents swimming side by side, the swarm of young ones between them. If one daring or uncontrolled swimmer spirals erratically away from the school, a parent catches him in its mouth and carries him to the midst of the flock, spitting him back where he will be safe. Even when the little ones assume angel shape at about two weeks and are eating and swimming independently, they tend to hover near the parents, who show a kind of absorbed preoccupation for them—something akin to pride and love.

This is the ideal family and events often happen just this way, but at any time during the described sequence, the young may be eaten. One pair may raise several spawnings beautifully, only to eat the next.

Blackjaw Mouthbreeder: *Tilapia macrocephala*

T. macrocephala is one of the mouthbreeders, as you may have gathered from its name. The male takes the eggs in his mouth, keeping them there until the young can swim. He must not be frightened at this crucial time, or he will discard the eggs and forget all about them! Artificial hatching can be done, however, with the use of an airstone and frequent agitation to move the eggs and turn them, like an old mother turkey might do.

This fish needs plenty of food. It is not as bad-tempered as some others, but must be fed well. It reaches a good size, up to 6 or 7 inches (15–18cm) but will probably stay smaller in the aquarium.

Color is interesting: the body is mainly silver with black markings which change from time to time in intensity and shape. The fins and tail have a blue-red blush.

Temperature should be 70°–85°F (22°–30°C); they're not particular about pH.

Discus: *Symphosodon discus*

In the early 1930s, a sensation was caused by the introduction of this spectacular fish from the Amazon.

It is pancake round and flattened like an angelfish. It stands tall and regal, and gives us all we could hope for in color, especially the male at breeding time. Mature size is usually 5–6 inches (13–15cm) long.

There are three species, green, brown, and blue, which are closely related. The primary difference is in the color.

The brown is most often seen: over a rich brown background, lightning-blue stripes run a wavy horizontal pattern. There is usually a touch of red on the dorsal and anal fin edges, the pectorals, and the eye.

These beauties are not difficult to keep if their requirements are met. The catch comes when one realizes that keeping Discus means faithful adherence to the proper schedule: once a week topping-off of 25 percent of the water, mainly live foods, frequent water testing to maintain the proper pH. Temperature about 80°–82°F (28°–30°C); pH 6.6 to 7.0 (slightly acid to neutral); and relatively soft water needed.

They are shy, gentle fish. Their tank should be well planted with tall, soft plants. No rocks or other hard-surfaced decorations should be used because they startle easily and may bash into things, causing abscesses which may not heal. It is much better to keep them alone in a large (10 gallon or 40 liter) tank. This would be the minimum size to use, and it is best to use the tall shape.

If you want to use other species with them, choose those that will not compete with the slow, dainty Discus for food. Since Discus have small mouths, your range of possibilities for tankmates is rather wide; they can be quite a bit smaller and still in no danger of being eaten.

Discus spawn much like angelfishes. A fairly peaceful courtship is followed by placement of the eggs in neat rows on some vertical object. They should be allowed to choose their own mates, again like the angels.

When the fry hatch, a strange thing happens. They find their way to the sides of their parents, and begin to feed on the copious amounts of body slime being produced for this purpose! Young have been raised on substitute formulas, but even at the risk of having the fry eaten by their parents, better results are had by leaving them to their natural way.

In less than a week, the babies can take newly hatched brine shrimp. As with all very young fish, feed them often.

If you are sure the water is clean and the proper acidity and degree of hardness, and still your discus seem not to prosper, try giving them more privacy. Cover the ends of the tank, as well as the back. Add a heavier planting. They are worth the trouble!

Egyptian Mouthbreeder: *Haplochromis multicolor*

Cleopatra in all her splendor would not rival this little fish from Egypt. Its name, *multicolor,* is fitting. In the dealer's tanks it may not show to particular advantage, but given the proper conditions—necessary, of course, to bring out the beauty in any fish—this one is very pretty. Over a silvery-blue ground, the scales show individually, having brown centers. There is a little dark tab at the upper part of the gill cover, and a dark pattern running down the side. Males have a reddish area at the tip of the anal fin. Fins and tail are well spangled with light blue.

They are occasionally kept in community tanks, for they are not as cross as some other Mouthbreeders, but watch them. As they develop toward maturity they may decide to make the world safe for Mouthbreeders everywhere, and clean out any residents small enough to conquer.

The Egyptian Mouthbreeder reaches a mature size of 4–8 inches (10 1/2–26cm). The best temperature range is 75°–85°F (22°–30°C).

Feed them well when conditioning for spawning. The female, who incubates the eggs, will not eat during the ten days she carries them. Even if netted, she will not relinquish the eggs, but she should be left in peace to complete her task. The male is only a hazard during incubation, so he should be removed.

The female faithfully guards the young after they are free-swimming. It's almost startling, even when you know what to expect, seeing the little fish dart into their mother's mouth at any sign of danger. She seems to become frustrated after they grow too large to contain in her mouth, and may begin to eat them. This can occur any time from three to seven days after their first release from her mouth.

Firemouth: *Cichlasoma meeki*

If you only try one cichlid, this one should be considered. It would be a shame to miss the color and drama of this totally engaging fellow.

Reaching a length of 4 inches (10 1/2cm) or a little more, it has a very pretty curve to its fins and tail, and the male develops a long, exaggerated point at the tips of the fins. Body color is basic olive, but there are generous sprinkles of light blue dots, and red on fins and tail. The outstanding characteristic is the lower mouth and belly color: they glow with the most intense fiery red imaginable. This color is, of course, at its best at breeding time, but can always be seen. The female also shares this distinction.

Breeding is basically the same with all the pit-digging cichlids. The male usually drives the female away and cares for the young.

He will attack any invader, be it fish or keeper's finger, and can most often be expected to be a devoted father. This is one of those mentioned that hovers over the young at night, gathering them into a quivering little mass at evening, and staying over them until morning, when he gathers every one up and moves them to another pit. This goes on all day, until time for bed, usually at the same pit. This is true of most fish which care for their young; when the fry become too difficult to control and keep in one place, the parent may become confused or angry and eat them. Always watch closely. Sometimes the little ones can stay with parent or parents until the tank becomes too crowded; other times parents must be removed at free-swimming time.

Best temperature for these fish: 80°F (28°C).

Jack Dempsey: *Cichlasoma biocellatum*

You guessed it—this one has *earned* its common name! The Jack Dempsey was one of the first cichlids to be kept by hobbyists—it is pretty, hardy, and has quite a personality.

A sweet, pleasant, community fish it is not.

There is no denying it is handsome. A dark background is lavishly decorated with blue dots. The shape is very like that of a firemouth, but with a large rounded tail. As it matures the colors become darker and fluctuate less.

The Jack Dempsey is one of the more intelligent fishes, becoming quite a pet. It is also one of the long-lived types. We had a beautiful pair for over seven years. The female died at that age, and the male lived for two more years, getting tamer as time went on.

A wide temperature range is tolerated—70°–90°F (21°–33°C), but the general rule should be to keep temperature around 78°–80°F (26°–27°C).

Mature size is 4–6 inches (approximately 10–15 1/2cm).

Jewel Fish: *Hemichromis bimaculatus*

A sparkly little (around 4 inch, a little over 10cm) beauty, this one has what might be called an aggressive temperament. Like so many of the more fierce-tempered fishes, it is a good parent. That is not to say it's a good spouse. All the cautions advised in the section on cichlids apply here. The eggs can be taken from the parents and raised artificially, but it does seem that the more ferocious the fish, the more tenderly the babes are nurtured.

If your fish spawn once, most often they'll spawn again. If you do lose a crop of eggs due to egg-eating, chances are good of starting over again, this time raising the little ones yourself.

The usual arrangement, with heavy planting, lots of hiding places, and a flower pot or two is advised, and do watch for too-heavy fighting at mating time. Temperature should be 72°–80°F (22°–28°C).

The colors flash brighter and dimmer with emotion, and the jewel fish is beautiful at times. At other times, he may not be especially outstanding, but the characteristic that gave it the common name, the jewels of blue, are always present in varying degrees.

Sexes can be distinguished in this way: even though the female may be at times a littler brighter, the male has larger, brighter jewels on his gill covers, and those on his tail form a balanced pattern all the way across, rather than being just on the top half of the tail, as they are in the female.

By the time the young are two months old, they realize they are fierce jewel fish, and start to fight. They need a large rearing tank, and plenty of food and cover. They will eat virtually any food, but live food always produces a brighter, better-colored fish.

They are found in most of the tropical parts of Africa.

Oscar: *Astronotus ocellatus*

The most important requirement for the oscar is a large, roomy tank, for this one can reach 8–10 inches (28–33cm). It grows fairly fast if properly fed and will eat almost anything.

In profile, its most distinctive feature is revealed (Fig. 7-13). The fins and tail are completely opaque. The body texture is not shiny, as in most scaled fishes, but has a matte finish. Basic color is chocolate, with markings and dots in orange. A round black dot at the base of the tail is bordered with orange.

In distress or fright they do a slow barrel-roll, another unusual feature. Oscars become very good pets. One friend, whose daughter was a victim of severe allergies, presented her with a tank of baby oscars. Five years later, even though the allergies had nearly disappeared, the oscars were still her cherished pets.

Being able to love and care for them had helped the little girl through a very difficult time in her life.

In Florida, oscars are being introduced to every freshwater fishing area bordering the Gulf of Mexico. They are said to be the fightingest gamefish in this hemisphere.

Oscars are good parents, but must have a large tank, 50–100 gallon capacity. Eggs are laid in strands. The best temperature range is 75°–85°F (24°–32°C).

If all goes well, you may one day be able to collect your own oscars in the southernmost parts of the country.

BETTAS

Betta splendens

No fish could be considered more dramatic than the Betta, or Siamese fighting fish (color Fig. 3). He is just that—a fighting fish, used like fighting cocks for wagering and sport in Siam, now Thailand.

Fig. 7-13   Oscar: *A. ocellatus.*

Pefectly peaceful with other types of fishes, a male Betta will suddenly spread his fins, arch his back, ruff out his gills, and flood himself with brilliant color at the approach of another male Betta or the sight of his beautiful self in a mirror. He will strut proudly back and forth, threatening and villifying in fish body-language. If the other fish is real, and not a reflection, the two of them will proceed to tear all the vertical fins to shreds, biting out a few scales as well. They may fight for hours until one surrenders, a pathetic stub of his former self. If the damage is confined to the fins, healing is surprisingly quick, but damaged scales or gills may mean the start of fungus, which can kill the fish.

If one fight could establish supremacy of one male, obviating any necessity of further fights, it would be nice, but this doesn't happen. Two or more males in a tank just means constant whacking away at one another.

From the original, metallic olive-green wild Betta, a most impressive range of colors has been developed: the famous and very rare black; all shades of blue and green, with or without metallic sheen; bright or deep red; flesh-colored body with wine red fins and tail—the Cambodian; albino; and mixtures of these colors, such as blue body with red fins, or actually variegated.

The Siamese fighting fish is very hardy and can be kept in a pint (1/2 liter) container, but it's better to use a larger one to enjoy the graceful swimming movements. One requirement, however, is rigid; for the most color and best performance and breeding, 80°F (27°C) is the temperature: no more, no less. They will live at lower or higher temperatures, but not as long nor as well. Any middle-register pH will do, for fighters are tolerant of most kinds of water, but they do like that just-right temperature.

Mosquito larvae are preferred to all other foods, but any live food small enough for them to swallow and all dry foods are welcomed. Best color, health, and vigor are obtained with a high ratio of live food.

A single male can be part of the community tank, where it adds color and flair while behaving as the most peaceful of fishes. It is a slow, graceful swimmer, which can be bullied by more aggressive mates. The females, while not so long-finned, also have good color and are usually peaceful; you may find an occasional hussy who makes life miserable for her mate, but this doesn't happen often. It's better to keep several females, rather than one, in a community tank with one male, because he'll want to bully her, whether he wants to spawn or not.

Which brings us to one of the most lovely, graceful spawning procedures in all ichthyology.

Use a 5- or 10-gallon (20–40 liter) tank, water at a temperature of 80°F (27°C), pH not important, depth 6–8 inches (15–25cm). You may have to adapt a standard heater-thermostat to the shallow water by hanging it outside the lip of a partially filled quart jar. *Keep the tank covered closely to keep out dust, scum, and drafts.* Condition the pair on live food. Be sure there are hiding places for the female: floating plants are helpful, and add a couple of flower pots, with the drainage holes enlarged and smoothed, for they like to dash through full-tilt. A filter isn't really necessary and shouldn't be run when there are eggs or babies, anyway, but a gently running airstone is a very good idea.

Allow a mature young male to establish himself. When he seems to be comfortable and confident, float a jar containing the ripe female. When a female is quite ready for spawning, her belly will be round and full (ripe), and a little round bump, looking just like an egg, will be seen at her vent. Almost invariably, at sight of her he will immediately build a nest of floating bubbles against her container, while spreading his fins, coloring deeply, strutting, always near, to allow her full view of his wonderfulness! Upon her release, he will hurry over to the site he really prefers and build a new bubble nest; the other was just a sample for her inspiration. She will explore the tank, giving passing glances to the busy male, while her trips about the tank just accidentally bring her nearer and nearer to the building site. On rare occasions, practiced females may join in the building, offering a few bubbles here and there, but they do not seem to last. Her assistance, if it is allowed by the male, is a mere gesture. The males are able to coat the bubbles with a substance that makes them last longer.

When the male is satisfied with the nest, he boldly resumes his courting, putting on a splendid show, with far more color and spreading of fins than even that used to impress another male. There is a great deal of shivering of the anal fin, the better to exhibit its color and size.

She reciprocates, joining in a rhapsodic ballet of motion and passion; altogether a dreamlike ritual that is one of nature's most lovely sights. At last he urges her under the nest, where he curves his body around hers; as they sink together through the water, eggs are released and fertilized. This will be repeated many times, until all the eggs are gone. He, and sometimes she, gathers the eggs, spitting each mouthful into the nest. If the female assists in the placing of the eggs, the male will impatiently snatch them from wherever she put them and tuck them in with the ones he retrieved, poking most of them into the same little spot until they are a tiny white mound. Since the nest often extends over a 6-inch area, this looks a little silly, but he seems to think it's important to have them all in exactly the right place.

At this time you must be on hand. When the eggs are all gathered, the cad has no further use for her, and chases and bullies her unmercifully, often even killing her. For his own peace, the safety of the eggs, and her security, she must be removed to where she can recover from any splits or nips in her fins. Sometimes he is a rather enthusiastic lover, but if there is only a little biting, that's par for the course.

Alone with his work, the male constantly cares for the eggs and nest, adding new bubbles, replacing fallen eggs, and threatening you with instant annihilation whenever you look in. In thirty-six hours, the eggs will have hatched and you will see tiny babies hanging in the nest, falling out and being replaced by the father, or zooming out from the nest like mad tadpoles, trying their wings.

He will soon lose patience with them, so as soon as you see that they are beginning to leave the nest, remove him, for he will eat them when he cannot keep them in the nest.

When the fry start swimming, sprinkle *infusoria* powder on the water surface, use an *infusoria* culture, or dried, powdered egg yolk. Within three days to a week, they can take newly hatched brine shrimp.

At all times keep a close cover over the tank; do not allow a draft, which will kill the young fish. Be sure there is no scum on the water surface; they are tiny and will be unable to break scum for their first breaths of air. When feeding, open the cover as little as possible.

Bettas are easy to spawn and raise; just observe the few precautions given here.

At about six to eight weeks the males, who can be distinguished by the more pointed dorsal fins, will begin to fight. They should be raised in separate containers: some use 8-ounce jars, but this is a little conservative; I prefer quart jars, which makes for a little less cleaning and gives them room to be comfortable.

LIVEBEARERS

Xiphorus sp.
Molleinesia sp.
Lebistes reticulatus

Livebearing fishes, those having their young alive, are interesting for many reasons: the platys, swordtails, mollies, and guppies are very colorful, easy to increase, and fine examples for youngsters just beginning to learn how propagation takes place. One word of caution: many livebearers, unless very well nourished, tend to eat their young as fast as they are born—not such a good illustration for children. To help avoid this problem, always supply plenty of live food, such as brine shrimp, supplemented with several varieties of dry food. Use a well-planted tank with plenty of floating plants or spawning mops.

It's best to isolate gravid, or pregnant, females from others when they are ready to deliver. When the stomach is full-to-bursting, showing a dark area near the vent where you can often see the little ones' eyes through the translucent skin, the mother is about ready. They can complicate matters for you, for they seem to be able to defer parturition at will. When moving them, treat them gently; they really are in a "delicate condition"! Some keepers prefer not to move a female at this time, for it is risky—they isolate her either well before time, or net out all the other fishes. Following these few tips, there is little likelihood of cannibalism, but remember: plenty of live food.

Nearly all the livebearers are tropical or semitropical, needing warmer tanks— between 74° and 80°F (23°–27°C).

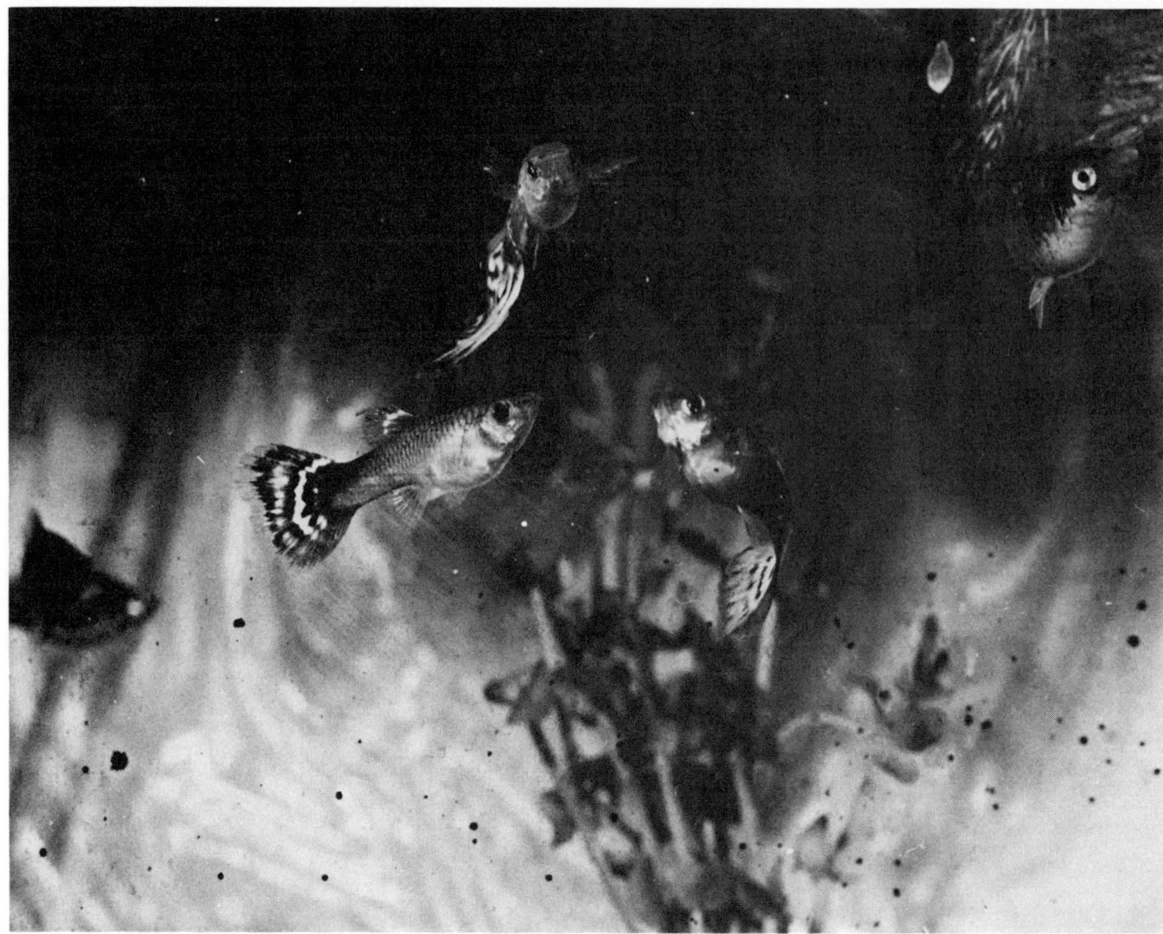

Fig. 7-14 Guppies: *L. reticulatus.*

Some may get a bit crabby. The males of swordtails, *Xiphorus* species, some-times are scrappy with other males, and can bully the females if there are not several females to each male. Mollies, *Molleinesia* species, have this same tendency.

The platy, another *Xiphorus* species, is a very desirable fish for the community tank. It is pretty, good-tempered, and hardy, but will eat its young unless very well fed and in a heavily planted tank. This one is best kept with other fishes, such as mollies, who like a little salt in the water: approximately a teaspoonful to 2 gallons (8 liters) of water works well because they seem to be healthier and more alert. Platys and swordtails come in a wide range of colors: all the reds, blues, yellows and variegated. The best temperature is 75°F (24°C).

Guppies, *Lebistes reticulatus,* have come a long way from the greenish little fish first found in Venezuela and Trinidad. Every color is available, as well as black and a sort of enamel white. The tail of the male is large and very colorful (Fig. 7-14): more color is being developed in the tails of females, as well. Every shape of tail, from long, square veiltail to pointed pintail, can be seen. The males

Fig. 7-15 Mollies: *Molleinesia* species. These green, wild-type mollies have been acclimated to saltwater.

constantly court the females, spreading and quivering their lovely tails. Guppies are perfectly peaceful. The best temperature for them is 75°–80°F (24°–27°C).

One fertilization enables a female to deliver several litters, approximately four weeks apart. Males grow much larger if raised separately from females as early as sexual differences appear.

Mollies may be grayish green, silver and black mottled, or flat-black—an attractive foil that gives added accent to the brightly colored fishes (Fig. 7-15). Boiled spinach or some flake food prepared for greens-loving fishes is eagerly accepted, as are all live foods. Mollies need greens and live foods, but will happily eat anything. Keep at a temperature of 75°–80°F (24°–27°C). Add one or two teaspoons of aquarium salt to each gallon (4 liters) of water.

Males of the livebearers have a gonopodium, with which the female is fertilized internally. The eggs then incubate in her brood pouch, to be born fully developed and swimming.

SHINERS

Notropis sp.

We mention only a few of the many types of shiners here; virtually all of them are of a size and temperament to recommend them highly.

Most of them are blessed with good color, and the main factor in deciding which ones to keep is which ones you are able to find!

Widely distributed throughout all but the arid parts of North America, some favor clear streams, some like the shallow edges of rivers, some prefer weedy ditches. So if you find a pretty, active, shiny small fish of the shiner type, try it: you'll probably like it!

Azurine Shiner: *N. lutrensis*

Rapidly becoming one of the most popular aquarium fishes, this elegant North American native is in more demand every day.

Several years ago, a group of country youngsters in central Missouri developed quite a thriving business, collecting and selling "redheads," as they called them. Their only overhead was a minnow trap and a few soda crackers and biscuit crumbs from the safe. These ambitious children may have played an important role in bringing *N. lutrensis* to the attention of the aquarium world, for the shiners' popularity accelerated rapidly from that time.

Some of the shiners found their way to an aquarium shop, where I saw them prominently displayed, with a tag on the tank proclaiming "Imperial Tetras—$2.95 each"! A gyp? Not really. The only dishonesty was in the name—they're not tetras, but a realistic analysis of the cost of collecting and transporting the minnows establishes reason for a good price, *if* you can find them! They are not widespread and, once found, never plentiful. Another point: they were some of the prettiest fish in the store!

Look for *N. lutrensis* in small midwestern streams directly above or below a riffle (where water runs swiftly over gravel) in very shallow water, 2–18 inches deep. They can be seined, but willingly enter a baited minnow trap. This is the better method, for with seining there is often injury to scales and fins. They will be dancing and flashing in small schools, each group featuring one to three unusually brightly colored specimens. All, even the females, have good color and will color up very well with good feeding and proper water conditions, but there is always a small percentage of both male and female super-fish to each group.

A program of selective breeding would surely produce an even more outstanding fish. A few capable hobbyists are at work on this project now and interesting results should soon come about.

Always check your local Conservation Commission for any regulations you should observe, and get property owners' permission. Incidentally, your local Conservation Commission is a good place to look for help and advice.

Most newly collected fish are under great stress, which means a higher than usual oxygen requirement. Pay careful attention to covering holding and transportation containers, for they will try to jump out of the small space back into their home waters, even when those waters are miles behind them!

No fish has accumulated more common names. In the area around the Moreau River in Missouri, the colloquial name is red head minnow; south, in the bootheel of Missouri, perch-nurses. Legend says "they keep care" of the perch's (local name for bluegill) nest of eggs when he is occupied otherwise, and "mind the young'uns when they hatch." You guessed it—their real interest is in a fine meal of eggs and young.

In Illinois it's "Bloodyhead" (yuck!) and down toward Texas, "Rainbow Minnow."

I have always preferred azurine shiner, which came about when our neighbor in the Ozarks saw the "minners" I had been keeping in a large wooden water-trough. "My, them's purty, sort of Azurine, like a early mornin' sky!" They were azurines from that moment, for me, and the name has spread—I encounter it frequently now. Hearing it, I remember the old lady's wrinkled face and soft, dreaming eyes: "Azurine, like a early mornin' sky!"

The overall color truly is a light, shining azure, with deep blue and glowing pink-red vertical shoulder marks, a reddish cap on top of the head, reddish tail and fins.

The body is deeper and fatter than most shiners and minnows. It can reach 4 inches (10cm) in length, with 3 more common.

Very playful, gentle, and active. When resting, they school closely in a charming drift, but at feeding time each man is for himself—they are quick, voracious eaters. Perfectly peaceful, these fish can be kept with gouramis, angels, and Bettas without nipping threadlike or trailing fins.

Omnivorous, they take any dry or live food. One trait, either good or bad, depending on whether you want snails: even a heavy population of snails will be dead within two days of the shiners' introduction into the tank. They especially relish the ramshorn species.

For shiners, they are relatively long-lived; I had a dozen azurines for three years. They would have lived longer but for my mistake. A dealer had told me that as much as 10 percent new water could be added to the tank without bothering to use Water-Rite. He was partially right: the angels, gouramis, and cats were unaffected, but all the azurines died. I can say authoritatively that they are very sensitive to the smallest trace of chlorine!

They survive midwestern winters and summers, from freezing to 90°F or even more, but ideal temperature is 65°–75°F (18°–25°C). They are usually found in water having a pH of 7.4 or thereabouts: any change should be made very gradually, say over two weeks' time, but it's best to just give them their preferred pH.

As do other very active fishes, they need well-aerated water, and though in their native streams they experience seasonal low, murky water, this won't do in a closed system; they soon fall victim to velvet or fungus infections.

This may lead the reader to think azurines are delicate. Actually they are very hardy once acclimated to confinement, and this is easily done. Just read the pH of their native water, duplicate it in a well-covered tank, keep a good filter going, feed them well, and be proud of owning one of our most beautiful natives.

Georgia Shiner: *N. hypsetopterus*

Another member of the *Notropis* family that's receiving more attention is the Georgia shiner. The same story applies to this one as to *N. lutrensis;* temperament and requirements are the same, but this one runs a little smaller, not over 3 inches (7 1/2cm), and has a more limited range. He is found mainly in parts of Florida and Georgia, and prefers a temperature of 50°–90°F (11°–33°C).

Their home water is usually not so alkaline as that of the azurines, so always observe the precaution of testing pH to be sure.

The body is a bright coppery-brown with yellow fins, red dorsal with a blurry black marking, and a dashing black and gold band running the length of the body. The anal and dorsal fins are larger than those seen in other *Notropis* species.

SILVERSIDES

Labidesthes sicculus
Menidia audens

All of the several species of silversides share the same features that would interest an aquarist. They are surpassingly beautiful, with long, slender narrow bodies with large bright silver eyes, two dorsal fins, a lateral streak of even more dazzling silver, and an overall look of animated slivers of glass. Another feature of interest—they practically self-destruct if handled! They can be trapped in the trusty glass minnow trap and transported from trap to carrying container with a large dipping implement, and thence to the tank. Never use a net, which always kills them. Once in the tank, silversides are hardy, peaceful pets, willing to eat whatever is offered, congregating in shimmering drifts.

Being topminnows, they take flake foods especially well and love wingless fruitflies.

If you are willing to use elaborate care in capture and transport, you will have a beautiful addition to the tank.

They are not especially difficult to find. Clear streams, river edges, lakes, and reservoirs are home to them. They're distributed over most of the United States, either naturally or as introduced forage for gamefishes.

REDBELLY DACE

Chrosomus sp.

Said by many to be the most colorful of the native minnows, the redbelly does make a fine aquarium pet, filling all requirements for temperament, size, eating habits, and performance. They are playful, peaceful, and pretty, attaining the great size of 4 inches (10cm) at the very outside.

The long, slender body is dark on the back with two dark lines running the length of the body, divided by a pale area. The upper line begins at the gill cover and extends to the base of the tail, which is clear or reddish. The lower line is broader, beginning at the nose and continuing through the eye to the base of the tail. The belly is always some shade of red, becoming positively fiery in spring at breeding time. Females are not as bright, but they're similar.

Not really very particular about water, they may be found in still, weedy ditches, ponds, or bogs, as well as clear running streams. For best color give them a well-planted tank and good clean water, gently circulated by a filter sytem.

Most dace feed mainly on algae and plant debris, and relish the dry flake foods prepared for plant-eating fishes, but they will take most foods. One of the finest aquarium fishes the United States can offer.

Ranges from the Great Lakes east, and south into Texas.

CREEK CHUB

Semotilus atromaculatus

Not a particularly colorful fish, the creek chub has a long, typical minnow body, silvery beneath, dark slate blue above, and divided by a lateral black line from nose to base of tail. There is a distinctive dark spot at the base of the dorsal and a fainter one at the base of the tail. Reaching a length of 4 inches (10cm) and sometimes more, this fish is hardy, good tempered, and eats anything.

This minnow is recommended because of its unusually playful habits. All the minnows are known for this characteristic, but the creek chub is outstanding in that it invents and plays games! We first noticed this several years back, and have since found it is an ingrained tendency in the type.

We had bought a vial of small rough opals in Mexico, and scattered a few in the tank of native fishes. The five chubs, who always had played chasing games, developed a very complicated ritual. One would pick up the brightest opal in his mouth and swim in a figure-eight pattern, chased by the others. After several passes, he would drop the stone exactly where it had been, and would hide himself behind a nearby rock. The others would make several passes, one finally picking it up, to repeat the swim-pattern, the drop, then the concealment behind the rock, bumping the hiding fish out, who joined the game at the front of the tank. This might go on for several hours. The fish were all so nearly the same size that we could not ascertain whether there was a definite sequence governing whose turn it was to be "it," but we believe closer observation would have revealed an even more intricate set of rules than first appeared.

A common minnow, found in streams all over the eastern and southern United States, the creek chub is easily trapped in a glass minnow trap.

HORNYHEAD CHUB

Hybopis biguttata

A name well deserved! There are rough little points on the top of the head, which some authorities believe are used to defend nesting territory. We have kept these fishes and have never seen the "horns" used.

In contrast to many minnows, which are egg-scatterers, spawning casually without preparation of a nest and caring not what becomes of the young, the hornyhead builds an oblong mound of gravel, which is defended from all other male hornyheads. Females are welcomed and several may contribute to the sizable mass of eggs, which are protected fiercely.

Other minnows are permitted to share the nest site, and several varieties may be seen spawning while the industrious hornyhead is still carrying stones for the nest. Choosing just the right size, he picks them up in his mouth, and may carry them for some distance.

A fat, blunt-headed fellow, he has a dark olive back and silvery belly, with a dark spot at the base of the tail. The head is slightly flattened on the top; males develop a reddish area here, adorned with the famous points, really more of a sandpapery than a horny appearance.

Reaching 6 inches (15 1/2cm), but usually less, this chub is found in clear, spring-fed streams at depths of 3–12 inches (7 1/2–30cm). Concentrated mainly in the Missouri and Arkansas Ozarks, he is less common elsewhere.

Where you find hornyheads, look also for Ozark minnows, *Dionda nubila;* bleeding shiners, *Notropis zonatus;* and various kinds of darters, *Percidae* species.

One of the more determined jumpers—keep the tank tightly covered.

BOWFIN

Amia calva

A long, slim, cylindrical body; long dorsal fin ending at the tail, which is also rounded; a mouth full of catlike teeth: this is the bowfin, one of prehistory's escapees. Fossils of the bowfin have been found in many parts of the world, and it appears he has changed but little.

The mottled, brownish color is not outstanding, but the males do have a black spot on the tail surrounded with bright orange.

A hungry fellow, he should be kept only with fish his size or larger.

Bowfins are found throughout the eastern half of the United States, concentrated more in the southern parts in sluggish waters.

The male is one of the most devoted parents, excavating a nest for the eggs and young among weed roots and gravel, a sort of tunnellike affair, and protecting and shepherding the little ones until they are close to 4 inches (10cm) long. Spawning is usually in May, so June is a good time to look for them. Mature size is 12 inches or more (30cm).

Offer live foods at first, gradually encouraging them to take bits of meat and angle worms. Dry foods are seldom accepted.

An auxiliary breathing organ enables the bowfin to live in water other fishes cannot tolerate. This is not a recommendation that he be kept in such conditions, just a comment on his hardiness and a clue as to where he may be found.

PICKEREL

Grass Pickerel: *Esox americanus*
Chain Pickerel: *E. niger*

Ranging from the Great Lakes, the St. Lawrence River, and south through Ohio and Missouri, the pickerels can be found in the slower running, more weedy parts of streams and rivers.

An extremely long, slim, streamlined body, underslung jaw, and large, intelligent eyes marked it as a predatory fish. The mouth is well supplied with teeth, used to seize and swallow whatever it can encompass. Not a fish to keep with smaller neighbors, but is so attractive it's worth considering if you should happen to find one. Just keep it with larger tankmates, and feed generously on live food, such as daphnia, mature brine shrimp, mealworms, and angleworms, and gradually teach it to take floating flake food.

The long body is marked with wavy dark areas, with a dark vertical greenish streak running through the eye (grass pickerel). The chain pickerel is similar, but the markings are in a more organized, chainlike pattern.

In both, the mouth is long and flattened, almost ducklike.

In late March or April the adults, varying from 12–14 inches (30–40cm), gather in shallow weedy areas at the edges of streams to spawn. After a great deal of splashing the eggs are scattered and deserted. Late May and June is a good time to look for small specimens.

GARS

Lepisosteus sp.

The feeding and spawning habits of the gars are very similar to those of the grass pickerel, with all the same cautions applicable: they are hungry, formidable fish. They are even vaguely similar, the gar having less pattern over the body, and a longer, more flattened mouth.

Lepisosteus means bony-scaled fish. The arrangement of the individual scales is fascinating; a perfect set of chainmail jackets each fish, for each of the scales is extremely hard and is furnished with a little hook which snaps securely into the next, making an almost impregnable suit of armor!

Gars are found in lakes, rivers, and streams in most parts of the Midwest and South to Louisiana and Florida, where there are stories of 20-foot (over 5 meter) alligator gars!

SUCKERS

There are so many different family names for suckers we won't attempt to offer them here; the important thing is to mention that they are fine aquarium inhabitants, rivaling the automatically accepted tropical catfishes as scavengers.

They are usually silver. Depending on variety, they may have reddish or yellowish fins; sometimes, as with the Mortimer Snerd-faced hog sucker, showing a brownish mottled pattern.

The most distinctive feature is the protruding sucker-mouth, placed low on the head, for slurping through the mud and sand in its quest for algae, small insects, and whatever else might be available.

Though reaching a good size in the wild, often over a foot in length, they tend to stay small in the tank, going about their bustling, busy work constantly.

We have found them to be hardy and undemanding if they are not handled with nets or—Heaven forbid—hands, which encourages fungus.

Easily seined in clean midwest streams; a plentiful fish.

Since spawning takes place early in spring, little ones are to be found in May, June, and July.

DARTERS

Percidae sp.
P. caprodes
Etheostoma caeruleum

When we say a fish is a member of the *Percidae* family, we're talking about the perch family; walleye and sauger, two rather large game fishes, are perches.

The darters are the tinies of the perch family, the largest being the log perch, *P. caprodes,* who may grow to 6 inches (15 1/2cm). Most darters stay around 2–3 inches (5–7 1/2cm)—good aquarium size.

They look and behave like little lizards, hopping and darting around the stream bottom looking for small live foods, with a lively, intelligent manner that is very attractive. Many, such as the rainbow darter, *E. caeruleum,* are brilliantly colored, with blue, red, and yellow patterns, almost garish in the intensity and variety of color. There are two dorsal fins, which in the rainbow are lavishly colored. The tail is squared, with rounded corners.

Two requirements may not be ignored if darters are to thrive for you: well oxygenated water with a good current, and live foods which will sink to the bottom, like brine shrimp. This is really all they ask.

If the transporting container is not large, with a good amount of space at the top for air, you will not reach home with the darters alive. One to a gallon-size (4 liter) container would be a safe bet if you are not more than two or three hours from the tank. More can be kept if a battery-driven airstone is used, or a few oxygen tablets.

Anything worth having, like an outstandingly colorful fish, is often a little extra trouble, but this is a fine tank fish, worth a bit of special consideration.

Most are found in shallow, fast-running water of clean streams, over most of the eastern half of the United States. See the chapter on collecting for a good method of capture.

They are sometimes sold in aquarium shops. Remember to insist on an extra big take-home bag if the clerk doesn't realize the need for it. A handy rule: any fish with an especially large gill area probably needs more oxygen than another the same size.

MOTTLED SCULPIN

Cottidae sp.

A mottled sculpin looks like a grossly exaggerated darter. The head is large and flattened with a wide mouth, large eyes at the top of the head, and broad, big gills. The pectoral fins are rounded and winglike, usually patterned with dark blotches, as is the entire body. There are two fins on the back, the rearmost one being the longest, continuing almost to the rounded tail. All fins are patterned instead of clear, which shows off their good size. This is a bottom fish, found hiding among gravel in swift, clean streams, eating insects, crustaceans, and whatever else it can catch.

Fishermen discard them if they are accidentally seined when collecting bait minnows, saying they kill minnows in the bait bucket. This is indirectly true, for the sculpin uses so much oxygen with those highly developed gills that both he and the minnows cannot survive in an already crowded area.

Give him plenty of well-aerated water, a clean gravelly bottom, and you'll be rewarded with an interesting little monster in your tank: a monster in looks, not size—most often runs 2–4 inches (5–10cm).

SUNFISH OR BREAM

Green Sunfish: *Lepomis cyanellus*
Red-ear Sunfish: *L. microlopus*
Punkinseed: *L. gibbosus*
Long-eared Sunfish: *L. megalotis*
Bluegill: *L. macrochirus*

As you can see, there are many members of the sunfish family. Those listed and shown in Figures 7-16 through 7-18 are only a representative few and, though their physical characteristics vary somewhat, their feeding and living habits are so nearly alike that we have placed them all in one section.

Here is one kind of fish that can be easily caught for the aquarium by the simple method of angling with rod and lure. Seining is really the preferred method of capture when it's possible, however. Maybe I should confess that my sole purpose in joining the family on fishing trips has always been to claim anything small and pretty enough for our tanks at home.

The hardy little sunfish, if handled with *wet hands* when removing him from the hook, takes up where he left off when put in a suitable tank. He is aggressive, alert, and intelligent. Many of the types outshine the exotic Discus and scats for color and personality. This is a daring statement, but you'll see.

Some of the pygmy sunfish mature at 1 1/2 inches (4cm), and the ones mentioned above seldom exceed 8 inches (23cm) in the wild. They will stay well under this size in your tank unless you are an unusually considerate host. Mine have always been fed the same diet as angels, gouramis, and minnows of all types, and have stayed under 5 inches (13cm), even considering they often live for many years. They eagerly strike at any floating surface food, dry, granulated, or live, and whack into pellets or frozen foods as they sink. This is a long way to say they will eat anything, except plants, but should, of course, be offered a good varied diet. If you would see a happy sunfish, drop in some angle worms.

Sunfish occur naturally or are stocked in virtually all streams, lakes, and ponds of the United States.

A wide variety of colors and patterns is seen in sunfish, and spawning colors are even more intense!

My personal favorite is the punkinseed, *L. gibbosus*. Its colors are a fish-keeper's dream. The body is more roundish and compressed than others of the species, background color is greenish-olive on back, overlaid by purple-violet, with orange specks on sides, the gill covers and belly orange. An overall feature is blue lightning streaks, mostly on the head region. The typical sunfish gill flap is bright orange.

Fig. 7-16   Bluegill: *L. macrochirus.*

Fig. 7-17   Green sunfish: *L. cya-nellus.*

Fig. 7-18   Long-eared sunfish: *L. megalotis.*

In the aquarium, different species of sunfish will cross—but only occasionally, when there are no mates to be found within the species. Spawning is similar to some of the cichlids, with the male establishing a territory, cleaning a round depression in the sand, and spawning as many females as he can attract. He then guards the nest and newly hatched young to a free-swimming stage, at which time he forgets all this propagate-the-species business, and begins to look upon the kids as hors d'oeuvres. They should be removed for safety and can take newly hatched brine shrimp as a first food.

We once had a single male punkinseed who entered into an ill-fated romance with a pretty female dwarf gourami—as good a choice as might be made under the circumstances, since she looked very much like a sunfish. The courtship was filled with dashing after one another, rubbing sides fondly, showing the finest, most jewellike colors, and all went well until the time came to go to the meticulously cleaned nest in the sand. Gouramis spawn in bubble-nests, blown by the male, which float on the surface like gobs of soap foam. Sunfish always spawn on the sand. Frantically, she tried to tell him that he must start blowing bubbles, fast! Urgently, he attempted to coax her to the only reasonable place for a sunfish and his mate to spawn, the sand.

Sadly, they realized that East and West, in this case, could never meet, she being from India, he being a Missouri fish.

Sunfish are sometimes described as being terrible tempered; this might be so if there is not enough territory or the food is inappropriate, but I have found these species to be completely peaceful, with their little family scraps amounting to no more than a few feints and passes that are not carried through.

If you add sunfish to a tank already containing some, there will be a great spreading of gill covers and fins, and small fights take place until territories are again delineated, but if the tank is big enough, peace will return. I don't mean for you to think I'm talking about huge tanks: I've kept four small sunfish, two black bullhead cats, five shiners, and two darters in a 10-gallon (40 liter) tank for years with no trouble. Just watch to see that each fish has enough room; otherwise there will be constant fighting. Despite this, sunfish are basically peaceful and can live with angels and the gentle gouramis. They need only good water, a little cover, such as driftwood, plants, and rocks, and they will be ideal tank citizens.

CATFISH

Ictalurus sp.
Noturus sp.

Our native American catfish are greedy, dumb, lazy, and altogether engaging! The frantic, lustful greed displayed at feeding time, the honest, direct, nononsense sloth, the unabashed cowardliness, are somehow refreshing to see.

Fig. 7-19   South American catfish, species uncertain. Closely resembles native North American bullhead types.

Baby cats are about as cute as can be, with the soft fleshy whiskers surrounding the mouth, the scaleless skin, the round, soft-looking fins.

We have many species of catfish in North America, widely distributed through lakes, ponds, and streams. Many of them reach very respectable sizes, some species being reported at over a hundred pounds!

Spawning occurs in protected dens in the spring, and the male guards the eggs and young until they reach about an inch and a half (under 4cm), when they scurry for cover and will be hard to find.

My favorite collecting method comes into play here; sitting in the water at the edge of a gravel stream, I relax, listening to the redwing blackbirds offering liquid, tranquil calls to one another. Idly turning over stone after stone, I see mayfly nymphs clinging to them, and little crawdads scuttle away in alarm. I carefully replace each stone as it was, for each one is some tiny body's home.

Suddenly something black shoots from one stone to the cover of another. What? A tadpole? Eagerly now the bits of gravel are snatched up, as the little black slithery thing dodges among them. Finally I get lucky: another quick grab, and it swims into the pool of water in my cupped palm—a miniature, whiskered catfish! Its round silvery eyes stare in fright. It looks like such a helpless baby that it probably doesn't even know it has a set of daggerlike weapons: the dorsal and pectoral fins, which look so soft, each has a stiff, pointed forespine which can give a pretty good sting!

Handling the cats is safe if you don't grasp them in such a way as to squeeze down on the spines, and the little ones don't represent much of a menace.

The most common cats are the bullheads, *Ictalurus* species, and the young ones will probably be black, but can be mottled shades of yellow and brown. If they are able to get enough food, they will finally grow so large they will have to be returned to the stream, for an insatiable appetite drives them to swallow anything small enough to get into their big mouths.

The tadpole madtom, *Noturus* species, is a miniature type cat. It only reaches 4–6 inches (10–15 1/2cm), and is a fine and dedicated scavenger for the tank, not growing so large. Even though there are several species of *Noturus,* they can be easily recognized by the distinctive fin structure. Our native cats all have a single dorsal fin forward on the back, and down toward the tail a smaller, soft, rounded fin can be seen. In the madtom, this fin is a part of the tail, forming a continuous fin. Some show a slight indentation just before the tail begins, but it's always one with the tail.

There is one other interesting characteristic that should be pointed out: the madtom has a poison gland at the base of the pectoral spine, and can deliver a rather painful jab. Again, just be careful. The pretty corydoras cats are equipped in similar fashion, and no one gets particularly excited.

They're very easy to feed; just offer a variety of anything. They are extremely hardy and undemanding.

THE CURIOUS CREATURES ●

AFRICAN CLAWED FROG

Xenopis laevis

They really are! Clawed, that is. They look like miniature frogs at first, gray-brown, hind feet large for such small frogs, with an active, beguilingly awkward way of dashing frantically here and there (Fig. 7-20). They stuff their large mouths with a hasty motion of both "hands" and are truly attractive in their ways.

A basking raft or island is not necessary here—their trips to the surface are quick and furtive, as if they are sure there is a wading-bird lurking in ambush. In their native African ponds and canals, there would be!

Being air-breathers, they don't compete with fishes for oxygen.

It's fun to teach them to eat freeze-dried tubefex chunks from your hand.

One quick chomp on the lump of food and they push at your fingers with their little hands to tear a piece loose, then scramble into and over your hand, looking for more. At these times you may think you feel a faint scratching sensation —you do! The claws, nearly invisible in the small frogs, quickly grow, black and shiny, into very respectable 3/4-inch (2cm) talons on a 4–5 inch (10 1/2–12 1/2cm) specimen! To the keeper, they are merely a curiosity, for the claws are not used to attack fishes. Any weak, sick fish will be torn apart and eaten, but healthy fish too large to gulp down whole are perfectly safe. Your hand could sustain a good scratch, however, if you should try to hold onto a mature frog. Strictly self-defense.

Each frog selects at least one and maybe two den-sites, which are excavated under a rock and guarded (no biting, just shy little feints).

Preferred temperature is 75°–80°F (24°–29°C). Temperature down to 70°F

Fig. 7-20   African clawed frog: *X. laevis.*

(22°C) won't cause illness, but the bright activity is not present, and they don't show off well.

The frogs are enthusiastic eaters, accepting frozen brine shrimp, live angleworms, and pieces of raw fish, all preferred in small chunks. They especially like angleworms, wolfing down whole as many as you are willing to offer.

CRAYFISH

Decapoda: *Cambarus* sp.

We called them crawdads, and rescued them from Granddaddy's bait bucket, making pets of them. The big ones, up to 4 or 5 inches for lake crayfish, could give a respectable pinch, but the little ones were harmless and we loved the armor-plated little guys.

They can be collected with minnow traps (rarely) or seined, but it's the smaller ones—1 1/2 inches and under (less than 4cm)—that you want, and they are best captured by hand.

Fig. 7-21   Jack the Snipper, a crayfish: *Cambarus* sp., posing for his portrait.

Seat yourself comfortably at the edge of a stream in 3–4 inches of water. Lift stones, replacing each one as it was. Most of the stones will be the roofs of crawdad dens and if you are stealthy enough, you can grab or net them before they're alarmed. They run from danger by snapping their tail-flippers, which rapidly propel them backward.

Colors and patterns vary widely, some being quite colorful, with shades of brown, yellow, red, green, and orange. The antennae are long and graceful, constantly waving through the water. Vibrations are picked up through them—they are the ears of the animal, and also seem to function as tasting organs.

There are five pairs of walking legs (Fig. 7-21), the first pair being large pincers, which hold larger bits of food and serve as defense and offense in the many fights, especially between males. If a fore pincer is lost, the one behind it develops larger to take its place.

The smaller pincers, which form the feet of the other pairs of legs, are in use constantly, feeling through the sand, tasting, and tucking food into the mouth, located under the thorax. Sometimes food is passed from one pincer to another, thence into the mouth. This is a smooth, efficient operation; the tiny "hands" never miss.

There are many species of crayfish throughout North America, with habitat preferences from wet fields, to swamps, to dark caves, to lakes, but the one described here is probably the most common, and most easily found in virtually any gravel stream in eastern and central North America.

Smaller crawdads don't eat plants, but scissor algae cleanly off the leaves. They pick up and work over every grain of sand. They will eat dead portions of leaves.

A little 1-inch (2 1/2cm) crawdad had a very predictable routine, always covering the same territory every day. Part of that routine involved the cleaning of a fortuitously positioned cryptocoryne leaf. It was so situated that he could step up onto the stem, and walk along the center of the leaf, working all the way. As he neared the end of the leaf, it slowly bent down, delivering him back to the sand, where he stepped off and continued on his route, for all the world like a bored executive stepping off the elevator he used every day.

If more than one is kept, they should be basically the same size, so no one bullies another. The uneasy truce is evident in their behavior, which becomes highly stylized. A form of courtesy develops, with no one coming too close to another. Gatherings take place: in our favorite domestic tank we had four small crawdads, all about the same size. At intervals during the day, usually midmorning and late evening, the four would abandon work, form a square, each evenly spaced from the other, and several minutes would be spent waving antennae and foreclaws. Finally one would politely begin to back away, still waving. The others would follow suit, still maintaining their spacing. When they felt they had reached a safe distance, each turned back to work.

Dens are excavated under rocks or plants, uprooting the latter and toppling the former if they are not solidly placed on the bottoms—not just on the sand. If inviting rock arrangements are offered, the landscaping won't be disturbed too much (Fig. 7-22).

Crawdads never quite finish work on their homes. Even after the sand is carried out and bulldozed into piles with the large claws, constant maintenance is necessary. There is endless bustling back and forth, reshaping the rampart at the entrance, shoving it into an ever neater heap, carrying out just a few more grains of sand clutched against the chest, cleaning, cleaning.

As growth progresses, the skin is shed. Remove empty skins, for they will dissolve and harden the water.

Females carry the round black eggs attached to the swimmerets under her abdomen, where she fans them until they hatch. She can be picked up and put into a container for closer examination—the eggs will not be disturbed.

Fig. 7-22   Jack on his front porch, enjoying a kernel of sweet corn.

Crawdads get hungrier and more ambitious at 2 1/2 inches (6 1/2cm) and above. They may nip bottom-resting fishes, or hang in the plants midway in the tank, big claws at the ready, grabbing clumsily at passersby. I don't believe they could capture a strong, healthy fish, but there may come a time when a return to the creek is indicated.

Good, amusing creatures, they add a dimension of entertainment not available from any other aquarium inhabitant.

FRESHWATER CLAMS

Pelecypoda order

Clams of many different species lie half-buried in the gravel and mud of streams throughout North America, living on microscopic plant and animal life, which they filter from the water.

Adult size may be from 3/10 inch (4–5mm) for the *Eupera singleyi* and *Pisidium dubium,* to 6 inches or more (over 15cm) for the *Anodonta grandis, Proptera alata,* and *Elliptia crassidens.* These are only a few of the species to be found. Once sought after as a source of mother-of-pearl, they are no longer harvested in this country.

Useful as water conditioners in the stream, and excellent on the half shell, escalloped (see Fig. 1-10), they are not for the tank, unless you are willing to check for vital signs every day. They may die without warning (how does a clam give warning?) and foul the tank.

There is another point to consider: clams go through a parasitic stage when, as larvae called *Glocida,* they are encysted on the bodies, fins, and gills of fishes.

FRESHWATER JELLYFISH

Craspedacusta sowerbyi

With a great deal of luck, you may see freshwater jellyfish. *C. sowerbyi,* the only species of jellyfish known in North America, is colorless, but in sunshine it will reflect prismatic colors, just as its marine relatives, which it resembles, do.

Shaped like half an orange floating cut side down, they are usually 1/2 inch or less (around 1cm) but we have seen them as big as an inch across (2 1/2cm, approximately) in the Lake of the Ozarks. They will live for a time in a tank, and are most interesting to watch. Harmless to all but newly hatched egglayers.

FRESHWATER SPONGES

Porifera family

Sometimes you'll see freshwater sponge colonies in large, gelatinous round clumps on the stems of the more sturdy water plants. They are basically colorless, but may appear either brownish (from debris in the water) or greenish (from algae growing in the tissues).

They live on microscopic plant and animal life, and play their part in keeping the water clean. However, they are not suitable for an aquarium, as they would sooner or later disintegrate, making a complete tank overhaul necessary.

RED-SPOTTED NEWTS, EFTS, AND SALAMANDERS

Notophthalmus viridescens

Native to eastern North America and the Great Plains, this rough-skinned little fellow will be 4 inches (10 1/2cm) or a little less at maturity; a good size for the terrarium.

Some of the newts are vivid in color. The red eft (name given to the sub-adult phase of the red-spotted newt) starts life in spring as an egg, sticking to the leaves of some water plant. It hatches into a fairylike, slender green creature with feathery gills. After three to four months in the water it transforms into its terrestial form: the red eft.

The color varies from one to another, but usually is a bright red.

Some individuals completely skip this adolescent stage, spending their lives in the water.

During its two or three years on land the red eft eats insects and worms, until one fine spring day it returns to water, where it mates and remains after assuming a more sedate color, usually some shade of brown or olive.

The alert little efts are easily kept in terraria or bog-tanks, or aquariums half to three-quarters full of water, featuring an island or emergent cliff for the inhabitants to use for climbing and basking. They eat any insect or worm, and will not touch any food not live and moving.

They will make little burrows for themselves and, when not curled up asleep in their tiny bedrooms, are busily searching the terrain and water for food.

Remember that you will be having to secure live food during the winter, because in your home there is no dormant, or hibernation, period. (See Ch. 5, Live Foods.)

Always provide both land and water for salamanders, newts, and efts.

Several types of salamanders are offered by pet shops (Fig. 7-23). Some can be expected to spend most of their time in the water, where they cruise around looking for food, nip at any passing fishes, indulge in scrambling mock-battles and, periodically, shed their skins!

The skins do not grow with the animal, and must be shed as body growth progresses. The salamander peels it off over its head like a tight T-shirt, briskly rolls it into a ball, and pops it into its mouth! When they are growing well, the skin is shed frequently enough for the performance to be seen many times.

Efts, newts, and salamanders are interesting pets, and often very pretty.

Fig. 7-23   One of the types of salamanders commonly seen in pet shops.

SNAILS

Planorbis corneus
Physa **sp.**
Ampullaria cuprina

Both loved and hated, snails are credited with being fine scavengers and condemned as messy plant eaters who manufacture more droppings to the proportion of algae and leftover food disposed of than they should.

As with any other water creature, the right place and time is the key.

They do make lots of droppings; they constantly eat and, naturally, they also make a bit of humus in the process. They eat fish eggs, becoming real slow-motion speed demons when they smell their favorite snack. Plants are sometimes attacked. Some types propagate at a rather impractical rate. You can't count on any snails to keep algae off the glass. They will eat algae, but only in a staggery little path. For a perfectly clean glass, it's the same old story—YOU clean it.

Snails are often the intermediate hosts of some fish diseases and parasites; I've never found this to be a problem, but it is one more point to consider. Every life-form introduced into the tank is a potential Typhoid Mary: this would also include live food like mosquito larvae, daphnia, and so on.

And for the plus side: they do plod along and seek out food other scavengers miss. Any dead animal matter that may have escaped notice of the keeper is sought out and cleaned up. If you like to grow Madagascar lace-leaf plant (*Aponogeton fenestralis*), snails are useful for keeping the delicate "lace" clean of algae, which is anathema to these beautiful plants. Some hobbyists say all their plants are more healthy when snails are present and this is a valid point. I have noticed plants tend to be more thrifty with snails present, provided they are not the voracious leaf-chomping types.

It's a good idea to add a few snails to the compartments Bettas inhabit; Bettas, being natural top-fish, aren't great about cleaning up every bit of food on the bottom of their barracks or tanks. In our Betta Barracks, we gave two red snails to each fish, to act as janitors. Three of the compartments are as clean as a kitchen floor, but in one the fine multicolor Betta exercised his war instinct by killing his custodians. The plastic floor of his cell is littered with uneaten food until I get around to cleaning it myself.

When the population rises to untidy proportions, you can resort to treachery. Trap enthusiastic plant eaters with lettuce. Weight pieces of leaf on the bottom. Snails especially like lettuce, and soon collect for the feast. You can then send snails and riddled leaf down the garbage disposal. This is a merciful, quick method of dispatch.

The attractive red ramshorn snail (*Planorbis corneus*) glues little globs of gelatin-containing eggs to glass sides and plants. You can scrub them off, but most of the newly hatched young are eaten by fish anyway. They are considered nutritious fish food.

Some of the native snails are interesting. There is one found in most streams all over the country—it is widespread, but not especially plentiful in any one place. It has the usual pointed brown shell, but when it exposes its body on the glass aquarium side, we see a feature that is totally wasted in its home stream, where there are no glass sides to climb, and no hood lite for backlighting. In such a situation, this snail's body is a living white opal! All the colors of a fine white opal are present in the slimy little fellow's body—quite a surprise!

In describing the domestic snails, not all latin names are given. Some, so far as I know, have no names, others have been given several—authorities disagree over them.

There is a creek snail with such a long, narrow spire that it looks like a pointy stick. It's really rather a useful denizen; it burrows in the sand, and reaches buried particles of food.

Several other types are very similar, and are said by some to hybridize. These are triangular in profile. They are commonly called pond snails (*Physa*). The shells are smooth and brown. Be observant when collecting. The types that are slow moving, with triangular antennae, are voracious plant eaters. Those with slender antennae who move at a faster rate will leave the plants alone. They are pretty good at gleaning after the fishes.

A good one for outdoor ponds is the Japanese live-bearing snail. I say ponds because they prefer cool water, and a heated tropical aquarium is just too warm for them. The young are born perfect miniatures of their parents, with fully hardened shells. You need a pair of these—males are distinguished by their slightly shorter left antennae. One fertilization lasts a lifetime.

These are rather large fellows, and are used in the Orient as food.

The "mystery snail" is so-called because it isn't known whether it is dimorphic (changing sex according to need) or hermaphroditic (both sexes in one individual). It's one of the larger types, reaching the size of a small apple. The color may be deep brown, or shades of brown stripes, which follow the direction of the spiral, really a pretty tortoise-shell effect. Keep it well scrubbed: because of its particular shell composition, algae loves to grow on it, making it look like a fuzzy green golf ball.

It's amusing to watch them when they need air. An inch or less from the surface, a siphon is extended out of the water, and the snail gravely pumps its shell like a tiny bellows until enough air is taken on, then it either lets go and allows itself to sink, or turns downward, to chug along contentedly, continuing the constant search for goodies.

There are several look-alikes who are plant eaters. Be sure you get *Ampullaria cuprina*. This one has a slightly higher spire, with distinctly rounded turns. The crease between the turns is deep and sharp. The plant eaters have a low spire and no crease.

Ampullaria cuprina leaves plants alone, but is such a large citizen and eats so enthusiastically it does make a lot of droppings. However, it is better to have humus than fermented food lying in the sand!

Egglaying is unique: when the mother reaches a diameter of 1–1 1/2 inches (2 1/2–4cm) he-she, or she, climbs out of the water. The tank should be well covered, because the search for just the right spot for the precious eggs may carry the prospective parent to its death somewhere far from the tank.

Above the waterline, an aerosol-like foam is extruded, which hardens to look like an oblong pinkish-white plaster of Paris glob.

The little ones hatch in approximately two weeks, depending on temperature and humidity, and fall into the water. Since their shells do not harden immediately, some may fall prey to fish. This can be remedied by floating a plastic lid beneath the egg-case. In the few hours required for the shells to harden, the little snails will be trying their speed on the lid. By the time they find their way to the water, they are ready to trundle around, doing their snaily business in relative safety.

The humidity must be high around the egg cases, or the case will harden to such a degree the babies can't break out when the time comes, and they will be forever trapped. Usually, in a covered tank, humidity is sufficient. In an open tank, you can fasten pieces of absorbent string extending from above the cases, across them into the water. The wicking action will supply extra moisture.

Again, in an uncovered tank you may lose your pretty snail mother-to-be: she's a rover.

Most snails can be stimulated to lay eggs by certain foods. A favorite *Cuprina* of ours, who had been named Ruth-Robert by the children after our long explanation of why a mother snail and a daddy snail weren't needed to get more of these particular snails, illustrated this to us one spring. We had been cleaning wild mushrooms. One was so riddled with little bugs we dropped it into Ruth-Robert's community tank. The fish eagerly picked all the bugs out. We noticed Ruth-Robert making all speed for the mushroom, which she devoured in short order. We were astonished, for this type ignores plants, and it hadn't occurred to us she might be interested in fungus. The next day we offered another small piece of mushroom, with the same results; she motored gratefully over and ate

Fig. 7-24   Surinam frog: *Pipa pipa*.

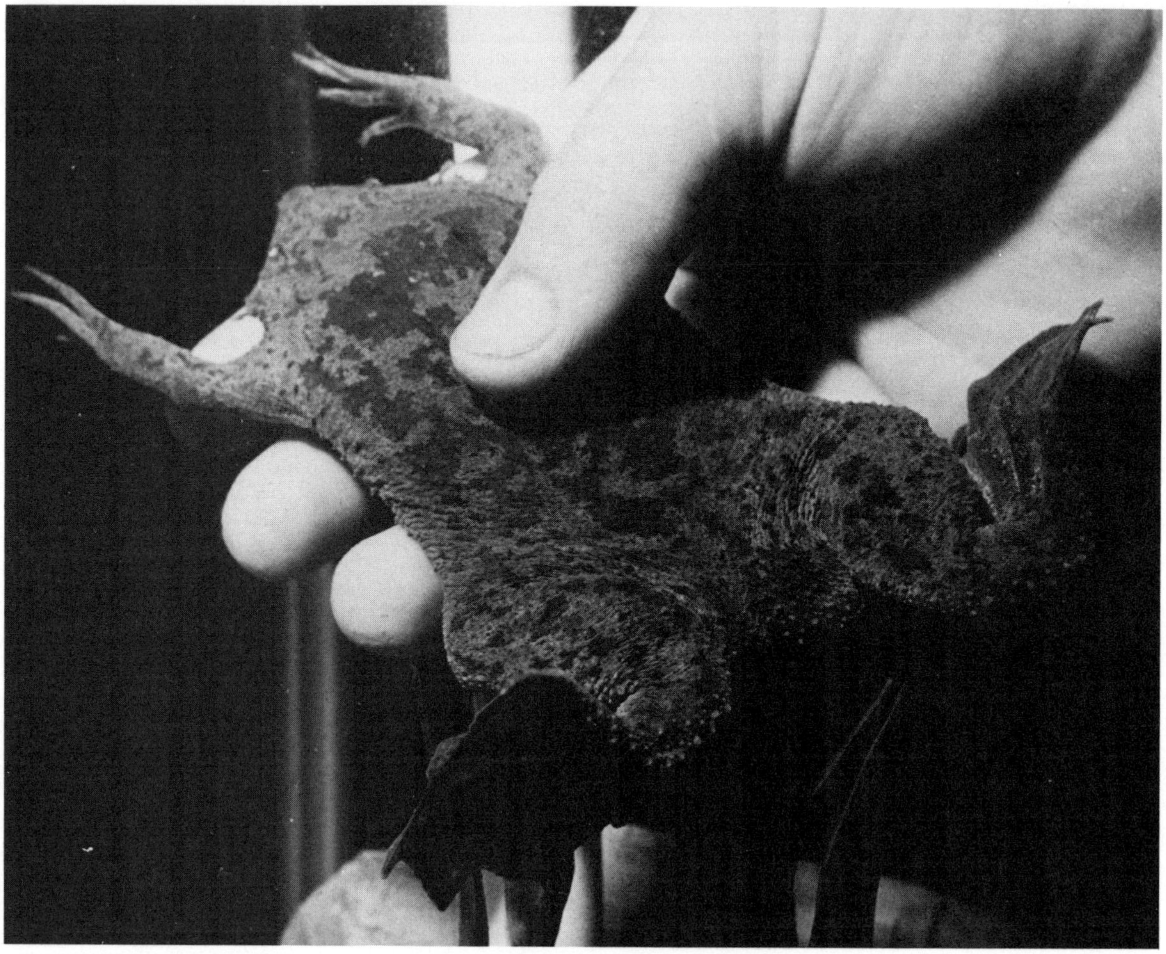

it all. They can eat rather large amounts when it's something they especially enjoy.

Two days later she began plastering a fine egg case above the waterline on the side glass, and every four to six days thereafter for a total of three cases! We had boarded her for over a year, and this was the first time she had offered to lay eggs. Two months later we repeated the mushroom experiment, and again egg-laying was induced. The white of a hard-boiled egg is helpful in this way also.

Some fishes kill snails—guppies, some cichlids, an occasional Betta. In this case, remove dead snails to prevent contamination of the water.

Snails are useful and interesting in the proper setting. They are not for the spawning tanks of egglayers, but fine for cleaning up once the eggs have hatched; they won't touch young fish.

They are certainly not necessary to the health of a tank. Whether to use them is just one more decision for you to make.

There is so much to choose from—consider all the available possibilities to make your aquarium, or more likely, aquaria—interesting and efficient.

SURINAM FROG

Pipa pipa

Surinam frogs, or toads as they are sometimes erroneously called, eat small fish and other aquatic animals, but can be coaxed to eat bits of liver or meat offered on a straw. Try moving or quivering it—they react more to movement than sight. Hand feeding does not encourage them to be tame; nothing you do is likely to encourage them to do anything in particular—they don't seem to be possessed of great intellect.

Six to eight inches (15 1/2–25cm) is the size most often seen, with the former much more likely. The best temperature is 75°–80°F (24°–29°C).

In a unique method of reproduction, the male spreads the fertilized eggs over the back of the female, which has thickened and softened in preparation. The eggs become encysted under the skin, and after approximately seventy-eight to eighty days (depending on temperature) the little ones push open their trap-doors, hopping into the world perfect replicas of their parents.

Surinams are night explorers, leaving the aquarium through any aperture for a moonlight hop. Since their bodies are very flat (Fig. 7-24), and they will nudge and pry at cracks to escape, be especially careful to secure the cover. Vinyl screening on a close-fitting frame is effective. Their quarters should feature a raft or emergent crook of driftwood for basking and resting.

They are pretty expensive, around 15–20 dollars; decidedly novel.

WATER SCORPIONS AND WATERBUGS

Slender Scorpion: *Ranatra fusca*
Flat Waterbug: *Belostoma fluminea*
Giant Waterbug: *Lethocerus americanus*

Water scorpions take several forms. Some look quite a lot like a stinkbug, broad and flat. Others strongly resemble walking sticks. All have strong, sharp-tipped catching arms, with which they catch and hold sick, weak small fish or bits of meat or worms. A piece of red beef will be sucked white in a short time: a good way to study their feeding habits is to offer the meat, see them grasp and eat, suck its juices and discard it, to wave their arms for more.

We had a specimen of *Belostoma fluminea*; J. Horrible Bugg was his name for obvious reasons. Broad, roundish, and flat, his back was covered with neatly arranged eggs, which he carried for about a week and a half. When they hatched they were perfect miniatures of their dad.

At the same time, we collected a pair of slender scorpions, *Ranatra fusca*. I say "pair" as a blind guess—they may not have been a mated pair, but I have never seen just one. Always there will be two, close together.

They were most interesting in the tank, quickly becoming very tame. They reached above the water surface to wave their catching arms whenever we came near. The arms would gesture insistently until we handed them each a bit of meat.

J. Horrible didn't seem quite so tame; it was he who swam over and bit me on the arm while I was cleaning the tank. It didn't hurt quite as much as a wasp sting, but the reaction was similar—it swelled rather nicely and was feverish for two weeks.

The scorpions, both *R. fusca* and *B. fluminea*, seemed to be basically scavengers. The only live food they ever caught in our tank was a dying minnow that I had already decided to remove.

Be cautious about waterbugs—many can give a really bad bite. The giant waterbug, *Lethocerus americanus*, is well known for this and can catch healthy fishes. It grows large, up to three inches (7 1/2cm) long, and can fly. It is often seen congregating around outdoor lights.

ELMER: FROM LOWLY TADPOLE TO HANDSOME FROG

R. catesbeiana are common over the eastern half of North America. Eggs are laid in shallow, still, or slow-moving water in a large, gelatinous mass in springtime. They hatch in four days to three weeks, depending on temperature, which also influences development of the tadpoles, who may take from five months to two years to become frogs.

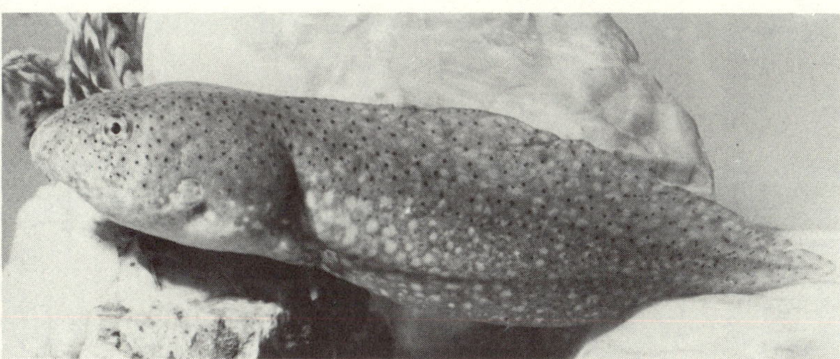

Fig. 7-25 Bullfrog, *Rana catesbeiana* tadpole, about 3 inches long. We had rescued him from a fast-drying puddle near a creek. At this stage, he was just a blob of a critter with a long tail. We named him Elmer, and on a diet of boiled lettuce, cut fish, and other greens and soft foods, he grew quickly.

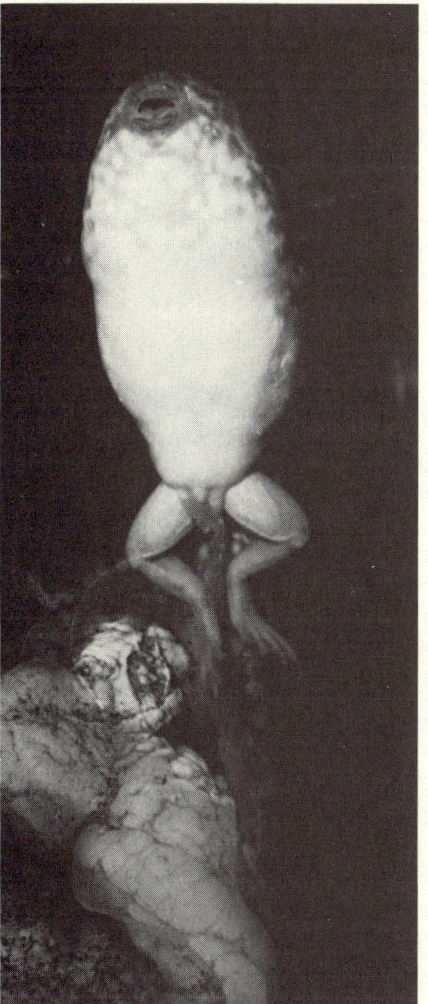

Fig. 7-26 Developing hind legs. For several days they trailed uselessly before he began to use them to perch on plants and stones, teetering precariously, for he lacked stabilizing front legs.

Fig. 7-27 The front legs appeared in a miraculous manner—inside the skin of Elmer's chest. We could see them moving around and occasionally an elbow would stick out of an opening in his side. After several days of this, fully developed arms sprang forth as though from sleeves. His eyes were beginning to assume froglike bulges.

It's the bullfrog that sings that famous barroom-barroom bass chorus on summer nights. They can be heard for long distances, for the voice is very strong, each one having its individual pitch.

Fig. 7-28   The head looks more froglike: the round mouth broadens into a smile, the eyes take on more form, the tail is being absorbed, and the legs are larger and stronger. At this point, the lungs begin to function and more time is spent out of water.

Fig. 7-29   Eleven days later, the tail is almost gone. Elmer begins to be more shy. We have observed that fish and other creatures do not seem overly fond of tadpoles, but relish frogs. Could it be that the tadpole's tail has a bad flavor, and it is only after its disappearance that the frog becomes really vulnerable?

Fig. 7-30   Time for Elmer to leave his aquarium home and return to the stream where he was born. With tail gone, Elmer has become a handsome frog. At this point, he has not been eating, living on the fat of his tail. He is now a predator and must have nothing less than live food, predominantly insects. Other frogs, snails, and small fishes will also be welcomed.

Fig. 7-31   Pearl gourami: *Tricogaster leeri*. A fine community tank member. Spawns like the Bettas, but there is no fighting; same water requirements as the Betta.

Fig. 7-32   Cardinal tetra. Needs fairly soft water; 6.6 to 6.8 pH; temperature 75°–80°F (24°–27°C).

Fig. 7-33 *Scatophagus argus*. Offer a diet high in greens of all kinds; needs some salt in water; pH never below 7.4.

Fig. 7-34 Leaf fish: *Polycentrus* species. Has a large mouth, likes all live foods.

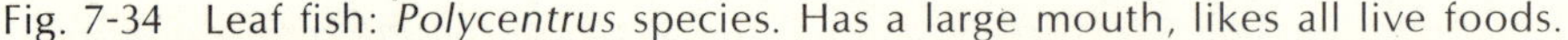

176

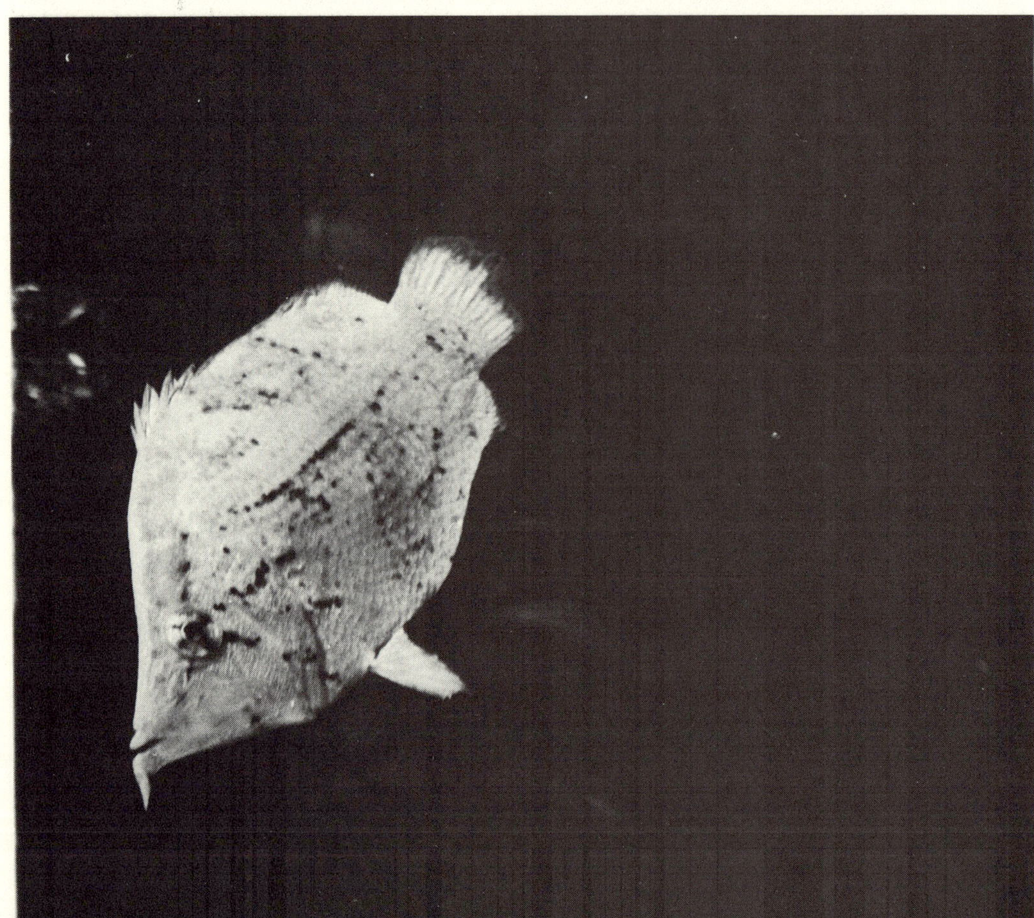

Fig. 7-35   Piranha: *Serrasalmus* species.

Fig. 7-36   Bleeding heart tetra: *Hyphessobrycon erythrostigmata*.

Fig. 7-37 Blind cave tetra: *Astyanax mexicanus.*

Fig. 7-38 Tiger barbs: *Barbus tetrazona.*

Fig. 7-39   Banjo catfish: *Bunocephalus* species.

Fig. 7-40   Elephant nose: *Gnathonemus* species.

Fig. 7-41 Kissing gourami: *Helostoma temmincki.*

Fig. 7-42 Silver dollar fish: *Metynnis roosevelti Eigenmann.*

⑧ The Garden Pool

The best and most famous gardens in the world include water, either as a major or incidental feature. There are as many designs as there are tastes, from natural to formal to ultra-contemporary.

A reflecting pool can be made of half a barrel, sunk to its rim and encircled with stones and plants, a factory-made fiberglass free-form shape, or a plastic-lined hollow in the soil (Figs. 8-1 through 8-8).

Only one pool will be described at length here, a natural woodland pool with a waterfall. The same plan could be adapted to any shape or theme. Whatever type is decided upon, it should be carefully planned and executed. Nothing looks more forlorn than a pool that didn't quite fulfill its makers' hopes.

If it is to contain fish, there should be enough depth to assure protection from the hot sun and suddenly fluctuating temperatures. The depth should go well below the frost line for your geographical area, or the fish will be unable to survive the winter. Contact your local weather bureau for information on frost depths for your area.

Most of the prefabricated pools are unsuitable for wintering-over goldfish or other hardy fishes. If the pool is too small or shallow, plans should be made for bringing the fish indoors during freezing weather.

LOCATION

Overhanging trees, shrubs and flowers look lovely until the debris they shed clutters and fouls the pool. They also might give too much shade. Sunlight improves fish colors and assists waterplant growth. Any shade needed can be supplied by water lily pads, other water plants, and a few large-leafed water-edge plants that don't shed constantly. Mid or late afternoon shade is not a bad idea—especially in areas with very hot summers.

Resist the temptation to put the pool in a low-lying location, where wet weather runoff will fill it with trash or carry away fish and water plants.

Roses, fruit trees, or any other plant needing frequent spraying for pests or diseases should not be near your pool.

Be sure you can get a water hose to the pool, and a source of electricity should be near for recirculating pump, lighting, or the yearly cleanup.

Make sure traffic won't be obstructed in any way; one enthusiast found his new pool precluded the use of trucks or tractors by blocking the only entry to his backyard. Heavy plants and concrete for the new patio had to be dollied in on hand-trucks.

DESIGN

Keep the pool in character with the rest of your garden; a square, formal pool would seem out of place in a natural woodland setting, for instance.

A lovely feature being used in pool design of late has been the Psyche Couch —fashioned after the famous painting of Psyche regarding her reflection in a still pool, it's an overhanging stone or wooden ledge where one can comfortably sprawl and gaze into the water from the very best vantage point.

One good way to avoid complications is to make a scale drawing, showing the pool and its surroundings. Be sure it's all in proper proportion—not too grand, not too dinky.

For a free-form pool, lay a hose in the shape you like. Stand back and regard it from all angles. Go to another part of the yard, turn and look back. Does it still look right? Is the shape pleasing, natural, no crimps or ugly angles?

ZONING REGULATIONS

If your yard is already fenced, well and good. If it's not, check local ordinances. The powers that be may decree it must be fenced.

CONSTRUCTION

If using concrete, check the possibility of ordering a mixer-load delivered rather than mixing it yourself. Unless you are experienced in this sort of work, it would be far cheaper and more practical from all standpoints.

The pool shell must be poured and troweled or formed in one operation, for cracks and leaks will develop if two or three pourings are made.

When satisfied with the shape, dig a basin a little larger than the finished pool, allowing 3-inch (7 1/2cm) thickness for side walls, and 4–5 (10 1/3– 12 1/2cm) for the bottom. This would be for a small, 8–9 foot or under (2 1/2– 2 3/4 meters) pool; thickness increases proportionately for larger ones.

Decide whether you want a drain and/or overflow pipe at this point. After the excavating, the drain is the first thing installed. Considering the ease with which the electric sump-pump is used for draining, I'd suggest this as a great time and money saving. Also, drains do leak or get opened by careless or mischievous hands, and thereon follows disaster! Small pools don't always have an overflow pipe, but they are useful. Be sure any intake is screened.

The pool should have shallow areas and deep areas. It can be basin-shaped, as suggested, or straight-sided. Most easily constructed would be the basin, where forms are not necessary.

Reinforcing wire is now laid to line the entire basin, stopping exactly at the edges. For the size pool we are discussing, chicken wire is adequate. Rocks may be used to prop it up, so that it becomes the middle layer of the concrete shell.

Concrete is now poured in and troweled so as to force out any air holes, making an even, solid layer around, under, and on top of the reinforcing wire. Edging stones can be laid at this time, forced into place in the concrete edge, with more concrete between them. Extend the edging out, apron-style, for a foot or preferably more, for nice effect and to keep debris out of the pool.

The concrete is now covered with canvas and allowed to set for several days. Canvas must be kept damp to keep the concrete from drying too rapidly. A finish coat can be applied of finer mix. Larger pools can be given a white gunnite finish, because the water will have a beautiful blue color of its own (providing it's well kept!). Smaller pools can be painted green, blue, or some dramatic color, but think carefully about this. Paint can be applied after the finish coat is thoroughly set, dried, and cured. Use only paint made for pools. Since all pool paint will need refurbishing periodically, the most practical and long-lasting treatment is the sparkling white plaster finish, which holds up for years without needing attention.

The finish coat is not applied until the concrete is cured. Fill and drain six or seven times, letting it set for two days with each filling. A good scrubbing with each draining helps clear the concrete of alkaline substance, the reason for all this curing. Until it's cured, concrete turns water so alkaline nothing can live in it.

With your pool all done, you will have a mad impulse to fill it and buy fish and plants. Patience!

After curing and applying the finishing coat (if any), fill and let set for two or three days. Chlorine must dissipate and the water must warm. Surplus oxygen will collect in tiny bubbles on the sides and must be given a chance to settle out.

Plants can now be added. If there is no source of water plants near you, look through garden magazines for ads. Order as many catalogues as you can, and compare prices and selection. Read between the lines. Terms like "resists mildew" (Oops! So it gets mildew, does it?) and "collected" (dragged it out of some swamp in the wilderness—probably loaded with parasites and water-weeds) should make you cautious. Don't buy plants with ricky-ticky names:

they could be anything, and probably won't survive shipping, even if they are
alive when packed.

Most good companies will give the Latin names as well as the common ones,
with clear descriptions of flower (if any), mature size, and cultural requirements.

New and expensive isn't necessarily better. When perusing the catalogues,
you will begin to recognize a few names. Some water lilies and other pool plants
are standards that have shown superiority over the years, and are included
in nearly every catalog because they are always in demand by experienced
growers. Pay special attention to them.

Many water plants can be planted in gravel on the pool bottom, but maintenance is easier if they are planted in containers, then sunk to the proper depth.

Water lilies require very rich soil of a high organic content, and added commercial fertilizer besides. Order this special fertilizer when you order the plants,
and follow directions on the containers exactly.

Clay pots or wooden boxes make good containers for planting. It is best to
use old, well-washed clay pots, 10 inches or larger. Place a square of vinyl screen
over the drainage hole and over this a layer of pea-gravel (particles are the size
of peas or a little smaller); add rich soil, fertilized according to the directions
accompanying the tuber (usually one cup for a 10–14 inch pot). Plant the
dormant or semidormant tuber and cover with soil, ending with a 2-inch mulch
of gravel. The crown of the plant should be just visable above the mulch. Sink
the pots in the water to just cover the crown 3–4 inches. As growth progresses,
the pot is placed in deeper water, 8–10 inches being the best final depth for
most types.

Another plant very popular with water gardeners is the water hyacinth. A
heavy bloomer and fast grower, it is cheap and propagates so well it has become
the bane of Florida waterways, where it actually halts navigation. The heavy
root system helps keep down algae, conceals eggs and fry, and offers shelter,
shade and security to fish, who seem to enjoy rubbing against it. A floater, it
must have full sun for good growth and flowering. If conditions are not to its
liking, it fails to grow and flower, or just turns up its toes and disintegrates,
clogging intake pipes of filters and overflow valves. The flower spike only lasts
one day, but another is ready to replace it almost every day. Not winter hardy,
but easy to buy every spring.

Most of the aquarium plants are satisfactory for pools, but shade—protection
for fish and blooms—should be the main aim in water gardening. This indicates
water lilies and water hyacinth mainly, pointed up by a few accent plants like
sweet flag and Egyptian papyrus.

A pool can cost almost anything, from a few dollars to thousands; the very
expensive, large ones are designed and constructed by professionals, but a very
low investment, temporary pool may be made from a piece of plastic lining a

Fig. 8-1   Melanie holds a fiber-glass waterfall; under it is a pool form. Several pools can be linked together with waterfalls, the edges concealed by stones.

Fig. 8-2   Wayne Gmachl shows one of the free-form fiberglass bases.

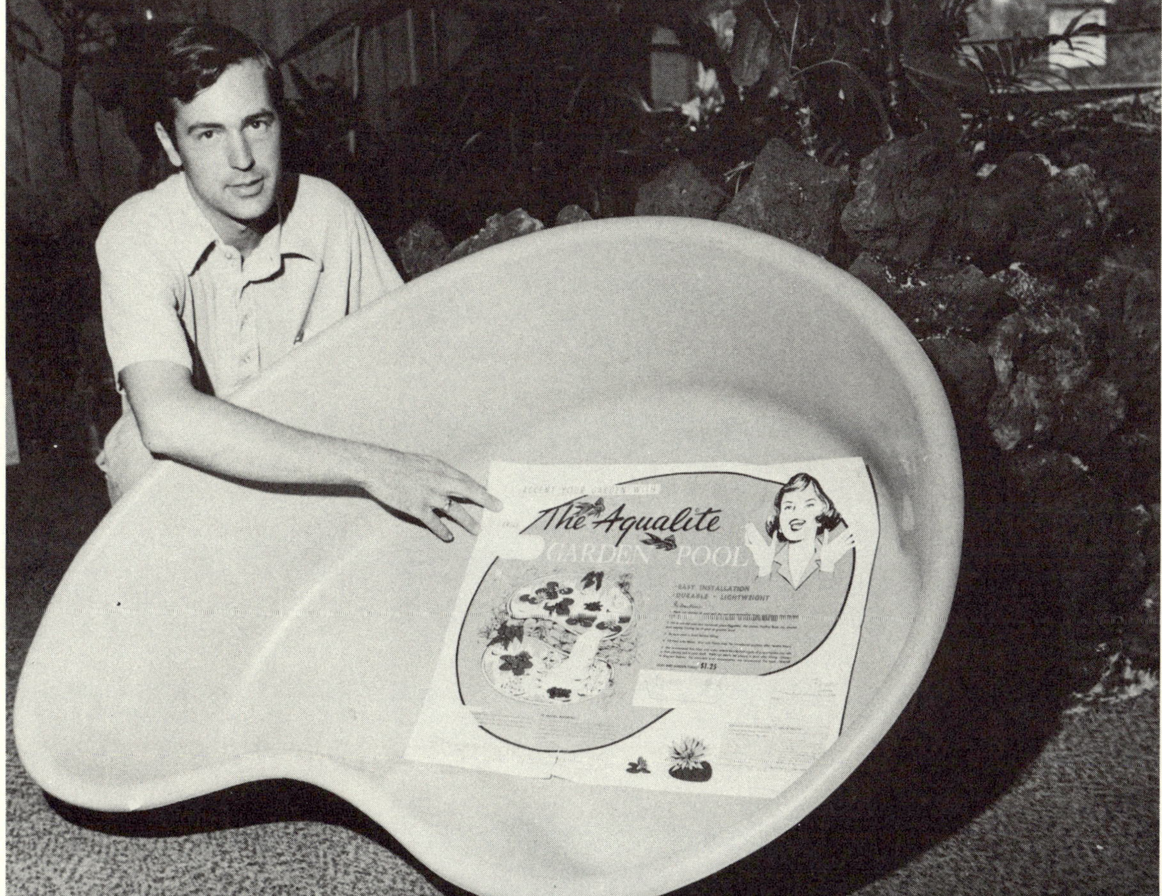

Fig. 8-3   The same base as shown in Fig. 8-2, installed in an indoor raised garden.

Fig. 8-4   Another fiberglass pool showing how easily edges can be concealed.

Fig. 8-5   The no-cost pool! A little work, and you have summer quarters for your goldfish.

Fig. 8-6   All we need for completion is some stonework.

Fig. 8-7   Some shade is helpful in keeping down green-water problems in a shallow pool.

Fig. 8-8   A formal koi pool. The koi, which look like large, brightly colored common goldfish, and are maintained the same way, make excellent pets. They are wintered-over in large tanks in the basement.

hole in the ground. A charming effect is gained by a little thoughtful rock-scaping, and a fountain could even be added.

Waterfalls and fountains are created with the help of submersible pumps, which sit invisibly under the water, recirculating the water through a plastic tube—which is concealed under rocks and plants—up, over, and splashing or trickling back down the stones, which you sweat and strain to install so that they look for all the world as if they had always been there, washed by that natural spring, which just happened to gush out in your backyard! Fountains are much simpler, for they only sit there and squirt water into the air, unless a more elaborate multioutlet fountain is wanted, in which case we return to the plastic pipe routine.

If your budget and back won't go for large stones, an even more convincing effect may be brought about by many smaller ones, cheaper to haul and place, which are fitted on several levels to resemble a large rock outcropping.

Pretty good fiberglass waterfalls are on the market, and can be used alone or in combination with a few stones, tree-trunk sections, driftwood, and so on (Fig. 8-1).

A favorite effect, the one we use ourselves, has a large dry creekbed of gravel running beside the pool, like our southern Missouri streambeds. There is a long mound of gravel near the end of the creekbed, which looks as if high water had left it there. Any gravel mulch should have an underlining of heavy black plastic to keep out weeds. This is available at building-supply houses and plant nurseries.

Pools need far less maintenance than, say, a bed of annual flowers, but some grooming should be done on the plants—removal of old flower heads and dead leaves—water level should be kept constant, and if there is no recirculating pump, watch for scum and floating leaves and skim them off with a hand-net.

Black aphids sometimes collect on floating or emergent leaves. Knock them into the water with a strong jet from the hose, where your friends the fish will enjoy them. Never use bug sprays if there are fish present.

In cold winter areas, float a barrel tied securely so that it won't damage the sides of the pool. This protects against ice damage.

If the quality of maintenance during the summer has been good or if there is a filter system, a yearly draining and cleaning may not be necessary.

Now, pull up a lawn-chair or recline on your Psyche Couch, and enjoy!

9 Diseases and Parasites

All plant and animal life is subject to illness or accident, and aquarium inhabitants are no exception, but a great deal of study has been and still is being done. Some aquarium stores offer diagnostic service and expert advice on treatment and prevention.

One such shop is Aqua-World in St. Louis, Missouri. John Schneiderhahn, an earnest, knowledgeable young man who owns the store and another elsewhere in the county, runs a fish disease clinic.

We were visiting there not long ago when a customer brought in a newly deceased fish and was greeted cordially by John—"Still killing them off, George?" George smiled lamely. "This one died twenty minutes ago, and some of the others looked peaked. Think you can help?"

The dead fish, a once brilliantly colored saltwater goby, was carried to a back room, where a well-equipped laboratory awaited. Jack Fournie, who is studying at St. Louis University for his Masters degree in Biology, with a specialty in Marine Parasitology, laid aside the preserved altum angel he had been dissecting.

"Hard to tell from just looking—I'll make some slides of the slime coating, conduct an autopsy, and see what we can find out."

Rows of formaldehyde-preserved specimens filled the shelves, and the work area featured several microscopes, some of them with cameras attached.

"So many diseases or parasites show similar symptoms, but the treatments are different. Shotgun treatments are usually ineffective, so it's necessary to know the real cause of the trouble.

"Many of the fishes I examine have fatty degeneration of the liver, but it is impossible to determine whether this was the primary or a secondary cause of death. It is problems such as these that make correct diagnoses and proper treatment somewhat difficult. Another factor, too often neglected, is environmental conditions. If they are poor, the fishes will be under stress, and their normal behavioral patterns may be altered. As a result, the fishes may appear to be diseased." He indicated a large yellow saltwater puffer in the tank behind us.

At Jack's gesture, the puffer lifted his upper lip, revealing razor sharp incisors in a comradely grin. "That fish looked diseased when his owner brought him in, but all he needed was good water conditions; proper pH and salinity has 'cured' it!"

This reminds us again that prevention is better than cure. Good housekeeping practices, proper diet, appropriate water and environmental conditions mean more to a fish than the best medicine ever developed.

People like John Schneiderhahn and Jack Fournie, who care enough to investigate trouble and offer solutions, have helped make the keeping of aquariums one of the leading hobbies in the world.

Modern medicine, treatments, and techniques are available to us, and make it possible to keep a healthy tank at all times, but certain considerations must be observed. *Prompt diagnosis and treatment are necessary;* don't wait for problems to gain a firm foothold. If your books on disease don't help, consult your aquarium store manager. Sometimes it is very beneficial to just stand at the counter and resolutely read labels on the medicine containers until you run across a clue!

When measuring dosage for any tank, bear in mind that only a bare 10-gallon tank contains 10 gallons (40 liters) of water. If there are rocks and sand, this must be taken into account. There may be a 2–3 gallon difference in a 10-gallon tank, with a more drastic variation as tank size increases.

Any handling or treatment is traumatic to a fish, and this problem is compounded by lowered resistance in a sick fish. Any good doctor should observe the patient after treatment. Shock reactions are likely, and without protection the other fishes could take advantage of a weakened tankmate or, if there is difficulty in resuming normal swimming and breathing, you may have to use artificial respiration, "swimming" the fish forward and backward with a gentle hand until it regains strength.

More than once, a fish has plunged to the bottom of the tank after being handled, there to suffocate, when a half-hour or so of first-aid could have saved it. In case of shock, keep the patient upright, keep it breathing.

Always follow directions exactly when using treatments of any kind. Remember to keep all preparations well out of the reach of children, and do not store them near medicines used by the family, where they might be used by accident!

Organize a little laboratory of your own, with a few most-likely-to-be-needed medicines in stock, especially if it might be inconvenient to make a quick trip to the store. Remember, delay can be disastrous!

In your lab, a strong magnifying glass, tweezers, a set of measuring spoons, a 4-cup measure, aquarium salt, a cheap high-intensity desk lamp, and a quantity of isopropyl alcohol for disinfecting nets and implements would be helpful. All but the lamp could be kept in a small box, so your "lab" wouldn't take much space or be in the way, but this little bit of planning does make things easier.

One more suggestion: an inexpensive microscope kit.

Beware the microscope! You will become so fascinated, studying all the little wigglies you'll find in fish-slime smears or drops of water, or thin slices of plant tissue, that you may find your own life has stopped and waited beside you, while you wandered through that tiny-beyond-tiny realm!

Keeping a log of your own descriptions of troubles and cures that did or did not work for you can become more and more valuable as you accumulate experience and knowledge, so you may want to include a notebook.

ICH

Ichthyophthirius multifiliis: in freshwater species
Cryptocaryon irritans: in saltwater species

Probably the most often encountered problem is ich, a disease that frequently develops in fish that have been chilled or mishandled in some manner. Some authorities declare firmly that no fish is immune to this protozoan parasite.

As with any disorder, proper diagnosis must be made. In this case it is a simple matter, for no other disease resembles the well-salted look of an ich-infested fish. At first only a few of the 1mm-size white specks appear, but soon they spread to cover the gills, fins, eyes, and the entire body. The unfortunate victim will scratch against rocks and plants, or hang dejectedly in one place, fins folded, shivering. Ich is fatal if not attended at once, but very easily treated.

The protozoa is perfectly safe as long as it is encysted under the skin of the fish, so it must be hastened on its life-cycle before it can stay long enough to kill its host.

Temperature is raised to 85° *gradually. Filtration is discontinued,* for the filter medium would remove the medication that is introduced at this time. *Aeration must be continued* through treatment. As soon as temperature is raised, medicine is added. If there are no catfish in the tank (cats don't tolerate salt well) sea-salt or aquarium salt is added—one rounded teaspoon (5ml) to each gallon (approx. 4 liters) of water is dissolved in a quart or so of water and poured in (mix well immediately). This does not harm plants, but it must be remembered salt does not dissipate, and can be expected to remain until water is changed. Since catfish are not often subject to ich, they can be removed to other quarters, to be returned to the tank after treatment is effected.

Acriflavine is another effective medicine, and should be used if there are tetras in the tank. For dosage follow label directions to the letter.

With the rise in temperature, the cysts leave their hosts and fall to the bottom, where they would divide into hundreds of baby ichs, who begin a free-swimming search for sustenance in the form of your cherished fish, but upon meeting with the salt or acriflavine, they perish.

All this takes less than a week. When the fish have shown no new infestation for two or three days, temperature can be slowly lowered to its usual level for their particular needs, and filtration resumed. If any new spots appear after this time, repeat the process, but if salt has been used do not add any more—it is still there. In another week or so, a 25 percent topping-off should be done, with a careful siphoning off of all bottom sediment. Cats should not be returned until this topping-off removes some of the salt.

Incidentally, there was some suspicion that the ich protozoan was capable of causing skin and/or intestinal disorders in humans. This has been dismissed as an obsolete speculation, but it only makes good sense to practice the usual clean-hands-before-dinner routine, as you would in any other situation.

For ich in saltwater tanks, remove infected fish to a 5 percent solution of methylene blue for five to seven days. This dye can be used in the marine aquarium, but it will tint coral, shells, and sand blue, which will persist for some time.

Figure 9-1 shows a *Naso lituratus* showing the peculiar texture indicative of saltwater ich.

A more modern and simple treatment specifies the use of malachite green, which is now widely available in aquarium shops. Follow label instructions carefully.

NEON DISEASE

Plistophora hyphessobryconis

This is a sporozoan disease most often seen in neon tetras, hence the name. Two small pale yellow spots appear, one above the other, at the base of the tail. The fish may live for some time, but finally a wasting of the body takes place and slow death follows.

An old and often repeated comment should be reemphasized here: find out what water conditions the particular fish requires and supply them. In this case, the beautiful little neon needs soft, slightly acid water. Some authorities have gone so far as to state neons do not contract this disease when kept under proper environmental conditions; others say correction of water conditions can arrest the disease.

If you see these symptoms in your fish, try correcting water hardness and pH, but the best method is to know the signs of a sick fish, and avoid buying from any tank wherein any of the fish show illness.

FIN AND TAIL ROT

Bacterial Infection

Fins and tails will begin to be eaten away, as if slowly dissolving from the outer edges. A vague, whitish scum is detectable at the site of attack.

Fig. 9-1 *Naso lituratus* heavily infected with *Cryptocaryon irritans,* the causative agent of salt-water "ich."

Several treatments have been recommended. Aureomycin can be used as an overall tank treatment, or affected fish can be dipped separately. Malachite green can also be used, as for fungus. Chloramphenicol is more effective for rather severe cases.

Don't let this one progress beyond bounds; it can destroy a fish.

VELVET

Oodinium limneticum: in freshwater species
Oodinium ocellatum: in saltwater species

Velvet, or rust as it is called by some, is a sneaky disease that can kill a fish before the unobservant keeper knows trouble is afoot.

This often happens with Bettas in particular, who will seem to have lost their vim and lie quietly for an unusually long time. In certain indirect light, an almost suedelike texture will be perceived about the head and back; in a few days the fish is dead.

It most often appears as a yellowish-brown slimy film near the dorsal area, which may not show up well under all lights. Spreading rapidly, it engulfs its host.

There are many treatments on the market, the best of these containing a solution of acriflavine.

Copper sulfate in solution is sometimes recommended for saltwater fishes and is very effective, but must be used very carefully, and brine shrimp should not be offered during this treatment. It seems they accumulate the copper in their bodies, delivering a fatal case of copper poisoning to any fish eating large quantities of them!

Treatment takes about five days, after which some topping-off should be done, followed by a final, *coup de gras* treatment in four more days and another topping off.

Discontinue filtration during treatment—maintain aeration and a temperature of 80°F (27°C).

Found most often on zebras, blind cavefish, white clouds, glass cats, rasboras, and extremely prevalant in marine fishes.

LYMPHOCYSTIS DISEASE

This is a common disease of marine fishes, showing itself in white, puffy-looking areas on fin, body, or mouth, actually grossly overgrown connective tissue cells. Causative agent is an intracellular virus (Fig. 9-2).

The patient should be treated in an isolation tank containing Penicillin G, 50 1. U/ml and streptomycin sulfate, .05 mg/ml to 5 gallons of sea water.

Ozone may prove to be effective, also. Using a Sanders' Ozonizer (which can be ordered from aquarium supply houses; a bit expensive), bubble ozone into the tank.

Fig. 9-2 *Holacanthus ciliaris* with lymphocystis disease.

TUBERCULOSIS

Mycobacterium piscium: in freshwater species
Mycobacterium marinum: in saltwater species

There are many specific causative agents in addition to these two, but symptoms are basically the same. It is sometimes referred to as "the wasting disease," a good description of the symptoms. Vigor declines, appetite diminishes, color fades, and the belly becomes progressively more hollow. These could also be manifestations of internal worms of one kind or another: only dissection can reveal the truth. For either problem, however, there is little hope of cure. One drug, Kanamycin, has been reported to be effective when administered in the food.

Best preventive measure; never buy hollow-bodied fish.

This form of tuberculosis does not affect humans.

POP-EYE

Exophthalmia

The eye looks as if there is fluid or air behind it in the socket forcing it to protrude, with one or both eyes affected. Many agents may cause it—developing larvae of some types of worms can make their home in an eye socket, causing swelling; an overactive airstone and high water temperature may cause the body fluids to become so saturated with gases that swelling takes place (in which case, reduce temperature, turn airstone to a slower rate, replace part of tank water); or kidney infections, bacteria, or drastic water changes, as from old to new water. A fish that has jumped out of water and lain several minutes before rescue may develop pop-eye.

Check over the conditions carefully: is temperature right, not unnecessarily high? Adjust airstone and filter rate. Wildly churning water will exhaust a fish, even if other disorders never appear. Don't shock the fish with large-volume water changes (belated advice on prevention, not cure). Keep the bottom clear of sediment, which is always a good propagating medium for bacteria.

On the chance the problem is due to worms, or trematodes, you may swab the eye with 5 percent Argyrol for freshwater fishes. For saltwater fishes, a dual treatment of 1 percent solution of silver nitrate, *followed immediately by one percent potassium dichromate.*

Some hobbyists are very enthusiastic about a newly introduced treatment involving salt and Maracyn (erythromycin). This antibiotic is used according to label directions, temperature kept around 78°F (26°C), and one teaspoon (5 ml) of iodized salt (table salt from the supermarket) is dissolved and added for every gallon of water. Continue treatment for one week, changing solution once during that time.

This last treatment was described to me by a friend, Charlotte Hopfinger, who raises and shows champion goldfish and has used it with success. The *Exophthalmia* was, in this case, thought to be environmental; the fish had jumped from its tank, and developed the malady shortly after.

FUNGUS

Sapralignia: external fungus

A white, cottony growth often appears at the site of a wound, bruise, or following any sudden temperature change or a case of ich.

Touch the affected areas with a cotton swab dipped in a one percent solution of malachite green. An overall infestation can be controlled by a sixty-second dip. There are many fungus cures on the market which work reasonably well—just treat as promptly as possible.

Mouth Fungus

Another cruel disease that has been virtually conquered recently. A white fluffy-looking area begins developing at the mouth, usually appearing in fish injured in fights or shipping. If treatment is delayed, the fungus will eat away the mouth tissues completely.

Aureomycin is the conquering hero here, as it is with many other formerly fatal diseases. Chlortetracycline is another recommended cure.

Follow directions on the label; it will not harm plants, and will dissipate of its own accord in a week or so.

Eye Fungus

Pterophyllum scalare, freshwater angels, seem to exhibit this problem more than other fishes. The eye gradually clouds and the disease can be fatal if left untreated. Poor housekeeping on the part of the aquarist may contribute to this problem. Should be treated promptly.

Follow the same method recommended for treatment of pop-eye in saltwater fishes: silver nitrate, followed by potassium dichromate.

Another treatment sometimes effective is ethromyacin (Maracin). Since several different causative agents may be at work here and diagnosis is difficult, more than one attempt at treatment may be necessary.

Itch

The only symptom to appear is the obvious discomfort of the fish as it tries to scratch itself against any object in the tank. Nearly always it's caused by accum-

Fig. 9-3   Sea horse with a microsporidial infection (light areas); caused by a *Glugea* species.

ulation of sediment and minerals, which creates ideal conditions for the prolif-eration of many kinds of organisms on the fishes' bodies.

Add permanganate of potash at the rate of 1/8 grain to the gallon (4 liters) of actual water content. Allow to stand for two or three hours, then siphon off one third to one half the water, cleaning the sediment out in the same operation. Replace with clean, dechlorinated water of the same temperature.

SPOROZOAN INFECTION

Microsporidea

"My fish just died—I couldn't see anything wrong with it!" This is one of the culprits that causes hobbyists to feel helpless. If there is visual manifestation, it will take the form of white bumps or knots on the fish's sides (Fig. 9-3). The internal organs are attacked, and death results unless treatment is instituted promptly. Very contagious to other fishes.

Quinine sulfate gallops to the rescue here—one gram dissolved in 100cc of acidic water (pH 5 or 6). This is enough to treat 10 gallons (40 liters) of water. Keep the solution in a dark place. Administer one third of the mixture on each of three days.

Sporozoan infections constitute a very complex area of fish diseases—even with dissection and microscopic examination, it's difficult to identify causative agents.

DROPSY

One of the sad facts of aquarium keeping is the realization that the keeper is not omnipotent, and can't always make a fish well. There is no sure cure for this malady, a bacterial infection which causes the fish's body to look bloated, with the scales standing out, looking as if they are loose. The eyes may have a pop-out look.

A possible cause is too high a temperature, and an airstone getting too heavy a charge of air, developing an overabundance of small bubbles. If damage has not been too extensive, correction of the cause may enable the fish to recover. If the water has indeed become super-saturated with oxygen and other gases, partial water replacement is advisable.

Dropsy seldom strikes in a clean tank of carefully fed fishes.

The good news is it is never epidemic, affecting one fish, without spreading. The bad news is that it's usually kinder to destroy any badly infected ones.

EXTERNAL PARASITES

Often the best treatment is the most direct and causes the fewest side effects. Any unwelcome stranger clinging to a fish may be plucked off with your trusty tweezers, and any wound left gently swabbed with a one-percent solution of malachite green.

Common sense must apply in all things, however, and if the invader seems so well entrenched that this treatment might injure the fish, try the method described for fish-lice.

FISH LICE

Argulus

Wafer-flat, 3/16-inch across, brownish or greenish and semitranslucent, lice look exactly like what they are (Fig. 9-4). There are chicken lice, people lice, dog

Fig. 9-4   Sea horse with fish lice of the genus *Argulus*.

lice, plant lice—apparently every living thing is accorded its own unique and special form of a louse.

Suspect a louse if you see one gill cover of a fish sticking out as if there might be an invader under it; they also will attach themselves to any part of a fresh or saltwater fish. A few individuals can be mechanically removed. If the hitchhiker is especially tough and hangs on so tenaciously you fear damage to the fish, touch it with a pencil or swab dipped in alcohol or a very strong salt solution; this may coerce it into loosening its hold.

A heavy population of them in a pool or very large tank, must be dealt with by three treatments, one week apart, of permanganate of potash, one grain to 8 gallons. This will send the lice into oblivion without harm to plants or fish.

The repeat treatments are necessary to wipe out any eggs hatching after the first or second treatment.

You may be able to see the eggs, which are yellow and deposited in long lines on some firm surface: a stone, glass, or plant stem. They are not harmed by chemical treatment and must hatch before you can get at them.

This rule should be followed when introducing any medicine into the water, but is most important with permanganate of potash: dissolve thoroughly in a quantity of water before using and, as always, measure carefully and accurately.

ANCHOR WORM

Lernaea species

Not a worm, but a crustacean, this varmint embeds its head in the tissues of a fish's body so deeply it may be impossible to remove mechanically. The body looks like a tiny glass rod, branched at the end, sticking out of the fish. The branches are egg-bearing cases. Found more often on collected fishes, particularly in North America.

One's first impulse is to pluck out the offender, but this rarely works. Safer to try this: either touch the anchor worm with a swab dipped into a 0.1 percent solution of potassium permanganate, or hold the fish in the net in such a way the protruding body of the parasite is immersed in a little puddle of the chemical, then use your tweezers. Treat the wound with a one percent solution of malachite green.

The chemical treatment suggested for a mass infestation of fish lice is effective, also, but use it very carefully.

LEECHES

Hirudinea

Many species of leeches are found throughout the world. They are not usually a real problem with aquarium fishes, as they prefer to prey upon each other, snails, small worms, and the like. As a child, swimming in the streams of the Missouri Ozarks, I have found small black ones, probably *erpobdellas*, hidden between my toes, feasting on my blood. A slightly painful swelling remained after removal, for apparently they, like so many other blood-suckers, inject an anticoagulant to facilitate feeding.

Leeches move inch-worm style, and can stretch or contract the flat body, which may be black, white, or shades of brown. Most are small, 1/2 inch (l l/2 cm) or under, but even in North America they can reach impressive proportions, the largest in my experience being a pair of brown and tan monsters, 12 and 14 inches (31 and 36cm) long! These were likely *Haemopsis* leeches, which can reach 18 inches (45cm). They were found swimming side by side, through mutual admiration, convenience, or coincidence I couldn't speculate, though some do mate and remain a pair.

Fig. 9-5   *Pterophyllum scalare* with a papilloma on the upper jaw. Causative agent is believed to be a virus.

Fig. 9-6   Oscar showing "hole in head" disease. Cause and cure are uncertain. Occasionally attacks older fishes, who show no distress and live on for years.

The bodies are unbelievably tough, bouncing back unharmed after being struck repeatedly by rocks.

For removal, use same method as described for anchor worms. A strong salt solution may also be used to stun them before taking them off, but this does not kill them. Drop them in a container of alcohol or some other strong chemical, not back into the water!

Remember to touch wounds left on fishes with malachite green (one percent solution, as usual).

Watch for little ones, carried tenderly on their mothers' stomach.

Examine all plants, whether bought or wild—leeches can be found hiding between leaves, especially at the base of stems.

In a tank or pond, leeches may be trapped by leaving a saucer or clay flower pot upside down overnight, and destroying the congregated beasties early the following morning. You could bait your trap with a bit of red meat. Continue until no more are found.

FLUKES

Gyrodactylidae: **Skin Parasite**
Dactyogyridae: **Gill Parasite**

Monogenetic trematodes, a term for "worm that needs no intermediate host for its own proliferation" are very common in marine and freshwater fishes. They can be seen with the aid of a strong magnifying glass, clinging to gills or skin. A smear of body slime, which becomes especially profuse in response to this parasite, placed on a microscope slide, reveals a profusion of flattish, wriggling worms.

The fish dashes madly from place to place, scratching itself, in great discomfort, and some slight bleeding may be seen.

Treatment is not difficult. The fish are dipped in a bath of one part glacial ascetic acid to five hundred parts water, each dip lasting twenty seconds, no longer. Repeat in two days.

Keep all sediment siphoned off the bottom of the tank.

HYDRA

Coelenterata

One of the polyps, hydra are fascinating creatures, reproducing like a plant. Simply growing new members like new branches of a tree, 1/16-inch (1.59mm) to 1/2-inch (12cm), occasionally a little larger, they look like tiny anemones and eat in much the same fashion. Hydra can travel, performing a slow sort of cartwheel operation, but seldom see the need, spending their time on glass tank sides or plants, waiting for lunch.

Interest in these strange creatures would be academic, if it weren't for their fondness for very small fish—say a newly hatched egglayer. Inside the body of the hydra is a neatly coiled grasping thread which shoots out, capturing tiny passersby, which are drawn into the stomach and devoured.

They may be destroyed by heat alone—a temperature of 85°F (30°C) for two or three days usually does them in. If they are resistant to heat, remove the fish and snails and add 2 teaspoons of household ammonia for each 4 gallons of water. In two hours hydra will be vanquished, most of the water can be siphoned off and replaced, and the fishes and snails returned. Any remaining ammonia becomes food for the plants.

Useful Books

Axelrod, Herbert A., and Vorderwinkler, William. *Color Guide to Tropical Fish.* New York and London: Sterling Publishing, 1955, 1958.

Axelrod, Herbert A., and Vorderwinkler, William. *Salt Water Aquarium Fish.* Jersey City: T.F.H. Publications, 1967.

Bellomy, Mildred B. *Sea Horses in Your Home.* Jersey City: T.F.H. Publications, n.d.

Dictionary of Fishes. St. Petersburg, Florida: Great Outdoors Publishing, 1967.

Frey, Hans. *Illustrated Dictionary of Tropical Fishes.* Jersey City: T.F.H. Publications, 1970.

Goldstein, Robert. *Diseases of Aquarium Fishes.* Jersey City: T.F.H. Publications, 1971.

Hass, Richard. *Know Your Aquarium.* New York: Pet Library, Ltd., n.d.

Herald, Earl. *Fishes of North America.* New York: Doubleday, 1972.

Hoffman, Glenn L., and Meyer, Fred P. *Parasites of Freshwater Fishes.* Jersey City: T.F.H. Publications, 1974.

Innes, William T. *Goldfish Varieties and Water Gardens.* Philadelphia: Innes Publishing, 1947, 1949.

Julian, T. W. *The Dell Encyclopedia of Tropical Fish.* New York: Delacorte Press, 1974.

O'Connell, R. F. *The Marine Aquarium for the Home Aquarist.* St. Petersburg, Florida: Great Outdoors Publishing, 1973.

Pflueger, Al. *Fisherman's Handbook.* Miami: Central Press, 1974.

Sterba, Gunter. *Dr. Sterba's Aquarium Handbook.* New York: The Pet Library, Ltd., 1973.

Van Duijn, C. Jr. *Diseases of Fishes.* 3d ed. London: Fakenham and Reading, 1973.

Zim, Herbert S., and Ingle, Lester. *Seashores* (Golden Nature Guides). New York: Western Publishing, Golden Press, 1947.

Zim, Herbert S., and Shoemaker, Hurst H. *Fishes—A Guide to Familiar American Species* (Golden Nature Guides). New York: Western Publishing, Golden Press, 1955.

Index

Page numbers in *italics* indicate information in illustrations.

Aeration, 24, 36
Aging water, 3, 27
Air pump, 27, 38, *38*
Airstone, 3, 4, *13*, 38
Algae, 3, 26
Alkalinity, 26
Amazon sword plant, 56
Anchor worm. *See
    Lernaea* sp.
Aphids, 63
Aquarium dealers, 51
Aquariums
    decorating, 24, 26–28,
        43–50
    types and sizes, 28, *32,
        33, 33*
    maintenance, 60–61
    setup, *28, 29, 46, 47*
Aquascope, 5, 6
Argulus (fish lice),
    198–200
Artificial sea salt, 4, 25, 27

Bacterial infection,
    192–193
Brine shrimp, 62–66
Buckets, collecting, 6,
    7, 13
Bunch plants, 58

Clover, four-leaf (water
    shamrocks), 57
Collecting, 3, *14, 17,
    18, 19*

Community tank, 21, 27,
    37, 40, 45
Coral, for decorating, 24
Cryptocaryon irritans,
    191–192, *193*
Crystalwort, 58–59

Daphnia, 67–68
Dip nets, 4, 5, 6, 13
Diseases and parasites,
    189–203
Dredging, 10
Driftwood, 50
Dropsy, 198
Duckweed, 58
Dwarf Madagascar lily, 59

Eelgrass, 56
Epoxy, 31
Exophthalmia, 195–196

Filtration, 3, 24, *28, 31,
    34, 35*
Fin and tail rot. *See*
    Bacterial infection
Float dipping, 4, *4, 5*
Flukes, 202
Food, 62–70
Freshwater aquariums, 29
Freshwater plants, 53–59,
    54, 55
Fruit flies, 68–69
Fungus, 196

Garden pools, 181–188
Gravel, 28, 31, 127

Hand-netting, 16, *17*
Heater, 25, 36, 38
Hood, *28,* 36
Hydra, 202–203
Hydrometer, *39*

Ich. *See Cryptocaryon
    irritans;
    Ichthyophthirius
    multifiliis*
*Ichthyophthirius
    multifiliis,* 191–192
Infusoria, 69
Itch, 196–197

Leeches, 200, 202
Lernaea sp. (anchor
    worm), 200
Lice. *See Argulus*
Lighting, 36
Live foods, 59–69
Lymphocystis, 194, *194*

Maintenance, 60–61
Mealworms, 69
Meat tenderizer, 7
Microsporidea. *See*
    Sporozoan infections
Minnow trap, 13, 16,
    18, 19
Mosquito larvae, 66–67

Neon disease. *See*
    Plistophora
    hyphessobryconis
Nets, 4–6, 13, 16, 17

Oodinium agents, as
    causes of disease,
    193–194

pH value, 26, 39
Plants, 24, 33, 52–59
    plastic, 24, 48, 49
Plistophora
    hyphessobryconis,
    192
Pop-eye. *See*
    Exophthalmia
Pump, 27, 38

Rocks, for decoration,
    3, 24

Salinity, 25
Saltwater plants, 52–53
Sand, 28, 31, 34
Scuba and skin diving,
    9, 10
Sea fan, 24, 36, 38, 43, 50
Sea horse tree, 29
Sea salt, 4, 25, 27
Seawater, 3, 4, 25, 27
Seining, 15, *15*
Setting up the aquarium,
    21, 29–51, *48, 49*
Shells, 3, 24, 49
Shrimp, 63–68
Spawning angelfish,
    131–138

Specific gravity, 25
Sporozoan infections,
    197–198

Temperature, 3, 25
Thermometer, 25, *39*
Thermostat, 25
Tuberculosis, 195

Velvet. *See Oodinium*
    agents

Water fern, 56–57
Waterite, 38, 149
Water wisteria, 57
Worms for food, 38, 69,
    70, 129, 149

SALTWATER ANIMALS AND FISHES

Abudefduf marginatus,
  80, 89
  saxatilis, 89
Acanthurus achilles,
  90–91, *91,* color Fig. 9
  coeruleus, 90
  olivaceous, 90
Amphiprion ephiprion,
  71–72, color Fig. 15
  sebae, 71–72
Anemonefish, 71–72, *94,*
  110, 110–112, color
  Fig. 15
Anemones, 71, 94, 110,
  111, 112, color Fig. 15
Angelfish, 46, 72–73,
  color Figs. 2, 5
Angelichthys ciliaris,
  72–73
  isabelita, 72–73
Anisotremus virginicus,
  79–80
Asteridae echinaster,
  105, 105–107

Balistapus aculaetus,
  92, 93
Balistes vetula, 93–94
Barracuda, 7
Blenny, *73,* 73–74
Bothus lunatus, 78–79
Boxfish, 74–75, 96
Burrfish, 74, color Fig. 6

Butterfly fish, 75, 96,
  color Figs. 7, 14

Catfish, 42
Chaetodipterus faber,
  89–90, color Fig. 1
Chaetodon capistratus, 75
  ocellatus, 75, color
  Fig. 14
Chasmodes saburrae, 73,
  73–74
Chelmon rostratus, 75, 96,
  color Fig. 7
Chilomycterus
  antennatus, 74
  antillarum, 74–75
  schoepfi, 74–75, color
  Fig. 6
Clams, 41
Clingerfish, 76
Clownfish, 71–72, *94,*
  110–112, color Fig. 15
Congridae, 107
Coquina, 41
Coral, 49, 52
Coris gaimardi, 95
Cowfish, 42, 76–77, *77*
Crabs, 98–99, color
  Fig. 13

Dacyllus aruanus, 78
  trimaculatus, 78
Damselfish, 12

Diplectrum formosum,
  84, *85*
Doratonatus megalepis,
  94, 95

Eels, 107–108, color Figs.
  8, 17
Elactinus oceanops, 79
Emblemaria pandionis, 73

Flounder, *78–79*

Giant seahorse, 42, color
  Fig. 11
Gobiesocidae, 76
Goby, 79
Gramma loreto, 87, color
  Fig. 12
Grunt, 79–80, *80*

Haemulon parrae, 88
  scirurus, 79–80
Hermit crabs, 21, color
  Fig. 13
Hippocampus hudsonius,
  101–103, 100–105
  zosterae, 100–105

Jawfish, 81
Jellyfish, 7, 41

Lactophrys cornutus, 76
  quadricornis, 76, *77*

Lionfish, 81–82, *83*, color
     Figs. 10, 18
Lobster, *113*

Mollies, 46
Moorish idol, 82
Muraenidae, 107–108, *109*

Nudibranch, 41

Octopus, 41, 99–100
Octopus vulgaris, 99–100
Ophiothrix spiculata,
     105–107, *106*
Opistognathus
     aurifrons, 81
     rhomaleus, 81
Opsanus beta, 92–93

Paralichthys stellatus, 78
Perch, saltwater, 84, *85*
Peterois antennata, 81–82,
     83, color Fig. 10
     volitans, 81, *83*, color
     Fig. 18

Pipefish, 84
Portuguese man-of-war, 7
Prionotus carolinus, 88–89
     tribulus, 88–89
Puffer, 42, 85–86, *86*

Remora remora, 86–87
Rhinomuraena, 107–108
Royal gramma, 87, color
     Fig. 12

Sailor's choice, 88
Sea anemone, 12, 27
Sea cucumber, 41
Sea hare, 41
Sea horse, 42, 63,
     100–105, *101–103*,
     color Fig. 11
Sea robin, 88–89
Sea slug, 41
Sea urchin, 7, *8*, 41, 97
Sergeant major, *80*, 89,
     color Fig. 5
Sharks, 7
Shellfish, *114*, *115*,
     116–117

Shrimp, 97
Spadefish, 89–90, color
     Fig. 1
Spheroides maculatus, 85
     spengleri, 85, *86*
Squirrel fish, 94
Starfish, 41, *105*, 105–107
Stenopus hispidus, 97–98
Stingeree, 41
Stingray, 7–8, *8*
Strongylocentrotus
     drobachiensis, 97
Surgeonfish, *90*, 90–91,
     color Fig. 9
Syngnathus fucus, 84
     scovelli, 84

Tang, 90–91, *91*
Toadfish, 92, 92–93
Triggerfish, *92*, 93–95

Wrasse, *94*, 95

Zanclus canescens, 82
     heniochus, 82

African clawed frog,
160–162, *161*
Amia calva, 152–153
Ampullaria cuprina,
167, 169
Angelfish, 37, 46, 50, 51,
131, *135,* 149, color
Fig. 16
Astronotus ocellatus,
141–142, *142*
Astyanax mexicanus, 178

Barb, *178*
Barbus tetrazona, 178
Bass, 42
Belostoma fluminea, 172
Betta, 37, 56, 66, *142,*
142–145, 149, 168,
color Fig. 3
Betta splendens, 142–145,
color Fig. 3
Blackjaw
mouthbreeder, 138
Black moor, 124, *124*
Bleeding shiner, 152
Blind cave fish, 178
Bloodyhead, 149
Bluegill, 44
Bowfin, 152–153
Bream, 156–158
Bunocephalus sp., *179*

Cambarus sp., 162–165

Carassius auratus,
119–129, *121,* color
Fig. 4
Cardinal tetra, 45, 46, *175*
Catfish, 44, 46, 158–160,
159, 179
Cave fish, 178
Celestial, *123*
Chrosomus sp., 151
Chubs, 151–152
Cichlasoma biocellatum,
140–141
meeki, 140
Cichlids, 131–138
Clams, 165
Corydoras, 160
Cottidae sp., 155–156
*Craspedacusta
sowerbyi,* 165
Crayfish, 44, 46, *162,*
162–164

Dace, 151
Danios, 46
Darters, 10, 44, 46,
154–155
Decapoda, *Cambarus*
sp., 162
Dionda nubila, 152
Discus, 132, 138, 156

Eels, 130–131
Efts, 166

Egyptian
mouthbreeder, 139
Elephant nose, 179
Esox americanus, 153
niger, 153
Etheostoma caeruleum,
154–155

Fire eel, 131
Firemouth, 46, 140
Frogs, 160, 171, *173–174*

Gars, 154
Georgia shiner, 150
Glow-lite tetra, 45
Gnathonemus sp., *179*
Goldfish, 57, 119–129,
color Fig. 4
Gourami, 46, 149, 158,
175, 180
Guppies, 46, 56, 145,
146, 147

Haplochromis multicolor,
139–140
*Helostoma
temmincki, 180*
*Hemichromis
bimaculatus,* 141
Hybopis biguttata, 152

Ictalurus sp., 158–160

Jack Dempsey, 140
Jellyfish, 165
Jewel fish, 141

Labidesthes sicculus,
    150–151
Leaf fish, *176*
Lebistes reticulatus,
    145–146, *146*
Leeches, 36
Lepisosteus sp., 154
Lepomis gibbosus,
    156–158
  cyanellus, 157
  macrochirus,
    156–158, *157*
  megalotis, 156–158, *157*
  microlopus, 156–158
Lethocerus
    americanus, 172
Livebearers, 145–147

Madtom, 160
Mastacembelidae sp.,
    130–131
Menidia audens, 150–151
Metynnis roosevelti
    Eigenmann, 180
Molleinesia sp., 145,
    146, *147*
Mollies, 46, 147
Mottled sculpin, 155

Newts, 69, 166
Notopthalmus
    viridescens, 166

Notropis
  hypsetopterus, 152
  lutrensis, 148
  zonatus, 152
Noturus sp., 158

Oranda, *122,* 122–123, *123*
Oscar, 46, 141–142

Pearl-scale oranda, *123*
Pelecypoda order, 165
Perch-nurse, 149
Percidae sp., 152, 154
  caprodes, 154–155
Physa sp., 167–171
Pickerel, 153
Pike, 42
Pipa pipa, 170, 171
Piranha, *177*
Planorbis corneus, 167
Platy, 46
Porifera family, 165–166
Pterophyllum altum,
    134–138
  eimekei, 134
  scalare, 133, 134

Rainbow minnow, 149
Rana catesbeiana, 173–174
Rasbora heteromorpha,
    129–130
Redbelly dace, 151
Red-cap oranda, *122*
Red-head minnow, 149
Red rasbora, 129–130

Salamanders, 69, 166,
    167, 170
Scatophagus argus, 176
Sculpin, 155
Semotilus atromaculatus,
    151–152
Shiners, 148–150
Shrimp, 97
Silver-dollar fish, 180
Silversides, 150–151
Snails, 149, 167–171
Spiny eel, 46, *130,*
    130–131
Sponges, 165–166
Suckers, 154
Sunfish, 46, 156–158, *157*
Surinam frog, *170,* 171
Swordtails, 145
Symphosodon discus, 138

Tadpoles, 173
Tetra, 46, 175, *177, 178*
Tilapia macrocephala, 138
Tricogaster leeni, 175
Trionx ferox, 62
Turtle, 62

Veiltails, 125, *125*

Waterbugs, 36, 125, 172
Water scorpions, 172

Xenopis laevis, 160, *161*
Xiphorus sp., 145–146